Fifth Edition

Introduction to Employment Law

Fundamentals for HR and business students

Kathy Daniels

This edition published in Great Britain and the United States in 2019 by Kogan Page Limited

2nd Floor, 45 Gee Street	c/o Martin P Hill Consulting	4737/23 Ansari Road
London EC1V 3RS	122 W 27th St, 10th Floor	Daryaganj
United Kingdom	New York NY 10001	New Delhi 110002
www.koganpage.com	USA	India

© Kogan Page, 2019

The right of Kathy Daniels to be identified as the author of this work has been asserted by her in accordance with the Copyright, Designs and Patents Act 1988.

ISBNs

HARDBACK   978 0 7494 9764 4
PAPERBACK   978 0 7494 8414 9
E-ISBN   978 0 7494 8415 6

British Library Cataloguing-in-Publication Data

A CIP record for this book is available from the British Library.

Library of Congress Cataloging-in-Publication Data

Names: Daniels, Kathy, author.
Title: Introduction to employment law : fundamentals for HR and business
    students / Kathy Daniels.
Other titles: Employment law
Description: [5th Edition]. | London ; New York : Kogan Page Limited, [2019]
    | Includes index.
Identifiers: LCCN 2018042623 (print) | LCCN 2018043219 (ebook) | ISBN
    9780749484156 (ebook) | ISBN 9780749484149 (pbk.)
Subjects: LCSH: Labor laws and legislation--Great Britain--Outlines,
    syllabi, etc.
Classification: LCC KD3009.6 (ebook) | LCC KD3009.6 .D36 2019 (print) | DDC
    344.4101--dc23

Typeset by Integra Software Services, Pondicherry
Print production managed by Jellyfish
Printed and bound in Great Britain by Ashford Colour Press Ltd.

CONTENTS

Contents

13   Study skills in employment law 263

LIST OF FIGURES AND TABLES

Figures

Tables

LIST OF LEGISLATION REFERRED TO

LIST OF CASES CITED

USEFUL WEBSITES

Acts of the UK Parliament
www.legislation.gov.uk

Advisory Conciliation and Arbitration Service
www.acas.org.uk

Central Arbitration Committee
www.gov.uk/government/organisations/central-arbitration-committee

Certification Officer
www.gov.uk/government/organisations/certification-officer

Chartered Institute of Personnel and Development
www.cipd.co.uk

Confederation of British Industry
www.cbi.org.uk

Court of Appeal Decisions
www.judiciary.gov.uk/court/court-of-appeal/

Court of Justice of the European Union
https://curia.europa.eu/jcms/jcms/j_6/en/

Department for Business, Energy and Industrial Strategy
www.gov.uk/government/organisations/department-for-business-energy-and-
industrial-strategy

Department for Education
www.gov.uk/government/organisation/department-for-education

Department for Work and Pensions
www.gov.uk/government/organisations/department-for-work-pensions

Employment Appeal Tribunal
www.gov.uk/courts-tribunals/employment-appeal-tribunal

Employment Tribunal judgments
www.gov.uk/employment-tribunal-decisions

Equality and Human Rights Commission
www.equalityhumanrights.org.uk

European Court of Human Rights
www.echr.coe.int

Health and Safety Executive
www.hse.gov.uk

Incorporated Council of Law Reporting
www.iclr.co.uk

Ministry of Justice
www.justice.gov.uk

Office for National Statistics
www.statistics.gov.uk

Scottish Law
www.scottishlaw.org.uk

Supreme Court judgments
www.supremecourt.uk/news/latest-judgments.html

Trades Union Congress
www.tuc.org.uk

Updates on recent rulings and developments in employment law
www.danielbarnett.co.uk

ABOUT THE AUTHOR

Kathy Daniels is Associate Professor and Associate Dean, Learning and Teaching, at Aston University, and teaches employment law and employee relations. She is also the lead tutor for employment law programmes at the Chartered Institute of Personnel and Development. She writes and presents extensively for a variety of organisations and law firms, specialising in employment law.

She is a lay member of the Employment Tribunals, sitting in Birmingham. Prior to these appointments she was a senior HR manager in the manufacturing sector.

PREFACE

It is nearly three years since the fourth edition of this book, and in that time there have been a significant number of changes in employment law. This book has been thoroughly revised to take account of all of those changes.

The book has been written specifically for non-lawyers. It presumes no prior knowledge of the subject and is particularly suitable, therefore, for those studying employment law as part of a non-law degree such as human resource management or business studies.

It covers the syllabus set by the Chartered Institute of Personnel and Development for the level 3 and 5 qualifications, and is particularly useful for students studying at this level. The book also covers the entire syllabus set by the Chartered Institute of Personnel and Development for its level 7 qualifications. Students studying at level 7 with no prior knowledge of employment law might find it useful to read this book as an introduction before progressing to further reading.

To make the subject of employment law more accessible for such students, legal cases referenced in the book are explained in some detail, bringing the subject to life and giving a clear illustration of each legal point in question.

In addition to understanding the facts of employment law, it is also important that students take time to examine the impact of employment law on organisations. To stimulate such evaluation, the book has a number of specific features that are discussed in the next section (starting on page xxix).

WALKTHROUGH OF TEXTBOOK FEATURES AND ONLINE RESOURCES

Chapter objectives

At the beginning of each chapter a bulleted set of chapter objectives summarises what you expect to learn from the chapter, helping you to track your progress.

CHAPTER OBJECTIVES

The objectives of this chapter are:

- to explore the purpose of employment law;
- to highlight the differences between criminal and civil law;
- to examine the sources of employment law;
- to define and explain terms commonly used in employment law;
- to determine the role of key institutions.

Examples to work through

At the end of each chapter are organisational scenarios, giving students the opportunity to apply the legislation they have learnt.

 Examples to work through

1 Is it true that employment law in the UK is primarily driven by initiatives from the EU? Justify your answer. To what extent will Brexit change employment law? What changes do you think most employers and employees want to see?

2 How much is employment law driven by the political stance of the government? In answering this question, explore the changes that the Coalition Government made to employment law.

3 Explore the various approaches that Acas uses to help resolve employment disputes. Which approaches seem to be most valuable for both the employer and the employee?

Case studies

A range of case studies give students the opportunity to apply the law in more detail, and are useful exam practice.

 Case study 2.1

On 20 January 2018 you dismissed Marjorie for gross misconduct. For a number of weeks you had been suspicious that an employee was stealing from the organisation, and following a series of investigations you worked out that Marjorie was the individual who was responsible.

You dismissed Marjorie three weeks before her wedding. After the wedding she was due to go on honeymoon for three weeks. You had heard that she was taken ill with malaria about two weeks after she returned from her honeymoon, but you have heard nothing more from her since.

Today you have received a copy of the ET1 that she has submitted to the Employment Tribunal. It was received at the tribunal on 24 April 2018. She had written a letter to the Employment Tribunal apologising for the delay in submitting her ET1 and blaming this on her wedding, honeymoon and illness. Having taken some advice you are aware that the Employment Tribunal might decide to accept her claim, even though it is out of time. However, you still decide to go ahead and request a preliminary hearing. You receive notification from the Employment Tribunal that a preliminary hearing will take place, but if it is decided that they can hear the claim a full hearing will follow immediately.

Outline the preparations that you need to take for: 1) the preliminary hearing; 2) the full hearing.

Task

In each chapter, a number of questions and activities will get you to reflect on what you have just read and encourage you to explore important concepts and issues in greater depth.

 Task

It is important that throughout your studies you keep abreast of the changes and developments in employment law. This can be achieved by reading such publications as the CIPD magazine *People Management*, reading quality newspapers, and browsing websites already listed for specific employment institutions. Decide now what will be your main sources of reference and be sure to make regular referrals to them.

Key learning points

At the end of each chapter, a bulleted list of the key learning points summarises the chapter and pulls out the most important points for you to remember.

 KEY LEARNING POINTS

1 Employment law is a rapidly changing area of law and the direction of changes is affected by the government of the UK.
2 Employment law is primarily governed by civil law, although there are situations in which criminal law might be applied. Civil law is based on the law of contract, tort and property.
3 Legislation is created by statute, common (case) law and the influence of codes of practice.
4 The UK is going to leave the EU, but until that happens European law has precedence over UK law.

Explore further

Explore further boxes contain suggestions for further reading and useful websites, encouraging you to delve further into areas of particular interest.

 Explore further

Look at recent changes in employment legislation in the UK. Distinguish which are the result of European directives and which are not. Are there underlying differences relating to the two sources of legislation? Now select any other member state of the EU. Contrast and compare key areas of legislation of this member state and of the UK. Are there any areas of commonality appearing? If not, how can that be explained?

Online resources for tutors at www.koganpage.com/introEL5

- PowerPoint slides – design your programme around these ready-made lectures.
- Lecturer's guide – including guidance on the activities and questions in the text.
- Additional case studies – these can be used as a classroom activity, for personal reflection and individual learning, or as the basis for assignments.
- Multiple-choice questions – a series of questions for each chapter to test your understanding of the text.

Online resources for students at www.koganpage.com/introEL5

- Annotated web links – access a wealth of useful information sources in order to develop your understanding of employment law issues.
- Multiple-choice questions – a series of questions for each chapter to test your understanding of the text.
- Summary of key points from each chapter.

01
The formation of employment law

CHAPTER OBJECTIVES

The objectives of this chapter are:

- to explore the purpose of employment law;
- to highlight the differences between criminal and civil law;
- to examine the sources of employment law;
- to define and explain terms commonly used in employment law;
- to determine the role of key institutions.

1.1 An introduction to employment law

The law in the UK is very broad. In this book we focus solely on the law that relates to the employment of individuals. The purpose of employment law is to regulate the relationship between the employer and employee.

Employment law is one of the fastest-changing areas of the law in the UK. In the past 50 years there has been a steady increase in the introduction of legislation. In 1979 the Conservative Government came into power with a reforming agenda. Under Margaret Thatcher's leadership it took the view that the balance of power in the employment relationship had swung too far in favour of the employee. The miners' strike in 1984/5 was a key example of this struggle for power. As a result of this concern over the balance of power, a series of new employment legislation was introduced in the 1980s and 1990s. One of the key elements of this was legislation that reduced the power of the trade unions and introduced new individual rights.

In 1997 the Labour Government returned to power. First, it opted into the Social Charter. The Social Charter is a declaration of member states of the European Union (EU) that brought in a level of basic rights (not just in relation to employment) as laid out in the 1957 Social Chapter (which is in the original Treaty of Rome). The basic rights include such things as a basic wage, the right to be consulted by employers and the right to join or not join a trade union. The signing of the charter led to the introduction of a series of changes in employment law. One of the first examples of this was the introduction of the National Minimum Wage in 1998.

It was also widely expected that the Labour Government would reverse much of the legislation introduced by the Conservative Government that curbed the powers of the trade unions. In fact, it did very little reversal, but did continue with the ongoing introduction of new legislation. There were specific themes to some of these introductions. For example, the concern over the increasing difficulty for employees in balancing home–work life led to the introduction of a number of pieces of legislation known as 'family friendly' policies.

In May 2010 a Coalition Government, formed by the Conservative and Liberal Democrat parties, took office. This government took office at a time when the UK was starting to emerge from a deep recession. A key objective of this government was to return the country to economic growth. The government was concerned that the extensive legislation that there was in relation to employment and other areas of business was excessive and burdensome – particularly for small and medium-sized organisations.

In its first year of office the Coalition Government embarked on a review of legislation, including employment law. The Coalition Government introduced a number of measures to make the Employment Tribunal System run more efficiently (some would argue that the measures have actually made it more difficult to bring a claim to the Employment Tribunal, making it easier for employers to act unlawfully without sanction). We will look at these measures in detail in Chapter 2.

In 2015 the Coalition Government was replaced by a Conservative Government. There have been some important changes to the law introduced by the Conservative Government, relating to areas such as industrial action, but the main challenge for it is the outcome of the referendum on EU membership, which took place on 23 June 2016. A majority of those who voted in the UK voted to leave the EU, and this process (Brexit) is currently in place – we will look at the impact of this in more detail later in this chapter.

In addition to the ongoing debates about Brexit the government commissioned Matthew Taylor (Chief Executive for the Royal Society of Arts) to chair a review of modern working practices. The report from this review was published in the summer of 2017 and is titled 'Good Work: The Taylor Review of Modern Working Practices'. In February 2018 the government announced four separate consultations, looking at how the recommendations of this review could be implemented.

The review is wide ranging but has a central theme of looking at the way people are working today. For example, we have an increased number of individuals working in the so-called 'gig economy', without a guarantee of hours of work or income. One recommendation from the review is that there is a new National Minimum Wage rate introduced for such individuals, giving them more pay to reflect their lack of security. In Chapter 3 of this book we look at the complexities of defining employment status. The review recommends that the definitions of employment status are reviewed. We await the outcome of the consultations, but we can be sure that there will be further change coming to employment law.

This relentless change, both in introducing and repealing legislation, has serious implications for those involved with employment law. Employers complain that there is a never-ending amount of bureaucracy to face, and human resource (HR) practitioners struggle to keep up with the changes. In this book we examine current legislation, anticipate some of the planned changes – and try to understand the impact on organisations of the major pieces of legislation.

 Explore further

Read the report from the Taylor review: 'Good Work: The Taylor Review of Modern Working Practices'. It can be found at https://www.gov.uk/ government/publications/good-work-the-taylor-review-of-modern-working-practices

 Task

As you have read, employment law is ever changing. Ensure that you keep abreast of these changes as you study. The CIPD website is an excellent source of information, especially the 'Employment Law' section, which is specifically for CIPD members.

It is clear that employment law is affected by a number of external factors, and one of these is the political party that is in government. In looking at the development of employment law it is important think about its purpose. Do we need employment law at all?

To answer that question we need to think about a situation where there is no law. Think for a moment of non-employment situations: if there is no law that says that murder is wrong do we become a dangerous society? If there is no law that puts a speed limit on the roads do fatalities increase?

The same reflections can be applied to employment law. If we have no law that stops employers from discriminating, or dismissing employees unfairly, does the workplace become a bad place to work? Do employees have no protection, and no job security? All societies need rules and agreed ways of working – that is what employment law brings to the workplace.

This stereotypical view might have been supported by policies in the past, but is certainly not as clear in today's political climate. It is certainly true, however, that the development of legislation does impact on the way that the employer and employee manage their relationship. Many employers would argue that employees now have too many rights. As we work through the book, think back to this point – and think about whether the balance in the employment relationship brought about by legislation is fair or not.

1.2 Criminal and civil law

Employment law is primarily governed by civil law. However, there is some criminal law that relates to employment matters, and for that reason the issue of criminal law cannot be ignored.

1.2.1 Criminal law

Criminal law focuses on the punishment of crimes, usually through proceedings brought by the Crown Prosecution Service. There is also the possibility of proceedings being brought by other bodies, such as the Health and Safety Executive. The punishment brought by criminal proceedings can be imprisonment or fines. In employment law the main cases of criminal law are brought through:

- The Trade Union and Labour Relations (Consolidation) Act 1992, some aspects of which relate to illegal activity during industrial action (we examine this in Chapter 10).
- The Data Protection Act 2018 – for improper use of confidential and personal data (we examine this in Chapter 11).
- The Health and Safety at Work Act 1974 – for criminal breaches of health and safety legislation (we examine these in Chapter 12).
- The Racial and Religious Hatred Act 2006, which makes it unlawful to incite racial hatred. Although the legislation relating to racial and religious discrimination (see Chapter 7) is likely to cover most situations in the workplace, there is the possibility that proceedings could be brought under this legislation as well.
- The Corporate Manslaughter and Corporate Homicide Act 2007, which allows companies and individual directors to be prosecuted if a fatality occurs as a result of serious breaches of health and safety responsibilities (see Chapter 12).

Criminal proceedings are usually first brought in the Magistrates' Court. Serious offences can be referred directly to the Crown Court. Appeals on issues of fact go to the Crown Court, whereas appeals on issues of law go to the High Court. From here any further appeals go to the Court of Appeal and then on to the Supreme Court. This structure is shown in Figure 1.1.

Figure 1.1 Structure of the criminal court system

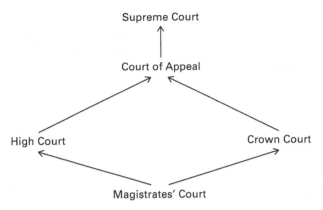

Examples of criminal cases relating to employment law are:

- *HSE v Compass Engineering Ltd and Kaltenbach Ltd* (2011)
  A breach of the Health and Safety at Work Act (1974) led to the Health and Safety Executive bringing a case against Compass Engineering and Kaltenbach. An employee looked to check work coming along a moving line and was dragged through a 12.5-centimetre gap. This occurred because of insufficient guarding. Compass (the employer) was fined £45,000 plus £24,000 costs and Kaltenbach (who installed the machinery) was fined £30,000 plus £16,000 costs.

- *R v The Mansfield Justices ex parte Sharkey and others* (1984) IRLR 496
  Nine striking miners, who were members of the Yorkshire National Union of Mineworkers, were arrested under the Public Order Act 1936. They were remanded on bail, with the condition that they did not visit any place for the purposes of picketing in relation to the existing employment dispute. They were allowed, however, to picket peacefully at their usual place of work.

- *R v Cotswold Geotechnical Holdings Ltd* (2011) Crown Court 020110037
  This was the first prosecution of corporate manslaughter under the Corporate Manslaughter and Corporate Homicide Act 2007. A young geologist was working with one of the directors of the company, taking soil samples from a trench that had been dug. The director left for the evening, leaving the geologist working alone. The sides of the trench collapsed, burying the geologist and killing him. The company was found negligent, in both the way that the trench had been dug and in leaving a young employee working there alone. It was fined £385,000.

 Task

During your studies take note of any employment cases you read that relate to criminal law. It is unlikely that you will find a great number of such cases, because most employment cases will relate to civil law.

1.2.2 Civil law

Most employment law will fall under the remit of civil law. Civil law is concerned with resolving a dispute between two parties. Most employment disputes will be resolved in the Employment Tribunal, which deals only with civil cases. In resolving the dispute a monetary award can be given to the wronged party (referred to as 'compensation' or 'damages'), and in some cases an injunction can be made. Civil law is based on the law of contract, of tort and of property.

Contract

In employment law a contract is made between the employer and the employees, consisting of a number of obligations on both sides of the agreement. If one of those obligations is breached in some way, there can be a dispute under the law of contract. For example:

- *Morrow v Safeway Stores plc* (2002) IRLR 9
  Morrow was a bakery production manager and had been criticised on a number of occasions for not doing her job correctly. On one occasion her manager gave her a public 'dressing down' in front of colleagues and a customer. She resigned and successfully claimed constructive dismissal, arguing that the humiliating treatment was a breach of her contract, namely the implied term of mutual trust and confidence.

Tort

A tort is a wrong, such as the wrong of negligence. If an employee is injured at work through the negligence of the employer (the employer has provided inadequate equipment, for example), a claim would be made based on the law of tort. For instance:

- *Walker v Northumberland County Council* (1995) IRLR 35
  In this case Walker was employed as a social worker by Northumberland County Council. Because of the stressful nature of his work, and the lack of support he received, he suffered a nervous breakdown. While he was absent from work due to this breakdown he agreed with his employers a series of measures to help him in his work. He returned to work, but the support agreed was withdrawn. Walker suffered a further breakdown. It was found that his employers had been negligent in not giving him the support that he needed to carry out his duties. (We examine this case in more detail in Chapter 12.)

Property

If an employee uses inventions designed at work – under the employer's copyright – for personal gain, there can be a claim under the law of property. For example:

- *Reiss Engineering v Harris* (1985) IRLR 23
  Harris was a sales manager working for a company that sold valves. Reiss Engineering did not have a research and design department, and had never de-

signed a valve or improvements or modifications to a valve. Harris invented a new type of valve. Reiss Engineering claimed that the patent for the new valve should belong to them because, they claimed, Harris had invented it during the course of his normal duties. The court held that it had not been part of Harris's normal duties to invent anything, and hence the patent belonged to Harris. (We examine this case in more detail in Chapter 11.)

In employment law most cases are first heard in an Employment Tribunal. If there is an appeal, which must be based on a point of law, it is referred to the Employment Appeal Tribunal. Any further appeal is directed to the Court of Appeal and then to the Supreme Court. This system is shown in Figure 1.2.

A civil law claim that is not related to employment is first brought in the County Court. Any appeal is then directed to the Court of Appeal and finally the Supreme Court. Not all employment-related issues must start in an Employment Tribunal. For example, certain cases of wrongful dismissal (see Chapter 9) can be brought in the County Court or the High Court, as well as in the Employment Tribunal (a wrongful dismissal claim with a value of £25,000 or more cannot be brought in the Employment Tribunal). This structure is shown in Figure 1.3.

Figure 1.2 Court system for employment-related claims

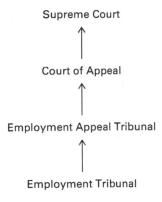

Figure 1.3 Court structure for civil claims

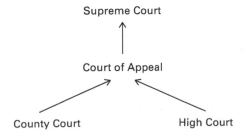

1.3 Sources of law

Legislation is created in a number of different ways, as set out below.

1.3.1 Statute

Statutes are Acts of Parliament, and they are the main source of legislation. A recent example of a statute is the Trade Union Act 2016.

An Act of Parliament has to go through a lengthy process before it is finally accepted as statute. Typically, it starts as a Green Paper, which is a consultation document. This Green Paper will pass through a number of parliamentary committees, depending on the range of its content. When all comments have been received and considered, it is issued as a White Paper, which is a statement of the government's policy. This White Paper (known as a bill) is then discussed and reviewed by the House of Commons, and then the House of Lords, before being finalised. It becomes a statute when it receives royal assent.

Some statutes are implemented immediately. However, it is more common for there to be a time lag between the royal assent and the enforcement of the content. This is usually for the practical reason that time is needed to implement the requirements. For example, the Trade Union Act 2016 received royal assent on 4 May 2016 but was not brought into force until 1 March 2017. Statute is created for a variety of reasons. Some are directly related to the political policies of the party in government – eg the National Minimum Wage Act 1998 was a result of a manifesto promise of the Labour Government to put in place a minimum basic wage (which was also driven by the signing of the Social Charter).

Some statute results from British membership of the EU – as we discuss later in this chapter. Some statute results from the need to address a growing area of legislation that has become difficult to manage. For example, the Equality Act 2010 replaced nine major pieces of discrimination legislation and more than 100 minor pieces of discrimination legislation, with the aim of making the whole area of discrimination legislation less complex.

Some statute results from concern regarding specific aspects of working life in the UK. For example, a significant part of the Employment Act 2002 related to family-friendly policies (which the Labour Government of 1997–2010 highlighted as a major concern). Prior to introducing this legislation the government undertook a survey of working life. It picked up on concerns about quality of family life and about the amount of time that parents were spending with their children. The content relating to maternity leave, paternity leave, adoption leave and flexible working were all intended to address this issue of the balance between working and family life.

1.3.2 Codes of practice

Codes of practice are not law, but if they are broken the court would expect to see a good reason for such a breach. They are, therefore, important and should be breached only if there is good reason for doing so. The most commonly quoted example of a code of practice, although not relevant to employment law, is the Highway Code.

Employment codes are issued by a number of bodies such as Acas (see section 1.5.1). An important code of practice (that we will look at in some detail in Chapter 8) is the Acas Code of Practice: Disciplinary and Grievance Procedures. If an employer does not follow this procedure when dismissing an employee, the dismissal will not be automatically unfair but the employer might struggle to persuade an employment tribunal that a fair process has been followed, and any compensation that is awarded can be increased by up to 25 per cent.

 Task

Look at the Acas website (www.acas.org.uk) and read one of the codes of practice that are there.

Become familiar with the style and content of codes of practice.

1.3.3 Common law

This is also known as case law and is law that is derived from judges' decisions, rather than being created by Parliament. Case law is law based on precedents following from judgments in previous cases. A precedent set by a court can be 'binding' or 'persuasive'.

It is 'binding' if it is set by the Court of Appeal, the Supreme Court or the Court of Justice of the European Union. This means that in any court hearing a case based on similar principles has to make its judgment in accordance with the principle that has already been set. This only changes if an appeal is made against a decision that results in a change in the decision, or if future statute alters the principle that has been set.

It is 'persuasive' if the judgment comes from the ruling of a lower level of court (eg the Employment Appeal Tribunal). In such a situation due respect must be given to a previous judgment but, if there is good reason, the principle of the ruling does not have to be followed.

Most cases give judgments specific to the person before them. For example, I could take a case to the Employment Tribunal saying that my contract of employment expressly stated that I should be paid my full holiday entitlement on leaving the company. The company did not pay that holiday pay. There is no dispute over the calculation of the holiday pay: the only issue is whether the money should have been paid. The tribunal reads my contract, agrees that the money is owed and orders that it should be paid. That judgment affects me alone. However, a case could be brought to the Court of Appeal where there is a disagreement over the legal definition of holiday pay (as defined in the Working Time Regulations 1998). In determining what the correct definition of holiday pay is, the Court of Appeal is determining how the law should be interpreted – and is setting a precedent that is then binding on any subsequent cases relating to the definition of holiday pay. This is case law.

Case law is interpreted by the most senior court in the relevant legal system, so if a decision is overturned by an appeal court that decision forms case law and not the decisions of previous courts. For example, if one of the parties thinks that the decision made in an Employment Tribunal is wrong, it can appeal to the Employment Appeal Tribunal (EAT). The EAT reviews the decision made by the Employment Tribunal and either supports it or changes it. If the EAT changes it, the EAT's interpretation takes precedence over the Employment Tribunal, and the case law is based on the EAT's decision.

If one party is unhappy with the reversal of the decision made by the EAT, he/she can appeal to the Court of Appeal. Any decision made by the Court of Appeal overrules the EAT. Ultimately, a decision of the Supreme Court overrules all previous decisions. As we will see later in this chapter, the only route of appeal beyond the Supreme Court is the Court of Justice of the European Union.

Note that case law cannot contradict statute.

1.4 The role of Europe

As already noted, the UK carried out a referendum on 23 June 2016 on the future of its membership of the EU, and the majority vote was for the UK to leave. That process is currently in place, with the UK due to leave the EU on 29 March 2019.

The government has created the European Union (Withdrawal) Bill 2018, which received royal assent in June 2018. This Bill means that all existing EU law will be copied across into domestic UK law the day after the UK leaves the EU. The UK will then be able to repeal or amend the law as it wants, and when it wants.

This is an important point. The day after Brexit employment law will not change (unless the UK makes a specific decision to change something). However, the difference will be that the UK can make changes if it wants to do so. For example, the Working Time Regulations 1998 were introduced because of the EU Working Time Directive. There is a limit on the working week of 48 hours (although employees can opt out from this limitation, as we will see in Chapter 5). Whilst the UK is part of the EU it cannot change the 48-hour limit. Once the UK is no longer part of the EU it will be able to change the 48 hours (subject to any limitations that are negotiated as part of the Brexit deal).

For now, however, the UK remains part of the EU and therefore it is important to understand the impact of this membership on employment law.

 Explore further

Keep up to date with developments relating to Brexit by going to www.cipd.co.uk and selecting 'Brexit Hub'. This is a selection of resources that the CIPD is developing to assist all those working in HR who need to know about Brexit.

The UK has been a member of the European Community (EC) since 1973. As already noted, the Labour Government signed the Social Charter on coming into power in 1997. The Social Charter is a declaration that the member state will adhere to a basic level of rights as spelled out in the 1957 Social Chapter. These basic rights include a right to a basic wage, the rights to join or not join a trade union, the right to strike, and the right to be consulted by employers. The Social Charter is important because it is the basis for many of the directives that have been introduced by the EC. (Note: although the Labour Government left office in 2010, the signing of the Social Charter remains and the UK still has to abide by the basic rights within this legislation.)

European law is given precedence over UK national law. Therefore, if there is any dispute between UK national law and European law, the European law will be enforced. There are four main sources of European law:

- Treaties are the primary source of all European law. A treaty is a framework within which a member state can implement legislation. The first treaty was the Treaty of Rome (1957), which created the European Economic Community (as it was then named). Subsequent treaties include the Maastricht Treaty (1992) and the Treaty of Amsterdam (1997).

- Regulations automatically become part of the national laws of the member state by virtue of treaties previously entered into. There might be a requirement for the member state to pass legislation to incorporate them. Examples of regulations are the Working Time Regulations 1998 and the Part-time Workers (Prevention of Less Favourable Treatment) Regulations 2000.

- Directives lay down objectives that the member state is 'directed' to implement by making them part of national law. The member state decides exactly how it will achieve this. There is usually a time period given in which to carry out the implementation, and there have been occasions on which an extension to this time period has been negotiated. If the member state does not implement the directive in the given time period, it can be forced to pay damages to any individual who has suffered loss as a result of the non-implementation. Examples of directives are the Working Time Directive 1993 and the Information and Consultation Directive 2002.

- Decisions relate to specific member states, individuals or organisations. They are binding.

Within the European Community, the European Commission and the European Parliament introduce new legislation. The Court of Justice of the European Union (formerly known as the European Court of Justice) has an important role in defining and interpreting EC law. The final court of appeal in a member state can refer a case to the Court of Justice for an interpretation of a specific aspect of European law. The Court of Justice makes the ruling and then returns it to the courts in the member state for that ruling to be acted upon.

A good example of this is *Kaltoft v The Municipality of Billund* (2014):

- *Kaltoft v The Municipality of Billund* (2014) EUECJ C-354/13
  This case was referred to the Court of Justice of the European Union by the Danish courts. Kaltoft was obese, and he argued that he had been dismissed from his job as a childminder because of his weight and that this was disability discrimination. The Court of Justice was asked to determine whether obesity

could be a disability. The court ruled that if obesity has reached the point where it causes physical or psychological limitations then it could be a disability, although obesity will not always be a disability. Just a short while later, this judgment was applied by the Northern Ireland Employment Tribunal in the case of *Bickerstaff v Butcher* (2015) NIIT/92/14 when the tribunal concluded that Bickerstaff, who had a body mass index of 48.5, was disabled and had suffered harassment.

 Task

Keep track of the Brexit discussions, and in particular any decisions that impact employment. A particular area to look out for is decisions relating to immigration. This will impact on the labour market that employers have available to them for recruitment purposes.

The Court of Justice carries out a number of additional functions, including:

- Hearing challenges that a member state has failed to fulfil some aspect of a treaty; an individual or a group of individuals can bring these challenges.
- Hearing complaints regarding the way in which European law has been interpreted and applied.

The European Court of Human Rights (ECHR), which is part of the Council of Europe, is the court that hears any claims that an individual, or group of individuals, has suffered a violation of the European Convention on Human Rights 1950. Much of this convention has been incorporated into the Human Rights Act 1998. In the same way as with the Court of Justice, any legislation of a member state that is found to be incompatible with European law is referred back to the government of the member state for amendments to be made to national legislation.

An example of a ruling by the ECHR is:

- *Barbulescu v Romania* (2017) ECHR 61496/08
  Barbulescu was asked by his employer to set up a company Yahoo Messenger account as a means for customers to communicate with the company. The company had a strict rule that no employee could use the company computers, telephone, fax and similar equipment for personal use. Barbulescu used the Yahoo Messenger account to send personal messages to his brother and girlfriend (when they were transcribed they amounted to around 45 pages of messages). He was dismissed. Barbulescu successfully argued that the employer had breached his privacy (Article 8 of the Human Rights Act 1998) by accessing his personal messages without first telling him that they were going to do so.

The Human Rights Act 1998 contains a number of articles that are explored in detail in Chapter 11.

Explore further

Look at recent changes in employment legislation in the UK. Distinguish which are the result of European directives and which are not. Are there underlying differences relating to the two sources of legislation? Now select any other member state of the EU. Contrast and compare key areas of legislation of this member state and of the UK. Are there any areas of commonality appearing? If not, how can that be explained?

1.5 Key institutions

There are a number of institutions within the UK that have a direct impact on the creation and workings of employment law. These include the following.

1.5.1 Acas

Acas (Advisory, Conciliation and Arbitration Service: www.acas.org.uk) is a service funded by the government but independent of any government control. Acas is run by a council of 12 members from business, unions and the independent sector. It has about 800 employees working from 11 regional offices and a head office in London. It has been in existence since 1974.

Acas is a service for both the employer and the employee. Its duty is to remain impartial and to try to help both sides find solutions to their difficulties. Specifically, the functions include:

- Advice – any person can phone Acas for advice about an employment-related matter. For example, an employer might phone to ask for information about recent developments in employment law, or an employee might phone asking for advice in taking a claim to the Employment Tribunal.

- Conciliation – the process of bringing both sides of a dispute together and helping them to find a solution to their difficulties. Acas might perform this role before any conflict has actually occurred, or when it has already commenced. Acas has statutory powers to offer conciliation when talks to resolve disputes break down. In particular, Acas tries to help both parties in an employment dispute to resolve the dispute before the case reaches the Employment Tribunal. All cases lodged with the Employment Tribunal are copied to Acas, and it will contact both parties and try to help them to reach an agreement. Acas also runs the Early Conciliation service, which almost all potential claimants to the Employment Tribunal must engage with before they can proceed in making a claim. We explore this service in some detail in Chapter 2.

- Arbitration – the process of bringing in an independent body (eg Acas) and letting it evaluate the situation and determine a solution. Although there is not always a legal requirement to implement the recommended solution, there is a moral obligation. This process can only work if both sides agree to be bound by the process of arbitration. Acas also works through the process of mediation. In mediation the mediator will suggest solutions to the problem, but the parties are not bound to accept any of the solutions.

- Training – Acas runs a significant amount of training sessions, aimed at both employers and employee representatives. As well as running national training events, Acas will work specifically with an organisation to provide tailored training sessions or consultancy advice.
- Research – Acas is involved in various areas of research relating to employment issues. This research is aimed at helping employers to run organisations more efficiently.

 Task

Look through the Acas website (www.acas. org.uk) and make sure you are familiar with the range of services that it provides. You might find it particularly interesting to read its annual report.

1.5.2 *The Central Arbitration Committee (CAC)*

The CAC (www.gov.uk/government/organisations/central-arbitration-committee) is an independent body with statutory powers whose specific role is to determine the outcome of applications relating to the statutory recognition or derecognition of trade unions for collective bargaining purposes (see Chapter 10). The CAC is also responsible for determining the outcome of disputes between employers and employees over the disclosure of information for collective bargaining purposes and in dealing with complaints relating to the establishment of works councils in the UK. All of these issues are looked at in more detail in Chapter 10.

The committee consists of a chairperson, 10 deputy chairpersons, 16 members representing workers and 16 members representing employers. The Secretary of State for Trade and Industry appoints the committee after consulting with Acas.

1.5.3 *The Equality and Human Rights Commission*

The Equality and Human Rights Commission (www.equalityhumanrights.com) was set up in October 2007 as a result of the Equality Act 2006, and replaced three former organisations:

- the EOC (Equal Opportunities Commission);
- the CRE (Commission for Racial Equality);
- the DRC (Disability Rights Commission).

The three former organisations had all worked to combat discrimination but, with the growing range of discrimination legislation (explored in Chapters 6 and 7), it was perceived that there was a need for one organisation that covered all aspects of discrimination. It was also considered that one organisation would be able to have greater impact than three separate organisations.

The role of the key institution relating to health and safety (the Health and Safety Executive) is detailed in Chapter 12. It is important to note that both the employer and the employee can seek advice and support from all the bodies outlined in this chapter. They operate without bias and are not permitted to promote the interests of one side of the employment relationship.

1.6 Explanation of common terms

There are some standard terms used in employment law that it is important to understand (you can also refer to the Glossary at the end of this book, which defines a wide range of terms used in employment law):

- An *Act* is always cited in a standard way – that is, the name of the Act followed by the date the Act was passed. For example: the Equality Act 2010. Capital letters should be used for each word – so it should be Equality Act 2010 not equality act 2010.
- The person who brings a case to a tribunal is called the *claimant*.
- The employer who defends a case in the tribunal is called the *respondent*.
- The person who brings a case to the appeal court is called the *appellant*.
- A case is always described as one party '*versus*' the other party, and the date it was heard in the court follows in parentheses (round brackets). For example: *Delaney v Staples* (1992).
- If a case is brought by the state it is listed as *R v A N Other* (2003), where *R* stands for 'Regina' (the queen, as head of state).
- *Ex parte* literally means 'from a party' – meaning that only one party is making the initial application. So in the case *R v Secretary of State ex parte Equal Opportunities Commission* (1994), the challenge was coming from a party called the Equal Opportunities Commission.

When cases are cited in literature, only a brief description of the facts is usually given. To read the full report you must refer to the given source. For example, *Delaney v Staples* (1992) IRLR 191 means that the full script can be found in the *Industrial Relations Law Reports* (www.irsonline.co.uk). A case followed by 'ICR' is reported in the *Industrial Case Reports* (www.lawreports.co.uk). (The printed versions of these reports can be found in many university libraries.)

 Task

It is important that throughout your studies you keep abreast of the changes and developments in employment law. This can be achieved by reading such publications as the CIPD magazine *People Management*, reading quality newspapers, and browsing websites already listed for specific employment institutions. Decide now what will be your main sources of reference and be sure to make regular referrals to them.

KEY LEARNING POINTS

1 Employment law is a rapidly changing area of law and the direction of changes is affected by the government of the UK.

2 Employment law is primarily governed by civil law, although there are situations in which criminal law might be applied. Civil law is based on the law of contract, tort and property.

3 Legislation is created by statute, common (case) law and the influence of codes of practice.

4 The UK is going to leave the EU, but until that happens European law has precedence over UK law.

Useful websites

www.acas.org.uk – Advisory, Conciliation and Arbitration Service

www.gov.uk/government/organisations/department-for-business-innovation-skills – Department for Business, Innovation and Skills

www.gov.uk/government/organisations/central-arbitration-committee – Central Arbitration Committee

www.cbi.org.uk – Confederation of British Industry

www.cipd.co.uk – Chartered Institute of Personnel and Development

www.curia.europa.eu – Court of Justice of the European Union

www.gov.uk/government/organisations/department-for-education – Department for Education and Skills

www.echr.coe.int – European Court of Human Rights

www.equalityhumanrights.com – Equality and Human Rights Commission

www.tuc.org.uk – Trades Union Congress

It is important to note that some legislation and legal terms are different in Scotland from those in England and Wales. A number of the websites direct Scottish students to particularly relevant information. In addition, it might be helpful to access the following specific websites:

www.scottish.parliament.uk

www.scottishlaw.org.uk

Examples to work through

1   Is it true that employment law in the UK is primarily driven by initiatives from the EU? Justify your answer. To what extent will Brexit change employment law? What changes do you think most employers and employees want to see?

2   How much is employment law driven by the political stance of the government? In answering this question, explore the changes that the Coalition Government made to employment law.

3   Explore the various approaches that Acas uses to help resolve employment disputes. Which approaches seem to be most valuable for both the employer and the employee?

02
The Employment Tribunals and the Employment Appeal Tribunal

CHAPTER OBJECTIVES

The objectives of this chapter are:

- to analyse the history of the Employment Tribunals;
- to explain the operation of the Employment Tribunals;
- to explore recent changes to the Employment Tribunals;
- to outline the impact of the Employment Appeal Tribunal.

2.1 The history of the Employment Tribunals

The Employment Tribunals were created by the Industrial Training Act 1964 (and at this stage were named 'industrial tribunals'). They were initially created to hear appeals relating to the assessment of training levies under this 1964 Act. Over the next three years their brief was extended to include such things as the determination of the right to a redundancy payment and issues surrounding the lack of, or inaccuracy of, a written statement of terms and conditions of employment.

In the mid-1960s the government became concerned about the number of unofficial strikes, wage inflation and the general existence of restrictive practices in industry. It commissioned Lord Donovan to lead an investigation into these issues. As a result of the investigation, the Donovan Report was published in 1968 and gave a comprehensive overview of industrial relations at the time.

As part of the recommendations in the report, Donovan saw the need for an industrial tribunal system to which employees could bring their grievances. He described this system as needing to be easily accessible, informal, speedy and inexpensive.

At first the industrial tribunal system was just this. However, over the years the workload of the tribunals has increased significantly, and many believe the system has moved far from the ideal that Donovan initially described.

It is easy to see some of the key reasons that the workload increased so dramatically. When the Donovan Report was published, there was no legislation relating to unfair dismissal (introduced in 1971), sex discrimination (1975) or race discrimination (1976). Today, more than half of the claims to the Employment Tribunals relate to these areas of legislation. In total, the Employment Tribunals have jurisdiction to hear cases relating to over 80 pieces of legislation, the most common being unfair dismissal.

Despite this increasing workload it was still hoped that the Employment Tribunals system could meet Donovan's ideal. The idea was that an employee who felt he/she had been badly treated by an employer should have the means to get an independent judgment on the issue, quickly and without cost. How are those criteria being met today?

2.1.1 *Easily accessible*

The Donovan Report suggested that there should be Employment Tribunals operating in all major industrial centres, making them easily accessible. In 1971 Employment Tribunals were heard in 84 locations. Today there are 33 centres at which Employment Tribunals are heard. There is also the ability to hear cases almost anywhere if people have particular needs (eg disability) that make it difficult to attend a permanent centre. It is difficult, therefore, to give a specific number of centres, but the system is certainly still very accessible to those who want to use it.

Accessibility can also refer to the ease of registering a claim with the Employment Tribunals. The system is open to everyone, and the actual process of registering a claim is relatively straightforward (as we see in section 2.2). Forms to apply to the Employment Tribunals (ET1) are readily available at places such as Citizens' Advice (it is also possible to complete the ET1 online at www.gov.uk/employment-tribunals/make-a-claim).

2.1.2 *Informal*

This is maybe the area that now least meets the original Donovan ideal. There are definitely ways in which the Employment Tribunals system is much less formal than other court systems. There are no wigs and gowns, and the hearing rooms are less imposing than many courtrooms. In higher courts the parties are expected to present their case, and challenge the case of the opposite side. An unrepresented claimant who is struggling to explain his/her case in the Employment Tribunal is usually given some assistance by the Employment Judge to make sure that all facts are communicated (but the judge will not give any advice on how to put a case).

However, it is widely accepted that the Employment Tribunals have moved away from the picture of the potentially wronged employee presenting his/her grievance in a simple manner, with the employer responding to the accusations. It is now very common for one or both parties to be represented by solicitors or barristers, and the simple arguments are often weighed down by substantial legal arguments. This has impacted on the aspect of informality – but is probably inevitable, given the growing amount of legislation relating to employment issues.

2.1.3 Speedy

The original Donovan ideal was of a very quick resolution to the grievance. This allowed the employee and employer to put the issue behind them and continue with a good working relationship or, if the employee had left the employer, allowed the employee to resolve the issue and move on to find new employment.

All the Employment Tribunals have targets to hear claims speedily. However, the actual timing between the claim being lodged and the hearing taking place will vary depending on how many days the case is listed for, and also depending on where in the country the claim is to be heard (some centres are busier than others). The large number of claims that were seen a few years ago certainly slowed down the process. When fees were introduced and the number of claims dropped the process speeded up. Now fees have been removed we might start to see some slowing down again.

2.1.4 Inexpensive

This is a contentious issue. On 29 July 2013 fees were introduced to bring a claim to the Employment Tribunal. The fees were set at two levels (depending on the complexity of the case). The fees were paid in two stages, and in total were £390 for a straightforward claim (eg unlawful deduction from wages) and £1,200 for a more complex claim (eg unfair dismissal). There were also fees for other services, such as making a claim to the Employment Appeals Tribunal. There was a fee remission process for those who struggled to pay and met the criteria to have the fee waived.

From the very introduction of the fees, Unison, the trade union, challenged them in the courts. The first challenge came to the High Court in October 2013, with Unison putting forward a number of arguments primarily that:

1 The fees made it excessively difficult, if not impossible, to exercise rights set out in EU law to bring a claim.

2 The fees made it excessively difficult, if not impossible, to bring a claim because they had been set so high (the fees were higher than those charged to bring similar levels of legal claims).

3 In introducing the fees the government breached the Public Sector Equality Duty.

4 The fees were indirectly discriminatory. The argument here was that equal pay claims attract the higher level of fee. It is most likely that women will bring equal pay claims and, on average, women are paid less than men. Hence it was argued that this amounted to indirect sex discrimination.

There followed a number of additional court hearings, until the issue reached the Supreme Court in March 2017. The Supreme Court concluded that the fees restricted access to the courts, because of the level at which they had been set, and therefore breached a constitutional right. They noted the significant drop there had been in claims since the fees had been introduced (around 80 per cent) and they considered evidence that the remission scheme was not working. They also considered whether the introduction of the fees was actually encouraging employers to break the rules relating to employment.

Having considered all these points they ruled that the fees were unlawful. As a result, they were removed on 26 July 2017. The government has started a process of paying back the fees that claimants have paid over the four years that they were in place.

It is possible that the government will introduce a new approach to fees at some time in the future, maybe with much lower fees. However, at the time of writing there are no definite plans.

Although the removal of the fees does mean that bringing a claim to the Employment Tribunal is now free, there are other costs that can be incurred. If a claimant chooses to represent himself/herself, and many do, there are obviously no legal costs. If the claimant chooses to seek legal representation, legal aid is not available, and so the claimant must meet those costs. If the claimant is a member of a trade union, that union will typically represent the claimant, presuming that they do not feel the case is totally unfounded. In some cases the claimant might get representation or support from one of the bodies described in Chapter 1 – such as the Equality and Human Rights Commission.

In many courts the unsuccessful party has to meet all or part of the costs of the opposing side. In the Employment Tribunal this is unusual, although the tribunal must consider whether costs should be awarded if a party (or that party's representative) has acted vexatiously, abusively, disruptively or otherwise unreasonably in either the bringing or conducting of the proceedings. Costs can be awarded up to £20,000.

We can see, therefore, that there are ways in which the 'Donovan ideal' is far away from the reality of today. However, the Employment Tribunals are still a court at the lowest rung of the court hierarchy, and there is still a desire to ensure that the claimant is able to bring his/her case and present it in a simple format.

 Explore further

How relevant do you think the 'Donovan ideal' is for today's world of employment? Are the issues of accessibility, informality, speed and expense of primary importance? Any students particularly interested in this should read the original Donovan Report.

2.2 Early conciliation

As we noted briefly in Chapter 1, the process of early conciliation was introduced on 6 April 2014 as a result of the Enterprise and Regulatory Reform Act 2013. It became compulsory from 6 May 2014.

Unless the claim is for one of the following reasons, a claimant cannot make a claim to the Employment Tribunal without first engaging in the Early Conciliation process:

- The claim is against the Security Service, Secret Intelligence Service or GCHQ.
- Another person who the claimant is making the claim with already has an Early Conciliation number.
- The claim is against an insolvent employer.
- The claim involves multiple claimants.
- There is an application for interim relief.

The process of Early Conciliation starts by the claimant making contact with the service (run by Acas) either online or by telephone. At this stage all the claimant needs to do is give his/her name and contact details and the name and contact details of the employer he/she is making a claim against. He/she is then contacted within two working days by an Early Support Conciliation Officer who will explain the process and ask for more details about the claim. At this stage the potential claimant can state that he/she does not want to go any further with the Early Conciliation process and it comes to an end. The claimant is issued with an Early Conciliation Number and can then proceed to make a claim to the Employment Tribunal. It is clear, therefore, that there is no obligation to actually engage in conciliation.

If the claimant does want to proceed the claim is passed to a Conciliation Officer. This officer will contact the employer and will have one month to try to facilitate a settlement between the two parties. If the employer does not want to engage in conciliation the process comes to an end and the claimant is issued with an Early Conciliation Number.

If conciliation does take place it can be extended by up to two weeks if both parties agree. If a settlement is agreed then the claim goes no further. If no settlement is agreed, or if the employer refuses to engage with Early Conciliation, the claimant is issued with an Early Conciliation Number and can proceed with a claim to the Employment Tribunal.

It is important to note that, although the process is usually triggered by the claimant, the employer can also trigger the process. If the employer had identified that there was a dispute that was likely to lead to an Employment Tribunal claim it can trigger the process in exactly the same way as the claimant.

As we will see in section 2.3.1, a claim to the Employment Tribunal must be brought within a specified timescale (typically three months). When the Early Conciliation process is triggered the clock that is ticking away relating to this timescale is stopped. It does not start again until the process has ended and has been unsuccessful. If when the process has ended there is less than one month left to bring a claim to the Employment Tribunal this will always be extended so that the potential claimant has at least one month to bring a claim.

The Early Conciliation process is free.

 Explore further

Go to http://www.acas.org.uk/index. aspx?articleid=4028 to read more about the

Acas Early Conciliation process, as explained by Acas.

2.3 The process of the Employment Tribunals

The Employment Tribunal consists of an Employment Judge (previously called a chairperson) and two lay members. The Employment Judge is a fully qualified lawyer who either works full-time as an Employment Judge or practises law part-time. The lay members are appointed by the Secretary of State for Trade and Industry. They have extensive experience and knowledge of employment issues. In each Employment Tribunal one lay member will come from an 'employee' background (eg a trade union official) and one from an 'employer' background (eg an HR manager). The three members of the Employment Tribunal have an equal vote in deciding the outcome of each case.

Increasingly, the Employment Tribunal consists of just an Employment Judge. Unfair dismissal claims account for nearly half of all claims to the Employment Tribunal, and judges can now sit alone to hear these cases.

The Employment Tribunal only has jurisdiction to hear claims arising from employment in the UK. However, employees working overseas for a UK company might be covered by the Employment Tribunal process, depending on the nature of their contract.

- *Pervez v Macquarie Bank Ltd (London Branch) and Macquarie Group Limited* (2010) UKEAT/0246/10/CEA
  Pervez worked for a Hong Kong-based company and was seconded to work in London for an associated company. The secondment was not successful and he was told that the assignment would be terminated. Under the terms of his contract, he was required to resign if there were no other suitable roles available. There were none, but he refused to resign and hence he was dismissed. He brought various claims, including unfair dismissal.

  The Employment Tribunal found that it had no jurisdiction to hear the claim because the employer did not carry on business in England or Wales and the dismissal took place overseas. However, the EAT held that the phrase 'carry on business' had been assessed too narrowly. It ruled that the employer carried on business in England by seconding the claimant to work in London, and hence there was jurisdiction to hear the claim.

2.3.1 Bringing a claim to the Employment Tribunals

A claimant makes a claim to the Employment Tribunals by completing the claim form known as an ET1. This form must be lodged at the Employment Tribunals within three months of the alleged incident occurring.

For example, if the claimant is an employee who has been dismissed, the claim form must reach the Employment Tribunals within three months of the date of dismissal. If the claimant is alleging that an act of sex discrimination has occurred, the claim form must reach the Employment Tribunals within three months of the last date of the alleged act of discrimination.

There are certain claims where the three-month rule is extended. These include:

- unfair dismissal for unofficial industrial action (six months from date of dismissal);
- redundancy payment (six months from relevant date);
- equal pay (six months from termination of employment).

If the claim form is presented after this date, and the claimant can show a justifiable reason for the delay, the claim can be referred to a preliminary hearing of the Employment Tribunal to consider whether the reason is indeed justifiable and whether the case should go forward to a full hearing.

The Employment Tribunal does not readily extend the deadline; good reason has to be shown. An ignorance of employment rights or of the relevant time limits would rarely be seen as good reason. Potentially good reasons are that the claimant was too ill or distressed to make a claim, or that internal procedures within the organisation needed to be completed.

It is not possible to have clear rules on when a claim presented out of time could still be accepted, because the details of each claim will vary. The following cases illustrate this issue:

- *Avon County Council v Haywood-Hicks* (1978) ICR 646
  In this case the claimant was a polytechnic manager. He had been dismissed and he claimed it had been an unfair dismissal. His claim form was received by the Employment Tribunal six weeks after the three-month period had elapsed. He claimed that he was not aware of the existence of Employment Tribunals, and the possibility of bringing a claim, until he read an article in a newspaper. The Employment Tribunal ruled that he ought to have investigated his rights and ought to have claimed in time. They ruled that the idea that a well-educated and intelligent man had no idea of his rights 'offended their notion of common sense'. The time limit was therefore not extended in this case.

- *Shultz v Esso Petroleum Ltd* (1999) IRLR 488
  The claimant became depressed during the last six weeks of the three-month period for making a claim and claimed he was too depressed to instruct solicitors. The Employment Tribunal and the Employment Appeal Tribunal both found in favour of the respondent. However, the Court of Appeal held that it had not been practicable for the claimant to lodge a claim. The Court of Appeal stressed that the issue of practicability was paramount.

There are occasions when an employee is waiting for an internal appeals process to be completed before making a decision whether or not to make a claim to the Employment Tribunal. If the employer is slow at arranging an appeals hearing, and the process is not completed within three months of a dismissal, an Employment Tribunal might be prepared to extend the period for the claim to be made.

2.3.2 Responding to a claim in the Employment Tribunal

The relevant regional office of the Employment Tribunal receives the claim to the tribunal and a copy is sent to the respondent. The respondent is also sent a form known as an ET3 to complete and return to the Employment Tribunal within 28 days. Note that this is 28 days from the date that the form is sent, not the date that it is received. As well as confirming details of the claimant and the respondent, the ET3 requires the respondent to outline its defence of the claim. In accordance with the Employment Tribunal (Constitution and Rules of Procedure) Regulations 2013, if the respondent wants to request an extension to the time limit to make a response, it must do so within 28 days of receiving the claim form.

When the 28-day period has elapsed, the case will be listed for a hearing in the Employment Tribunal. If the respondent does not respond within the 28-day period, the case will still be listed, and the respondent has lost his/her right to take any further part in the proceedings. A copy of the completed ET3 is sent to the claimant by the Employment Tribunal.

The Employment Tribunal (Constitution and Rules of Procedure) Regulations 2013 prescribe that all claims and responses must be made on the ET1 and ET3 forms. The Employment Tribunals will reject any submissions that are not on these forms.

 Explore further

To find out more about the process of making and responding to a claim go to https://www.gov.uk/employment-tribunals – as well as explaining the process this is where individuals can make a claim, so this allows you to see the start of the process.

2.4 Preliminary hearing

There are circumstances in which a claim can be listed for some form of review prior to a full hearing. This is known as a preliminary hearing. Prior to 29 July 2013 there were two forms of hearings that could take place prior to a full hearing – a pre-hearing review and a case management discussion. These have now been merged into one, as a preliminary hearing.

The purpose of the preliminary hearing is to address points that need resolving before a full hearing can take place. So, for example, the hearing might consider whether an individual bringing a claim of disability discrimination is disabled, or whether someone who is alleging unfair dismissal is an employee (because non-employees cannot bring this claim).

In addition, the hearing might address arguments that the claim has no reasonable prospect of success. The Employment Judge running the hearing can strike out a claim, and can order a deposit to be paid by a claimant who wants to proceed with a claim that seems unlikely to succeed, or to be paid by a respondent who seems to be trying to defend the indefensible. The deposit cannot be more than £1,000, and it can be requested in relation to part of a claim. For example, if a claimant was bringing claims of unfair dismissal and race discrimination and the judge considered that the unfair dismissal claim had reasonable prospects of success whereas the race discrimination claim was unfounded, it could order a deposit to be paid just in relation to the discrimination claim. The claimant could then decide to just proceed with the unfair dismissal claim, or proceed with both and pay the deposit. The deposit is refunded if the party then goes on to win their case.

2.4.1 Settlement prior to the hearing

As already noted, copies of all ET1 and ET3 forms are sent to Acas, who have a statutory duty to try to facilitate a settlement. They will do this even though a settlement might have already been attempted through the Early Conciliation process.

It is usual for the conciliation to involve a payment of some financial sum, although reinstatement or re-engagement can occur in some cases. When both sides have agreed a settlement that is reached through Acas, it is confirmed on a form COT3 and the case is then withdrawn from the Employment Tribunal. The signing of the COT3 prohibits either side from pursuing any issue relating to the case.

Outside of the Acas process a settlement agreement can be reached (NB: prior to 29 July 2013 these agreements were referred to as compromise agreements; the change in name is hoped to make the purpose of the agreements clearer – this change was made as a result of the Enterprise and Regulatory Reform Act 2013). These agreements have the same status as a COT3 (ie the parties cannot take the claim any further) but are not negotiated through Acas. A settlement agreement must be in writing and can only be reached when the claimant has received advice from a relevant, independent adviser. An independent adviser is a qualified lawyer, a certified adviser from an independent trade union or a worker at an advice centre who has been certified as an adviser for this purpose.

The Enterprise and Regulatory Reform Act 2013 also introduced the new concept of 'confidential pre-termination negotiations'. This allows an employer to discuss a possible settlement with an employee prior to a termination of employment, without it being referred to as evidence should the situation subsequently result in an unfair dismissal claim. It could only be referred to if there had been 'improper behaviour' by one of the parties during the negotiations of the settlement.

Acas has produced a Code of Practice on Settlement Agreements and in this it defines 'improper behaviour' as the following (the list is said not to be inclusive):

- Harassment, bullying and intimidation, including through the use of offensive words or aggressive behaviour.
- Physical assault or the threat of assault.
- All forms of victimisation.
- Discrimination.
- Putting undue pressure on a party (for example, not allowing sufficient time to consider the terms).
- An employer saying that the employee will be dismissed if the settlement agreement is not accepted, if no form of disciplinary process has begun.
- An employee threatening to damage the employer's public reputation if the organisation does not accept the agreement (unless there is a whistleblowing issue).

 Explore further

The Acas Code of Practice on Settlement Agreements can be accessed at http://www. acas.org. uk/media/pdf/j/8/Acas-Code-of- Practice-on-Settlement-Agreements.pdf – read through this to gain more understanding of the process of reaching a settlement agreement.

2.5 Judicial mediation

Another way in which a claim can be settled before it is heard in the Employment Tribunal is through judicial mediation. An ET1 and ET3 are submitted in the usual way, and an Employment Judge decides, having read the documents, that it seems that the case could be resolved through mediation rather than through a full hearing. Judicial mediation is suggested to the two parties, and if they agree the regional Employment Judge makes the final decision as to whether the case is suitable for the process.

The two parties then come together with an Employment Judge who has been specifically trained in mediation. The judge facilitates the two parties in reaching a settlement, but does not give an opinion on the merits of the case. If the mediation is successful the claim goes no further. If it is not successful the claim is listed for a full hearing, in front of a different judge.

2.5.1 *Withdrawing a claim*

In addition, the claimant can withdraw his/her claim at any stage. The claimant simply has to inform the Employment Tribunal that there is no intention to pursue the claim further and does not have to give a reason for this decision.

2.6 The operation of the Employment Tribunals

Before the case is listed an Employment Judge will have reviewed the file and estimated how long the case will take to hear. A case might be listed for one day (or part day), but it is quite possible for a hearing to be listed for several days, especially if there are a group of claimants bringing a case against a respondent. Unless there are good reasons, all hearings are open to the public. Exceptions to this include situations where national security might be at risk or where a juvenile is involved in some way.

The Employment Tribunal will also send directions to the two parties. These typically set dates for the parties to prepare witness statements and documents, and to exchange them (we will look at this in more detail when we consider the preparation required for a tribunal hearing). If the parties do not comply with the directions they could be excluded from the hearing, or an 'unless order' can be given.

- *Riniker v City and Islington College Corporation* (2010) ET/0495/08/CEA
  Following a claim of unfair dismissal, the Employment Judge reviewed the case and issued the usual directions to both parties to disclose documents, exchange witness statements and for Riniker to prepare a schedule of loss. Riniker did not meet the requirements of the directions on a number of occasions.

  The Employment Judge then issued an 'unless order'. An 'unless order' requires a party to comply with specific directions by a certain date, and if the party does not do this the claim can then be struck out. Riniker still did not comply, but on the deadline day of the 'unless order' she wrote to the Employment Tribunal complaining about the 'unless order' and seeking to vary it. This request was reviewed by an Employment Judge, who considered the complaints. They were dismissed and hence her claim was struck out for non-compliance with the 'unless order'. The EAT later ruled that the judge had been entitled to issue the 'unless order', and hence dismissed Riniker's appeal.

After all the evidence has been presented, and all witnesses have been heard, the Employment Tribunal retires to reach a verdict. The verdict has to be a majority view, not necessarily a unanimous view. The Employment Judge's vote on the decision is not given more weight than the lay members. The Employment Tribunal can give its judgment in summary form (ie identifying just the key facts and concluding with the judgment) or give extended reasons.

Extended reasons give a thorough summary of the facts of the case, an explanation of the reasons behind the decision of the Employment Tribunal and a summary of the merits of the case. A party requiring extended reasons must request them within 14 days of the summary reasons being given. It is not unusual for summary reasons to be given before the parties leave the tribunal building. This will depend on the time available and the complexity of the case.

A decision will always be confirmed in writing to both parties. If the decision and reasons have been given orally then the reasons will only be given in writing if they are requested by one of the parties.

The decision of the Employment Tribunal is not only who has 'won' the case, but also what remedies are to be made. The remedies will vary according to the type of claim brought. For example, if the claim brought is for an unlawful deduction of wages, and the Employment Tribunal finds that there has been an unlawful deduction, the remedy will be to pay the money that has been unlawfully deducted.

If there is time after the judgment has been given, the Employment Tribunal can go on to consider the remedy. However, if there is no time, or if the Employment Tribunal wants the parties to provide it with documents that they do not have available, a separate remedy hearing will be arranged.

In cases such as unfair dismissal (when employment has ended) there are three remedy options available to the Employment Tribunal:

- Reinstatement – the employee returns to the job he/she had. This is a rare remedy because the relationship between the employee and the previous management is usually too badly damaged for a working relationship to be resumed. In addition, it is quite possible that the employee has gone on to find new employment while waiting for the hearing.

- Re-engagement – the employee returns to the company but in a different role. Again, this is rare because of the damage that has been done to the employment relationship.

- Compensation – the company is ordered to pay an amount of money to the employee. This is the most common remedy. Compensation consists of two elements, the basic award and the compensatory award. The basic award is calculated with reference to age and length of service (we will look at this in detail in Chapter 8). The compensatory award is determined by the Employment Tribunal, who considers issues such as the salary that the claimant has lost. Compensatory awards for unfair dismissal are currently (2018) capped at £83,682 or the employee's annual salary, whichever is lower. The alternative cap of the employee's annual salary was introduced to make claimants more realistic in the settlement process.

Task

Find out what preparations each party needs to make before a hearing. Looking at the Employment Tribunals section of the government website (www.gov.uk/employment-tribunals) will help in doing this.

2.7 Preparation for an Employment Tribunal hearing

As already noted, the claimant is required to submit an ET1 form. This starts the claim process. The ET1 is sent to the Employment Tribunal, not directly to the employer. The Employment Tribunal then sends a copy of the ET1 to the employer, along with a blank ET3 to be completed. As already noted, the ET3 must be completed and returned to the Employment Tribunal within 28 days.

The ET3 requires the employer to complete factual details such as the salary of the employee and the start date of employment. It also requires the employer to summarise the main points relating to the situation and the defence that is being put forward. An Employment Tribunal will not look favourably on an employer who presents a case in the actual hearing that differs from that which is summarised on the ET3. When the ET3 has been returned to the Employment Tribunal, the papers will be reviewed by an Employment Judge and a decision will be made as to whether the case should go directly to a full hearing or whether there is a need for a preliminary hearing.

Once the review of the papers has taken place, the Employment Tribunal will write to the parties, giving the date of the hearing and directions. The directions are likely to require:

- All witness statements to be written and exchanged with the other party within a specific timeframe. This is usually 14 days prior to the hearing. Witness statements also have to be sent to the Employment Tribunal within this timeframe. All witness statements should be included. The Employment Tribunal is entitled to refuse to hear any witness whose statement has not been submitted as required.

  (The taking of witness statements is an important process. It is important to ensure that only witnesses who have something relevant to say are included. For example, in a claim of unfair dismissal, those involved in the investigation, decision to dismiss and any appeal are clearly key. However, a line manager who can comment on something that happened a few years back that did not lead to the dismissal is not relevant. Witness statements should include all the evidence that the witness is going to give. Although some supplementary questions can be asked of the witness, this should be brief and should not be part of the substantial evidence.)

- A bundle of documents to be collated. One bundle is required, hence the employer and claimant have to co-operate over its collation. It is usual for the employer to take responsibility for putting the bundle together, because the employer usually has more resources available. The employer and claimant will usually contact each other with a list of documents that they propose to include. The documents should be presented in a folder or other format where the papers are kept in order, with all pages of the bundle numbered. It is usual to have an index at the front of the bundle.

- A schedule of loss to be produced by the claimant. This is a calculation of the compensation that the claimant is wanting as a result of the claim. If the claimant goes on to win the case this will be reviewed by the Employment Tribunal in a remedy hearing.

It is usual to number each paragraph of the witness statement, because this makes it easy to locate specific facts during cross-examination. It is also usual to refer to specific documents in the bundle while working through the statement. The witness should sign the statement.

On the day of the hearing the two parties arrive at the tribunal centre and sign in with the duty clerk. They will then be asked to wait in the appropriate waiting room. The clerk assigned to the case will come to the parties to check who is present, to determine whether the witnesses want to swear on the Bible or other holy book, or affirm, and to collect any papers that the parties have brought with them (although there should not really be any, as they should all have been submitted prior to the hearing).

When the tribunal is ready, the clerk will collect the parties and they will be taken into the tribunal room. The Employment Judge will then start with some introductions and deal with any preliminary issues. The hearing then commences. Each party takes it in turn to present their evidence. Each witness goes to the witness stand, affirms or swears on a holy book. It is usual for the tribunal to have read the witness statement prior to the hearing, but if they have not read it, or if they think it would be useful, they can ask a witness to read the statement. Each witness will be cross-examined by the other party, then the tribunal will ask any questions and then the witness's representative will be able to ask any final questions.

Once both sides have presented all of their evidence, each side will be given an opportunity to sum up their key points. In this summing-up the party should direct the Employment Tribunal to the key points of the case and to any relevant law. If the party is not represented by a lawyer and is representing herself/himself, the Employment Tribunal will not expect the party to refer to any law. The Employment Tribunal then adjourns and considers its decision.

 Task

Attend the local Employment Tribunal. Hearings typically start at 10 am, so arrive at least 15 minutes before. Explain to the clerk the purpose of your visit and ask advice for a suitable hearing to watch. Try to attend the full hearing and (if the decision is given that day) stay to hear the decision.

2.8 The role of the Employment Appeal Tribunal

If a party is dissatisfied with the outcome of a claim to the Employment Tribunal there are two options – to ask the tribunal to review the decision (a process referred to as reconsideration) or to make an appeal to the Employment Appeal Tribunal (EAT). A reconsideration can only be requested if there are specific points to be addressed – it cannot be requested just because the decision is not liked. An application for a reconsideration must be made within 14 days of the judgment being received.

- *Adeqbuji v Meteor Parking* (2010) UKEAT/1570/09
  Adeqbuji's claim to the Employment Tribunal was dismissed, but then fresh evidence came to light that could have changed the outcome. The EAT ruled that it was restricted to hearing appeals on points of law and that it could not hear the appeal. Rather, it recommended that Adeqbuji should apply to the tribunal for a reconsideration, given the new evidence.

Both the claimant and the respondent have the right to appeal against the decision of the Employment Tribunal. An appeal is referred to the EAT.

An appeal can only be made on a point of law or on a claim that the finding of the Employment Tribunal is 'perverse'. In addition, there can be an appeal if the decision has been subject to some fundamental flaw, such as when one member of the Employment Tribunal has been found to be known to one of the parties, or a member of the Employment Tribunal behaved in a way that clearly demonstrated bias, or if the Employment Tribunal refused to hear a witness, to allow cross-examination or to take note of a piece of relevant evidence. An appeal is also allowed if a member of the Employment Tribunal falls asleep during the hearing!

An appeal must be lodged within 42 days of the date that the extended reasons were sent to the appellant. The appeal is lodged by serving a notice of appeal along with a copy of the tribunal's decision and a copy of the extended reasons.

All appeals are listed for a preliminary hearing/directions (PHD). The main purpose of the PHD is to determine whether there are adequate grounds for appeal and, if there are, to give directions to both parties on preparation for the full appeal hearing.

In claiming that a finding was perverse, the appellant must show that the conclusion reached by the Employment Tribunal was one that no reasonable tribunal could have reached. This is very difficult to present successfully. For example:

- *Williams and others v Whitbread Beer Co Ltd* (1996) CA 22
  Williams was attending a works-related course and after a course session went to the hotel bar. He had a number of drinks and became loud and abusive to a fellow employee. When his manager told him to 'tone it down' he became loud and abusive towards his manager. Whitbread held a disciplinary hearing and Williams was summarily dismissed for gross misconduct.

  The Employment Tribunal found that the dismissal was not within the band of reasonable responses of a reasonable company, and hence concluded that the dismissal was unfair. Whitbread appealed and the appeal was upheld because the EAT concluded that a reasonable Employment Tribunal could have concluded that dismissal was a fair response.

  The Court of Appeal overturned the EAT's decision, stating that the role of the EAT was to determine whether the tribunal had reached a conclusion that no reasonable tribunal could have reached. They ruled that the tribunal's conclusion was reasonable, and even if it was not the conclusion the EAT would have reached, there was no evidence of 'perversity' and hence the decision of the Employment Tribunal had to stand.

An example of an appeal on a point of law can be found in:

- *Royal Bank of Scotland v McAdie* (2007) EAT 0208/06
  McAdie was dismissed on the grounds of ill health. However, she claimed that her dismissal was unfair because much of her illness had been caused by the poor way that her employer had dealt with grievances that she had raised. The Employment Tribunal agreed that her dismissal was unfair, because they concluded that no reasonable employer would have addressed the grievances in the way that they had been addressed, and the situation should therefore never have arisen.

  However, the EAT ruled that the ET had focused on the wrong point. Although it was certainly the case that there was a link between the grievance and the ill health, it did not mean that a dismissal could not be fair. The question was not whether the illness had been caused by the grievance, rather whether the dismissal could be fair. Given the situation of the long-term illness, it found that the dismissal was fair.

In 2007 Acas extended its conciliation services to cover certain categories of EAT cases, at the EAT's invitation. The type of cases where conciliation may be appropriate includes cases where:

- the employment relationship is ongoing;
- a case might be referred back to the Employment Tribunal;
- an appeal relates to monetary awards.

 Explore further

Many of the cases we will study in this book have been referred to appeal – some to a higher level of appeal than the Employment Appeal Tribunal. Look at a number of these cases and note the reasons that the appeals were made. What are the most common reasons that you encounter? Do you think there is any way in which the procedure of the Employment Tribunals ought to be changed in order to reduce the number of cases that go to appeal?

2.9 The number of claims to the Employment Tribunal

The number of claims to the Employment Tribunal has been of concern to successive governments. The concerns have partly been about the cost of running the tribunal service, but also about the amount of time that employers have been spending in defending claims. The Coalition Government, in particular, saw the fear of a tribunal claim being one of the reasons that small and medium-sized businesses were not prepared to make tough management decisions. Why had the number of claims grown so much?

- Every time new legislation is introduced, there are new claims that can be brought to the Employment Tribunal. For example, in October 2006 legislation making discrimination on the grounds of age unlawful was introduced. In 2010–11, 6,800 claims relating to age discrimination were made – claims that could not have been made prior to October 2006.

- Initiatives to reduce claims had not worked, or had actually resulted in more claims. For example, the Employment Act 2002 included statutory procedures to be followed when handling disciplinary or grievance situations in the workplace – these were introduced in 2004. One of the primary purposes of these two procedures was to push the resolution of differences in employment back into the workplace. The idea was that this would then reduce the number of claims to the Employment Tribunal because issues would be resolved without being escalated to this level.

   In February 2007 the Gibbons Report was published on research into the efficiency of the statutory procedures. The report concluded that the procedures had resulted in increased claims and that any advantages they might have brought had been outweighed by the problems.

   Part of the reason for the increased claims was the need for the courts to develop case law to clarify aspects of the legislation – for example, determining what constitutes raising a grievance. Another reason is that any failure to follow the dismissals and disciplinary procedure resulted in an automatically unfair dismissal – and employees brought claims on this basis that they could not have brought previously.

   The conclusions of the Gibbons Report were that the statutory procedures should be abolished. This happened in April 2009.

- It is certainly true that individuals are more aware of their rights. They might not be certain exactly what those rights are, but they know enough to be prompted to go and find out more. It is more likely, therefore, that individuals will think about the possibility of bringing a claim.

 Task

Read the Gibbons Report (available on the Department for Business, Innovation and Skills website) to understand the key concerns that were expressed.

2.9.1 *Solutions to the problem*

The government has addressed the increased number of claims in a variety of ways, as set out below.

Introducing fees

The introduction of fees, as already explained, has had a dramatic impact on the number of claims brought to the Employment Tribunal. Overall, the number of claims dropped by around 80 per cent. Now the fees have been removed there has been an increase in the number of claims, currently estimated to be around a 60 per cent increase. It certainly seems that fees deter claims, but if they are deterring legitimate claims (as it was feared they were) then they are not solving the problem.

Early conciliation

As we have already noted, a potential claimant has to engage with the Early Conciliation process before bringing a claim to the Employment Tribunal. The aim of this is to resolve problems at an earlier stage, so that they never become an issue before the tribunal.

Although there have also been other, more minor, changes to the Employment Tribunal system it does seem that these two solutions have had a significant effect.

Previous to these two changes there had been other attempts to reduce the number of claims, which were less successful, as follows.

2.9.2 *The Acas Arbitration Scheme*

The Employment Rights (Dispute Resolution) Act 1998 introduced a new scheme to try to reduce the pressure on the Employment Tribunal system. It is known as the Acas Arbitration Scheme. The scheme was launched in May 2001 and it was hoped that it would take the strain off the Employment Tribunal system. In reality it had little impact – handling very few cases each year. However, it is an important step and requires examination.

The Acas Arbitration Scheme only addresses unfair dismissal cases and claims made in relation to requests for flexible working. Although that limits its jurisdiction, we must remember that nearly half of all claims to the Employment Tribunals do relate to unfair dismissal.

The main advantage of the scheme is that it hears claims quickly, it is informal, and it is speedy – maybe going back to the Donovan ideal we examined in sections 2.1.2 and 2.1.3.

The initial lodging of the claim is still to the Employment Tribunals through submitting an ET1. If both parties agree, the claim may then be taken out of the Employment Tribunal process and directed to the Acas arbitration process. At that stage an Acas arbitrator (not an Acas member of staff but an independent person appointed by Acas who is deemed to have specialist relevant knowledge) is appointed to the case. The Acas arbitrator then arranges a time for the hearing as quickly as possible, with a target of being heard within a period of two months.

The hearings are conducted informally and as locally as possible to the parties. There is no cross-examination of witnesses (witness statements may be presented, but the witnesses are not questioned), no formal pleadings and the proceedings are confidential. The two parties simply explain their side of the case to the Acas arbitrator, bringing his/her attention to any relevant documents. Each party is also allowed the opportunity to comment on the other party's written submission. The Acas arbitrator then questions both parties and also seeks views on any remedy that might be awarded. Both parties are then invited to make closing statements. The Acas arbitrator determines the outcome. The decision is not given at the hearing, but is communicated to both parties in writing after the hearing.

The decision of the arbitrator is final – there is no route of appeal unless there is a challenge on the grounds of substantive jurisdiction or on grounds of serious irregularity.

Why has the system been so little used?

The limited focus of jurisdiction can be a problem. It is not unusual for a claim to relate to more than one area of legislation. For example, there could be a claim for unfair dismissal and unlawful deduction of wages. If such a claim went through the Acas arbitration route, only the part relating to unfair dismissal could be heard. The matter relating to unlawful deduction of wages would have to be referred to the Employment Tribunal, meaning that the parties would have to attend two hearings. This is unlikely to be popular with claimants or respondents.

In addition, if there are any disputes relating to the claim – eg was the claimant actually dismissed, was the claim to the Employment Tribunal made in time? etc – the Acas arbitrator cannot hear the claim. Again, it is not unusual for these types of issues to accompany a claim for unfair dismissal.

The potential to appeal is very limited. Although this means the claim is finalised more quickly, people might be apprehensive about committing themselves to a scheme in which there is no appeal – especially as there is an alternative (ie the Employment Tribunal) where there is the right of appeal.

The hearings are in private and hence representatives are not able to assess how effective the process is and decide if they want to use this route. In reality, this is a small issue because there have been so few hearings. However, a representative has a responsibility to give the best advice possible to his/her client. So he/she might find it difficult to recommend a process he/she has never seen in operation and knows relatively little about.

The Acas arbitrator is not required to be legally qualified. Although the Acas arbitrator will be thoroughly trained, and will have been selected for his/her depth of knowledge and experience, some claimants or respondents might feel uncomfortable that no formal legal qualification is required.

Whatever the reasons for the poor uptake, the scheme is currently under review. There could be alterations made to it, or it could simply be relaunched with more publicity and more explanation.

 Task

Relate the Acas Arbitration Scheme back to the 'Donovan ideal'. On the basis of that analysis, do you think the scheme is well designed?

What would you alter to make the scheme more attractive?

2.10 The Employment Tribunals (Constitution and Rules of Procedure) Regulations 2013 and 2016

As already noted, there have also been some less significant changes to the Employment Tribunal System. These were included in the 2001, 2004 and 2013 versions of the Employment Tribunals (Constitution and Rules of Procedure) Regulations, as well as the more recent 2016 version.

The key points to note from the 2013 regulations, in addition to those already explained in this chapter, are:

- An Employment Judge will carry out an initial review of all ET1 and ET3 forms. If the judge considers that either the claim or response has no reasonable prospect of success the parties will be informed. If neither party objects the case will be struck out.

- The tribunal will use written representations if they are received at least seven days prior to a hearing.

- All or part of a hearing can be conducted using electronic communication as long as the public and the parties to the hearing can see and hear what the tribunal can see and hear.

The 2016 regulations primarily addressed postponements. Although this is not reducing the number of claims, it is reducing the time that a claim can take to progress through the system. Since April 2016 both the claimant and the respondent have been limited to making two postponement requests. Any further request, or any request that is made less than seven days before the hearing (or at the hearing itself) will only be granted in exceptional circumstances. If a postponement is granted in these situations a tribunal has to consider awarding costs against the party that requested the postponement.

KEY LEARNING POINTS

1 The Employment Tribunal System was originally intended to be easily accessible, informal, speedy and inexpensive.
2 The Employment Tribunals have jurisdiction to hear cases relating to over 80 pieces of legislation, the most common being unfair dismissal.
3 Fees, which were introduced to bring a claim to the Employment Tribunal, have now been removed.
4 The Early Conciliation process must be engaged with in most cases, before proceeding to bring a claim to the Employment Tribunal.
5 A claimant lodging an ET1 at the tribunal starts the process of a claim to a tribunal. The respondent must reply to this claim within 28 days, using an ET3.
6 The Employment Appeal Tribunal reviews cases when there is dispute over a point of law, or the judgment of the Employment Tribunals is viewed as 'perverse'.

Examples to work through

1 In this chapter you have read about the introduction of fees to bring a claim to the Employment Tribunal. They have now been removed. Do you think there should be a fee or not? Justify your answer.

2 Do you think that the 'Donovan ideal' is relevant for organisations today? Justify your answer.

3 You have received a copy of an ET1 made by an ex-employee to the Employment Tribunals, which was received by them four months after he was dismissed. Explain how you should proceed.

 Case study 2.1

On 20 January 2018 you dismissed Marjorie for gross misconduct. For a number of weeks you had been suspicious that an employee was stealing from the organisation, and following a series of investigations you worked out that Marjorie was the individual who was responsible.

You dismissed Marjorie three weeks before her wedding. After the wedding she was due to go on honeymoon for three weeks. You had heard that she was taken ill with malaria about two weeks after she returned from her honeymoon, but you have heard nothing more from her since.

Today you have received a copy of the ET1 that she has submitted to the Employment Tribunal. It was received at the tribunal on 24 April 2018. She had written a letter to the Employment Tribunal apologising for the delay in submitting her ET1 and blaming this on her wedding, honeymoon and illness. Having taken some advice you are aware that the Employment Tribunal might decide to accept her claim, even though it is out of time. However, you still decide to go ahead and request a preliminary hearing. You receive notification from the Employment Tribunal that a preliminary hearing will take place, but if it is decided that they can hear the claim a full hearing will follow immediately.

Outline the preparations that you need to take for: 1) the preliminary hearing; 2) the full hearing.

03
Contract of employment

CHAPTER OBJECTIVES

The objectives of this chapter are:

- to describe and explain the tests used to determine employment status;
- to examine the component parts of the contract of employment;
- to outline the detail to be contained in the statement of initial employment particulars;
- to define and list the duties of the employee and the employer;
- to outline the concept of continuity of employment.

3.1 Who is an employee?

This is an important question, because much of the legal protection we look at in this book relates only to employees. For example, an employee can make a claim for unfair dismissal but someone else who is working in an organisation and who is not an employee cannot make a claim, even if their employment is terminated in exactly the same way. Some legislation extends to both employees and those working within an organisation without employment status – discrimination legislation is an example.

There are three alternatives for those who work in an organisation. They can be an employee, a worker or they can be providing their services on a self-employed basis. Section 230 (1) of the Employment Rights Act 1996 defines an employee as 'an individual who has entered into or works under a contract of employment'. Section 230 (3) of the same Act states that a worker is 'an individual who either works under a contract of employment or works under any other contract where that individual agrees to personally perform work or services for another party'.

Although these definitions are of some use, they do not tell us exactly who is an employee. This is primarily because situations of employment are very varied, particularly with the more flexible ways of working that many individuals have. Where there is any doubt over employment status, it is the responsibility of the courts (usually the Employment Tribunals) to take each individual case and to apply their judgment. They do this by applying tests that have been developed through case law. This task is often carried out in a preliminary hearing – to determine, for example, whether a claim for unfair dismissal can be heard because the respondent is claiming that the claimant was never an employee.

A variety of tests have been developed over the years by the courts to determine whether there is an employment relationship. The tests that are typically used today are the multiple test and the mutual obligations test, but we will start by looking at the other tests that have developed in order to gain some insight into how the approach to determining employment status has evolved.

3.1.1 Control test

This test originates from a judgment in 1881 in the case of *Yemens v Noakes*. The judge stated that 'An employee is subject to the command of his master as to the manner in which he shall do his work.'

The idea was that if a person was being told how to do his work, he was an employee. This is an outdated test for two main reasons. First, we have a much more skilled workforce than 120 years ago, and many employees are expected to work without specific instructions, using their skill and expertise. Second, an independent contractor could be told specifically what to do if hired for a specific project (eg a company could hire an electrician to help with a rewiring project and give very specific tasks).

3.1.2 Organisation test

In *Stevenson v MacDonald* (1952) 1 TLR 101 the judge, Lord Denning, stated that 'A person is an employee if that person is an integral part of the business.' This is of more use than the control test because it overcomes the problem of skilled people having control over their own work. However, it does not help us in the example of the electrician – if the company is carrying out a refurbishment project, completing the rewiring is an important part of the overall process. If there is no other electrician, the person who has been hired could be seen to be an 'integral part of the business' (under Lord Denning's ruling). This does not necessarily mean that he has become an employee.

3.1.3 Ordinary person test

In *Collins v Hertfordshire County Council* (1947) KB 598 the judge posed the question, 'Was a contract a contract of employment within the meaning which an ordinary person would give to those words?'

This is also known as the 'man in the street' test – in other words, what would ordinary common sense conclude? However, such a simple test does not give us any guidelines over what should be used to determine an employment relationship and what should not. On that basis, the test is of little help.

3.1.4 Economic reality test

Another approach to determining employment status starts by looking at the extent to which the individual is in business on his/her own account, rather than looking at whether there is an employment relationship. The focus here, therefore, is on payment methods, approach to paying tax, who pays for equipment, whether holiday and sick pay are paid – all aspects that typically suggest whether someone is an employee or is self-employed.

3.1.5 Multiple test

The experience of using the tests we have examined has shown the courts that it is not possible to focus on one particular aspect of the working relationship and to use that to determine whether or not there is an employment relationship. On that basis, the most commonly used test in the courts today is the multiple test.

In using the multiple test the courts look at every aspect of the relationship as described and use them to determine the nature of that relationship. The test was developed from the ruling in the following case:

- *Ready-Mixed Concrete v Minister of Pensions* (1968) ER 433
  Ready-Mixed Concrete decided to separate the making of concrete from the delivery of the concrete. It put in place a system of 'owner-drivers' – in other words, the delivery personnel would own their own vehicles and would be self-employed. In determining whether or not the drivers were self-employed the courts looked at a number of aspects of their employment. In favour of the drivers' being employees was:
  - they had to wear company uniforms (suggesting a level of control from the employer);
  - their lorries had to be available for company work at certain hours (an obligation to work);
  - they could only use the lorries for company business (again, suggesting a level of control);
  - they had to obey the foreman's orders (definitely an issue of control);
  - they could sell the lorries back to the company at an agreed valuation (not typical of an independent relationship).

In favour of the drivers' being self-employed was:
  - the drivers were responsible for the maintenance and running costs of the lorries (suggesting that the expenses of employment were their own);
  - the drivers could employ a substitute driver (there was no obligation on the driver to be personally available for work);
  - the drivers could own more than one lorry (suggesting that they could work for more than one employer);

– the drivers paid their own tax and NI contributions (an employer typically deducts tax and NI from the employee's pay).

Although there were factors suggesting both types of relationship, the court decided that there were three crucial conditions to meet for a contract of employment to exist:

- The employee must agree to provide his own work and skill.
- The employer must have some element of control.
- There must not be any term inconsistent with a contract of employment. (Inconsistency with a contract of employment could be such things as the employee being responsible for payment of his/her own tax and NI contributions – typically the employer deducts these from the employee's pay. However, that one point alone would not necessarily be enough to determine employment status.)

The court found that the drivers were self-employed. They were not required to provide their own work and skill and there were factors inconsistent with a contract of employment. In determining the nature of a working relationship in the courts today, those three crucial conditions are usually addressed and the decision is made based on the answer to them.

3.1.6 *Mutual obligations test*

The mutual obligations test is used alongside the multiple test by the courts today. It looks at the nature of the relationship between the employer and the person in question, and considers whether there is sufficient mutuality for an employment relationship to exist. There are two levels of mutuality to consider. First, is there an obligation to provide work (and an obligation to carry out that work)? Second, is there a promise of future work (both a promise to provide it [employer] and a promise to carry it out [employee])? The following case explains this test:

- *Carmichael v National Power* (2000) IRLR 43
  In this case Mrs Carmichael and her colleague worked at a power station as visitor guides. The work was part-time. The relationship between the women and National Power was described as that of a 'station guide on a casual as-required basis'. National Power argued, therefore, that the work was on a casual basis and that there was no obligation to provide work. It was also noted that on 17 occasions Mrs Carmichael had been unable to work and her colleague had been unable to work on eight occasions.
  The House of Lords found that there was no employment relationship because there was no obligation to provide work and no obligation to do work that was offered.

The use of the multiple and mutual obligations test was confirmed in the case of *Montgomery v Johnson Underwood Ltd* (2001) IRLR 269 in which the courts referred to the need for the employer to have control over the individual and for there to be mutual obligation as the 'irreducible minimum' for employment status to exist. A decision that seems to contrast with this is:

- *Cornwall County Council v Prater* (2006) EWCA Civ 102
  Prater was a teacher working with children who were unable to attend school. She worked under a series of contracts, with no obligation to take a

further contract once one had been completed – and the council was under no obligation to offer her any future contracts. There were some breaks between contracts, but both parties accepted that they would not be seen to break her continuity of employment if she were found to be an employee.

The Court of Appeal held that Prater was working under a series of contracts of employment and that they added together to give her sufficient service to accrue employment rights. They found that the case differed from Carmichael because each of the contracts was of a lengthy duration and she had always accepted the contracts that had been offered. The gaps between the contracts were seen to be a temporary cessation rather than ending and restarting the contractual relationship.

Another key difference between the Carmichael and Prater cases was what had happened in reality. Although both had started with an agreement that there was no obligation to do the work, in Prater's case she had regularly been offered work and she had always accepted it. In Carmichael's case she had refused a number of offers of work. Even if, when the contract is first agreed, there is no intention to have mutuality of obligation the Employment Tribunals would also look at what had actually happened. It could be that neither the employer nor the individual intended there to be an employment relationship, but it has developed into that over time.

A key question in determining employment status is whether an individual is required to do work personally:

- *Express and Echo Publications v Tanton* (1999) IRLR 367
  Tanton was allowed to provide a substitute if he was not available to work. This meant that he was not an employee, with the Court of Appeal stating that being obliged to work in person was an 'irreducible minimum' for employment status.

In some ways it could be argued that it is to the employer's advantage to have individuals who are not employees, because those individuals will have fewer employment rights. However, simply putting a term into a written contract that expressly states that an individual is not an employee or includes terms that suggest that there is not an employment relationship does not guarantee that an individual will not be an employee. If there is a dispute over employment status the courts will look at how the working relationship has actually been performed.

- *Redrow Homes (Yorkshire) Ltd v Buckborough and another* (2009) IRLR 34
  A contractual term allowing the employee to substitute another to do his work was part of the agreement. However, the courts found that this term was a sham because it was not intended that the substitution would ever occur and hence the individual was a worker and was able to claim holiday pay (which was the focus of the dispute).

3.1.7 Workers

So far, we have focused on the difference between an employee and someone who is self-employed. However, we have to note that there is also a 'worker' category that is referred to in some statute, effectively meaning that we have three options of status (employee, worker and self-employed).

Workers have less protection in law than employees, but more than self-employed people. For example, the law relating to the National Minimum Wage, working time and equal pay applies to workers.

The definition of a worker is not very clear, and does vary in different statutes. However, maybe the most effective way is to think of the economic reality test that we have already mentioned. If that test shows that the individual is in business on their own account, they are self-employed. However, if the person has to provide work personally for an individual they could be a worker, if they do not meet the definition of an employee.

The concept of a worker has come under more scrutiny in recent times, with a number of cases being brought where the individuals work in the so-called 'gig economy'. In almost all of these cases the individuals concerned have been told by the employer that they are working on a self-employed basis, but they have argued that they are employees.

- *Uber BV, Uber London Ltd and Uber Britannia Ltd v Aslam, Farrar, Dawson and others (2017) UKEAT 0056/17*
  Uber drivers argued that they were employees, although they were being treated as self-employed. Uber drivers log on to the Uber app when they are ready to work. They are then asked to do journeys as they are booked. If they refuse three journeys in a row they are compulsorily logged out of the Uber system for up 10 minutes. They have to do the work personally and they are clearly under the control of the employer. However, there are elements that are inconsistent with employment, such as having the choice of when to work. It was concluded that they were workers (they are planning to appeal this ruling at the Court of Appeal).

- *Pimlico Plumbers v Smith (2018) UKSC 29*
  Smith worked as a freelance plumber for Pimlico, but he argued that he was an employee. He was required to wear the Pimlico uniform, drive a van with the Pimlico logo and use suppliers from an approved supplier. He had to work a set number of hours per week, but he could choose when he was available for work. He had to do the work personally.
  Again, there were some elements that were inconsistent with employment but he did have to do work personally and he was under the control of the employer and therefore it was concluded that he was a worker.

- *Independent Workers Union of Great Britain v RooFoods t/a Deliveroo (2017) TUR1/985*
  Deliveroo cyclists argued that they were employees. They were required to wear the company uniform, and once they had said they were available for work they had to do the work that was given to them. However, they were allowed to ask someone else to cover their work for them, and they did do this from time to time.
  As there was not the obligation to do the work personally they were not workers, and were classed as self-employed.

3.1.8 The rights of employees, workers and the self-employed

As we have already noted, one of the reasons that it is important to get the right definition of employment status is because employees, workers and the self-employed have different rights. A summary of those rights can be found in Table 3.1.

Table 3.1 The rights of employees, workers and the self-employed

Right	Employee	Worker	Self-Employed
Make a claim of unfair dismissal	Yes	No	No
Receive holiday pay	Yes	Yes	No
Receive breaks as set out in the Working Time Regulations 1998	Yes	Yes	No
Be paid the National Minimum/Living Wage	Yes	Yes	No
Receive a Statutory Redundancy payment	Yes	No	No
Be protected against discrimination	Yes	Yes	Possibly
Be given a written statement of initial employment particulars	Yes	No	No
Be issued with an itemised pay slip	Yes	No	No
Receive statutory notice if the employer terminates the employment	Yes	No	No
Protected from unlawful deduction from wages	Yes	Yes	No
Be accompanied to a disciplinary or grievance meeting by a trade union representative or colleague	Yes	Yes	No
Protected under data protection legislation	Yes	Yes	Yes
Receive paid time off for antenatal care	Yes	No	No
Take statutory maternity/adoption/paternity/ shared parental leave	Yes	No	No
Make a request for flexible working	Yes	No	No
Receive paid time off for trade union duties	Yes	No	No
Have legal protection if making a protected disclosure	Yes	Yes	Possibly
Receive protection from health and safety legislation	Yes	Yes	Yes

 Explore further

Do you think that the courts have arrived at a satisfactory solution to the issue of deciding who is an employee? If not, what potential problems do you see with the current situation? What type of test might improve the current situation?

3.2 The contract of employment

The contract of employment describes the basis of the employment relationship. It can be in writing or it can be agreed orally. It is of great importance in the event of any dispute, because the contract of employment explains the way in which the employer and employee have agreed to work together. The contract of employment is a legal document and employers should therefore take care in determining the content. The terms of the contract of employment can be classified as: 1) express terms; 2) implied terms.

Express terms are terms that have been discussed and agreed between the employer and employee. They might not be in writing. It must be emphasised that express terms cannot diminish statutory rights. We examine statutory rights in more detail later in this chapter, but in essence they are rights expressed in law (in statute). So, for example, the National Minimum Wage (NMW) is determined by statute. Potentially, the employer can offer a wage of a lower level than the NMW and the employee can accept this. However, if the employee then challenges this wage in the court, the employer cannot argue that it is fair because it was agreed between the two parties – because it has diminished the employee's statutory rights.

Implied terms are those that have not been specifically agreed between the employer and employee but are derived from the following sources:

- collective agreements;
- statute;
- custom and practice;
- the courts;
- work rules.

3.3 Written statement of initial employment particulars

Sections 1 to 7 of the Employment Rights Act 1996 set out the right of all employees who work for an employer for at least one month to receive a written statement of initial employment particulars, no later than two months after the beginning of employment. The statement must include all of the following:

- the names of the employer and the employee;
- the date when employment began;
- the date when continuous service with the employer began (ie taking into account any previous service with the employer prior to this appointment);
- the job title, or a brief description of the job duties;
- the rate of remuneration, the way in which it is to be calculated (eg the terms of a bonus scheme) and the periods at which the employee will be paid – this includes all financial benefits as well as basic pay;
- terms and conditions relating to hours of work (eg this should include basic hours, shift patterns and rules regarding overtime);

- terms and conditions relating to holiday pay (eg this must specify the numbers of days' holiday to which the employee is entitled each year and the period in which it is to be taken);
- the place of work, or the employer's address if the employee will be moving between a number of places of work;
- terms and conditions relating to payments given if incapacitated due to sickness or injury;
- details of pension schemes;
- the length of notice the employee is required to give, and the employer is entitled to receive, to terminate the contract of employment;
- where the employment is not intended to be permanent, the period for which it is expected to continue, or if it is a fixed-term contract, the date it is to end;
- any collective agreements that will directly affect the employee including, where the employer is not a party, the persons by whom they were made;
- if the employee is required to work outside the UK for more than one month, the duration of the period of work outside the UK, the currency of the remuneration while abroad and any additional remuneration or benefits applicable to the work; in addition, any terms and conditions relating to the eventual return to the UK;
- details of disciplinary rules that apply to the employee;
- details of grievance procedures and the name of the person the employee should apply to if he/she is dissatisfied with any disciplinary decision or to air a grievance.

The employer can refer the employee to company documents, such as a staff handbook or intranet, to explain sickness absence schemes, disciplinary and grievance rules and a pension scheme.

 Task

Look at the statement of initial particulars issued by your organisation, or one with which you are familiar. Does it meet all of the criteria listed in section 3.3?

The items listed here are those that must be required to satisfy the requirements of the Employment Rights Act 1996. However, it is very likely that the employer will include additional clauses that are relevant to the employment of the individual concerned. Additional clauses could include:

- A probationary period, and what an employer will do if the employee is unsuccessful in achieving the targets set during the probationary period.
- A restrictive covenant (see Chapter 11).
- A prohibition on revealing confidential information (see Chapter 11).

- Terms relating to specific benefits, for example if an employee is assigned a company car there are likely to be terms setting out how it might be used, issues relating to insurance and issues relating to the replacement of the vehicle after a set period of time.

Despite this lengthy list of contents, the statement is not the full contract of employment; it is simply a statement of the main terms and conditions of employment. Indeed, it should be noted that the law does not actually require employees to sign the statement or to give any indication that they have received the statement (although it would certainly be good practice for the employer to ensure that there is a signed copy on file). The statement is the employer's version of the terms and conditions and is not an indication of any agreement being reached between the employer and the employee. If the employee works in accordance with the terms and conditions, it could be argued that the employer's version has contractual effect because of the lack of any challenge.

In practice, a court will usually accept that the statement is strong evidence of the terms agreed by the employer and employee. However, because the statement is not a contract, either party can challenge the accuracy of the statement – as happened in the following case.

- *System Floors (UK) Ltd v Daniel* (1985) IRLR 475
  Daniel brought a claim of unfair dismissal against System Floors. System Floors challenged his right to bring the claim, stating that he had insufficient continuity of service. They challenged the date when employment commenced, declaring that it was actually one week later than cited in the written statement of initial employment particulars. The EAT allowed the employer to show that the actual starting date was different from the one stated, although it did emphasise that it is a 'heavy burden' to show that actual terms differ from the statement.

3.4 Implied terms

The implied terms are just as important a part of the contract as the express terms. As already noted, they come from a variety of sources:

3.4.1 Collective agreements

A collective agreement is an agreement made between the employer and the employees' trade union or association following a collective bargaining process. As the term suggests, the agreement applies 'collectively' to all employees covered by the negotiating group. Typical topics for collective agreements are pay, bonus schemes, shift patterns, redundancy agreements, and disciplinary and grievance procedures.

A collective agreement can be incorporated (become part of) a contract of employment by express incorporation or implied incorporation.

Express incorporation

Here there is a clear statement that the employer and employee agree to be bound by a collective agreement. This is typically a statement within the collective agreement that expressly incorporates the collective agreement into the contract of employment. An example of express incorporation is found in the following case:

- *National Coal Board v Galley* (1958) 1 WLR 16
  The pit deputies working for the National Coal Board (NCB) had contracts of employment that stated that they were regulated by any national agreements. After negotiation with the trade unions a national agreement was revised and a clause requiring pit deputies to work on such days as reasonably practicable was inserted. This could potentially involve working on Saturdays. Galley refused to work on Saturdays and was held to be in breach of his contract. This was because his contract of employment stated that his employment was governed by national agreements and the revised collective agreement had been expressly incorporated into his contract.

Implied corporation

If there is no express term, an alternative is to claim that the collective agreement has been incorporated into a contract of employment by 'implication'. If the employer and employee have always conducted the employment relationship in accordance with the collective agreement, it can be implied that they agreed to be bound by that agreement. However, this is less certain than a term that has been expressly incorporated, because the intention to be bound by an agreement can always be challenged. For example:

- *Campbell v Union Carbide Ltd* (2002) EAT 0341/01
  Campbell was employed as a chemical plant operator, initially with ICI. ICI entered into a collective agreement with the recognised trade union that included a clause covering redundancy payments that was stated to be legally binding, and another clause headed 'Discretionary severance in non-redundancy cases'. The part of ICI in which Campbell worked was transferred to Union Carbide Ltd, along with all terms and conditions of employment. After a period of time Campbell was given notice of termination on the grounds of ill health. He claimed that he was entitled to payments under the 'discretionary severance in non-redundancy cases' clause because these payments had been made by the organisation in all previous cases when an employee had been terminated following a lengthy period of sickness absence. Union Carbide refused to make the payment, stressing that the payments were classed as 'discretionary'.

  The EAT ruled that although the payments had always been made, this did not give rise to incorporation by implication or evidence of a contractual term. The important question was whether there was evidence that both parties intended the payments to form a term of the contract. Because the payments had specifically been called 'discretionary' payments, it ruled that the employer had indicated that there was no intention for the payments to be contractual – and so there was no requirement to make the payments.

Task

What collective agreements exist in your organisation (or an organisation with which you are familiar)? Are they expressly incorporated into the contract of employment? If they are not, is there evidence that they have been incorporated by implication?

3.4.2 Statute

As already noted, a contract of employment cannot diminish any rights of the employee determined by statute. Any relevant statute automatically forms a part of the contract of employment. Two examples are:

- The National Minimum Wage Act 1998 (see Chapter 5): the employer must pay at least the minimum wage as determined by the Secretary of State.
- The Working Time Regulations 1998 (see Chapter 5): the employer must allow all employees covered by this legislation the breaks, holidays, rest periods and maximum weekly hours as laid out in the regulations.

3.4.3 Custom and practice

Before written particulars and written contracts of employment were widely used, custom and practice was of importance because looking at the 'way it has always been done' gave a good indication of the terms by which the employer and employee intended to be bound. Since the introduction of written documents, custom and practice has become less important.

However, it can still be argued that if there is a definite practice that is reasonable and is generally applied, it could form part of the contract of employment. In determining whether the practice has become part of the contract a full range of issues must be considered, including such issues as how long the custom has been in place, whether the policy regarding the custom has been brought to the attention of employees by management and whether there is evidence that both parties intended the custom to be part of the contract of employment.

Custom and practice can be useful in helping the courts to interpret a contractual term that is not clear. If we look back at the case of *Campbell v Union Carbide Ltd* we see the issue of custom and practice highlighted. Although Union Carbide had always paid the ill-health severance payment (evidence of custom and practice), it was judged not to have formed part of the contract because it was clearly highlighted as discretionary.

- *Shumba v Park Cakes Ltd (2013) EWCA Civ 974*
  The company paid enhanced redundancy payments, which were not specifically referred to in the employees' contracts but were in the HR manual. A group of employees were made redundant and not given the enhanced payments because the employer said they were not contractual.

They were found to be contractual through custom and practice. The payments had always been made, and it was reasonable for the employees to conclude that they would be entitled to them.

 Task

Are there any practices that could be incorporated by custom and practice into the contracts of employment in your organisation (or one with which you are familiar)? What are they?

Are they important to the organisation? Should they be expressly agreed between the employer and employee?

3.4.4 The courts

The role of the courts in determining implied terms has developed through a series of cases. The initial view was based on the 'officious bystander test' (derived from *Shirlaw v Southern Foundries* (1939) ER 113 – see Case Summaries, Chapter 3).

This test questioned whether a term would be implied if an officious bystander asked two parties who had a contract if a term that they had not specifically mentioned was part of the contract. If they replied 'of course', then the term was implied.

This is a very limited way of looking at implied terms and the courts now take a much wider view. One issue to be considered is 'reasonableness':

- *Courtaulds Northern Spinning Ltd v Sibson* (1988) ICR 451
  Sibson resigned from the trade union and, because the trade union operated a closed shop (all employees had to join the trade union – a practice no longer allowed in law), the trade union insisted he be moved to another site. Sibson was offered employment one mile from his current place of work, but he refused to go and resigned, claiming unfair and constructive dismissal (see Chapter 8). The Court of Appeal ruled that the agreement to move sites should be implied if it was satisfied that both parties would have agreed to it if they were being reasonable. It was judged that a move of one mile was reasonable and so there was no dismissal.

A more recent decision is:

- *Johnstone v Bloomsbury Health Authority* (1992) QB 333
  Johnstone was a senior house officer in a hospital. His contract gave a standard working week of 40 hours and he had to be available on call for an average of 48 hours each week. As we will see when we examine the duties of the employer, there is an implied term that the employer will take reasonable care of the employee's health and safety. In stating an average of 48 hours per week, it was actually possible for Johnstone to work over 100 hours

in a week, which breached that implied term. The Court of Appeal ruled that the right for the employer to request overtime work had to be limited by the implied term of care for the employee's health and safety. However, one judge dissented, declaring that however burdensome the requirements might be, they were express terms of the contract of employment.

In summary, the courts will look at all factors regarding the employment relationship and determine whether there is an implication that both parties would agree to be bound by the term under question. They will then look wider than this and consider whether the implied term is reasonable. They will also consider a wider approach and determine whether the implication of the term is necessary, or of benefit to, the contract of employment.

3.4.5 Work rules

Many organisations have a set of rules governing the way in which they require employees to act. These might cover such things as not smoking, not bringing alcohol or drugs on to the site, the correct way to wear uniforms, etc. Such rules are clearly devised by management and, unlike collective agreements, do not require any prior negotiation. If a rule has been expressly incorporated into a contract of employment, it will be contractual. For example, if the rule of not smoking on company premises is expressly written into a contract of employment, that requirement is contractual. However, if something is simply contained in the set of rules and is not referred to in any contractual documents, it is not part of that contract.

- *Artemis International Corporation Ltd* (2008) IRLR 629
  In this case the court found that an enhanced redundancy policy, which was contained within a staff handbook, and which was referred to in individual employment contracts, was a contractual term. In determining this it was particularly important that the redundancy calculation and method of payment were clearly set out and the policy was in a section headed 'entitlements'.

3.5 Implied terms of law

As well as terms that can be implied into the contract of employment, there are also obligations placed on both the employer and the employee by law. These obligations are implied into the contract of employment.

3.5.1 Duties on the employer

To pay wages

There is a duty of the employer to pay the employee during the period of employment.

- *Devonald v Rosser* (1906) KB 728
  The employer closed the works (tinplate) through lack of business. Two weeks later the employer gave all employees one month's notice of the termination of

this contract. Devonald claimed pay for the two weeks before the notice was given. This was granted because there was an implied duty that the employer would pay the employee.

To provide work

This duty is unclear. It is possible that the failure to provide work might be a breach of contract if earnings depend on work being provided (eg a sales person remunerated by commission) or the employee needs the opportunity to practise skills (eg a trainee).

- *William Hill Organisation Ltd v Tucker* (1998) IRLR 313
  Tucker had been involved in developing a new approach to betting. When he gave notice of his intention to resign, William Hill tried to put him on 'garden leave' (to stay away from work while on full pay) for six months. During that period he would not be allowed to work. Tucker challenged this on the basis that he needed to keep practising his skills and six months was too long a period to be away from work. He was successful in his claim.

- *SG&R Valuation Service Co v Boudrais and others* (2008) EWCA 1340
  Two directors of the company resigned with the intention of going to work for a competitor. Their employer put them on garden leave to delay the point at which they could join the competitor. The directors argued that the company had an obligation to provide them with work, and by not doing so (ie by putting them on garden leave) it had breached their contract of employment, meaning that they were no longer bound by any obligations imposed by the company. They were unsuccessful in their argument. The employer is required to provide work unless the actions of the employee have rendered it impossible to do so – as had happened here.

To provide references

An employer has a duty to take care when writing references. The following case highlights the difficulties that can arise in this area:

- *Spring v Guardian Assurance plc* (1994) IRLR 460
  Spring was a sales representative for an insurance company, which was sold to Guardian Assurance. At this time Spring decided to set up in business selling insurance for another organisation. Under the rules of the insurance business, Guardian Assurance was required to give a reference about Spring to the new organisation. The reference was written on the basis of information from Spring's previous superiors and included references to a serious case of mis-selling and suggested that Spring was not honest and was a man of little or no integrity. On this basis the new insurance company refused to accept Spring as selling for them and other insurance companies also rejected him.

  Spring brought an action in the High Court claiming damages for loss of earnings based on malicious falsehood, breach of an implied term of contract and negligence arising from the preparation of the reference.

  The High Court judge described the reference as a 'kiss of death' to Spring's career in insurance because it was so bad. It was found that the allegations of dishonesty were untrue – Spring had acted incompetently but not dishonestly. The judge found that there was no malicious action, because the reference writers genuinely believed Spring was a 'rogue'. However, it was accepted that Guardian Assurance had a duty to take due care over writing the reference and had been negligent because they had not checked that the allegations of dishonesty were true. They had thereby breached the duty of due care. This ruling was supported in the House of Lords.

This case confirms the duty of an employer in giving a reference. The employer must take every care to ensure that every detail written in a reference is correct. This must include checking the details before writing the reference. It is also the responsibility of the employer to ensure that the overall impression given by the reference is fair. It is therefore important to consider what is not included as well as what is.

The contractual right to receive a reference was also challenged in *Spring v Guardian Assurance*. In the House of Lords judgment the judges concluded that there was a duty when the kind of employment is such that a reference is normally required. In this instance, the insurance business requires that organisations seek a reference from previous employers and so it would seem that a contractual right for a reference could exist. However, if there is no requirement in the particular sector that a reference is provided then the employer is only under an obligation to provide a reference if there is a contractual requirement (either an express term or an implied term).

Although there is a clear requirement to state the truth in giving references, the truth must be related to matters that have been thoroughly investigated and are therefore believed to be true.

- *TSB Bank plc v Harris* (2000) IRLR 157
  Harris worked for the TSB. During her employment, there had been 17 complaints about her by customers. Surprisingly, Harris was unaware of these complaints. Harris applied for a job with the Prudential and they sought a reference from the TSB. In the reference the TSB stated that there had been 17 complaints against Harris: four had been upheld and eight were still under investigation. The Prudential declined to employ Harris. On hearing of the reference Harris resigned from the TSB and claimed unfair constructive dismissal (see Chapter 8). The EAT upheld Harris's claim, stating that the TSB had breached the implied term of trust and confidence by not ensuring that the complaints cited in the reference were fair and reasonable.

  In this case the TSB had reported the facts relating to Harris as they understood them. However, by not bringing the complaints to her attention they had not investigated them thoroughly and so they could not be certain they were true.

Although there might be a limited obligation to provide a reference, there is a clear requirement to ensure that the content is correct. However, in bringing a claim that a reference has damaged an employee's ability to seek alternative employment, the employee must be able to show that it was the reference that harmed his/her prospects and not any other factors.

Explore further

As we have seen in section 3.5, the giving of references is fraught with potential difficulties. Look in the HR and business press for any recent cases that have occurred relating to the giving of references. Are you able to draw up any guidelines on giving references that might be of use to your employer?

To take reasonable care for the health and safety of employees

We study this requirement in Chapter 12.

To indemnify the employee against all liabilities and losses incurred in the course of employment

A good example of this is expenses incurred when travelling on company business. Any legitimate business expense should be reimbursed by the employer.

To take reasonable steps to bring to the attention of employees rights of which they would not ordinarily be aware

There are instances where an employee could not be expected to be aware of a particular right. For example, this could be because it has been negotiated with a representative body and the employee was unaware of the negotiations.

- *Scally v Southern Health and Social Services Board* (1991) IRLR 522
  In this case a group of doctors working for the Health Service in Northern Ireland claimed they had not been advised of the ability to purchase extra years that would enhance their pension contributions. When the doctors did find out about the scheme they applied to join, but their application was rejected as being out of time. The House of Lords went on to rule that an employer has an obligation to make employees aware of their rights.

The employer is required to take reasonable steps. It might be deemed reasonable to put notices on a noticeboard. However, if there are employees who are rarely in the building (eg sales representatives who spend most of their time travelling to see customers), it could be argued that it is not a reasonable way of informing that group of employees. In the same way, it would not be sufficient to e-mail information to all employees if some did not have access to a computer.

To give effective support against bullying at work

This can also be linked to the duty to take reasonable care of the safety (and health) of employees. We examine the issues associated with bullying, and the employer's duties, in Chapter 7.

To respect the privacy of the employee

This is explored in Chapter 11.

To deal effectively with grievances

This is explored in Chapter 8.

To take care not to damage the relationship of trust and confidence that should exist between an employer and an employee

This requirement is one that falls on both the employer and the employee. The issue of trust and confidence is seen to be right at the heart of the contract of employment. If there is no trust and confidence, there can be no successful relationship. One of the first cases outlining this was:

- *Isle of Wight Tourist Board v Coombes* (1976) IRLR 413
  Mrs Coombes was the personal secretary to the director of the board. One day they had an argument and in the presence of another employee the director stated, 'She is an intolerable bitch on a Monday morning.' Mrs Coombes resigned and claimed constructive dismissal (see Chapter 8). She was successful in her claim because it was judged that the words of the director had shattered any trust and confidence in the relationship.

The breach of trust and confidence can also be between a group of employees and the employer:

- *Malik and another v Bank of Credit and Commerce International SA* (1997) IRLR 462
  The BCCI collapsed in 1991 after widespread allegations of fraudulent actions. Malik worked for BCCI and alleged that the employer conducting the business in a corrupt and dishonest manner amounted to a breach of the implied term of trust and confidence. The House of Lords held that Malik could bring a claim for damages relating to the stigma of working for BCCI, relating to any damage to future employment prospects.

- *Husain and another v Bank of Credit and Commerce International SA* (2002) EWCA Civ 82
  In this case, another two former employees of BCCI were unsuccessful in their claim for damages related to the stigma. The Court of Appeal ruled that although the actions of BCCI might well be a breach of trust and confidence, the inability of the individuals to find alternative work related more to personal factors, such as inflating their experience and knowledge on job applications.

 Explore further

The duty of trust and confidence is at the heart of any contract of employment. As we work through this book we will see other situations when this duty is breached. Read these cases carefully. Is there ever a case when the employment relationship has survived such a breach?

3.5.2 Duties on the employee

To obey all instructions of the employer

It should be noted that the instructions should be reasonable and they should be legal.

- *Ottoman Bank v Chakarian* (1930) AC 277
  The employer instructed Chakarian to remain in Constantinople, although he had previously been sentenced to death there. He disobeyed and this was found to be justified because the instruction had been unreasonable.
- *Morrish v Henley Ltd* (1973) ER 137
  The employee was instructed to falsify the accounts at the garage where he was employed. He refused and was dismissed. This was an unfair dismissal because the instruction was to carry out an illegal act.

To co-operate with the employer

A clear example of lack of co-operation is the taking of industrial action:

- *Secretary of State for Employment v ASLEF* (1972) QB 443
  ASLEF instructed its members to carry out a work-to-rule. The employees worked strictly according to the company's rules and caused considerable disruption. The Court of Appeal held that by carrying out the work-to-rule the employees were in breach of the implied term of co-operating with the employer. Lord Denning commented: 'Now I quite agree that a man is not bound positively to do more for his employer than his contract requires. He can withdraw his goodwill if he pleases. But what he must not do is wilfully obstruct the employer as he goes about his business.'

As we see in Chapter 10, employees do have the right to take industrial action if this action is taken in accordance with relevant legislation.

Fidelity

Employees must not carry out activities that clearly conflict with the duty that they owe to their employer. They must therefore not compete with the employer:

- *Imam-Sadeque v BlueBay Asset Management Ltd* (2013) IRLR 344
  The employee said he was going to leave, but that would mean that he would not be able to receive full benefit from his share options, which were worth £1.7 million. The employer agreed to give him full benefit in return for him agreeing not to enter into competition with the employer when he left. He did set up in competition, which was a breach of fidelity. He lost his share options as a result of breaching the contract, which was found to be fair.

To take reasonable care in carrying out the duties of their contract

If an employee injures another person or property in the course of his/her duties, the employee can be liable to indemnify the employer against any damages. In reality, the issue is typically dealt with through the employer's insurance:

- *Lister v Romford Ice and Cold Storage Ltd* (1956) AC 555
  Lister was a lorry driver who negligently injured a fellow employee (his father) when packing his lorry. The injured employee sought damages from Romford Ice and Cold Storage and was successful (the employer was responsible due to vicarious liability – see Chapter 7). The employer's insurers then brought an action against Lister, in the employer's name, claiming damages for the breach of the implied term that he would exercise reasonable care in carrying out his duties. This claim was allowed.

3.6 Continuity of employment

The qualification for certain employment rights is dependent on the employee having had a specific period of continuous employment. An example of this is the requirement to have two years' continuous service (one if the employee started work before 6 April 2012) before being able to make a claim of unfair dismissal (see Chapter 8).

Section 212 of the Employment Rights Act 1996 defines continuous service as including any week during which all or part of the employee's relationship with the employer is governed by a contract of employment. This section also allows for continuity of employment to continue although the contract is not in existence. These exceptional situations are:

- an employee is away from work following the contract ending or having resigned or having been dismissed, and is sick or injured, but is then taken back on within 26 weeks;
- a period of absence due to a temporary cessation of work;
- any period during which employment is regarded as continuing due to custom.

For example, it could be the custom of the employer to allow compassionate leave in certain situations that is unpaid. It should be noted that maternity legislation (see Chapter 5) allows for the continuity of employment during the period of maternity leave, and an employee who is absent due to long-term sickness also continues to accrue service. It should also be noted that an employee's continuity of employment is preserved when that employment is subject to a transfer of undertaking (see Chapter 9).

In all of these cases continuity of employment is preserved and the weeks during which work does not take place actually count towards the calculation of the period of continuous employment. There are also situations when continuity of employment is preserved, but the weeks when work does not take place do not count towards continuous employment. They are:

- a period of time when an employee is taking part in a strike;
- a period of time when an employee is locked out by the employer (this is when an employer refuses to provide work for the employees, with the aim of forcing them to accept certain terms and conditions of employment).

KEY LEARNING POINTS

1 There are a number of tests used by the courts to determine who is an employee. The most commonly used are the multiple test and the mutual obligations test.

2 The contract of employment consists of express and implied terms.

3 Express terms are those that have been discussed and agreed between the employer and employee.

4 The sources of implied terms are collective agreements, statute, custom and practice, the courts, work rules.

5 A written statement of initial employment particulars must be given to all employees within two months of commencing employment.

6 A collective agreement can be part of a contract of employment through express or implied incorporation.

7 A contract of employment cannot diminish any rights of the employee determined by statute.

8 The courts can determine whether a term is implied within a contract of employment through looking at a wide range of factors within the way the relationship between employer and employee is conducted.

9 Work rules are only incorporated into a contract of employment if they are specifically mentioned in that contract.

10 There are a series of duties on both the employer and the employee that have been imposed by law.

11 Continuity of employment includes any week when the relationship between the employee and the employer is governed by the contract of employment, although certain exceptions to this do apply.

 Case study 2.1

- *Shirlaw v Southern Foundries* (1939) ER 113 – A term is implied into a contract of employment when, if an officious bystander were to make a suggestion to the parties, they would reply, 'Oh, of course!'

- *Sagar v Ridehalgh* (1931) Ch 310 – Weavers who made an error received a deduction in pay. This was the custom and practice in the Lancashire mills, and was therefore seen as an implied contractual term.

- *Mears v Safecar Security Ltd* (1982) IRLR 183 – There was a dispute over whether the employee was entitled to sick pay. The employer had never paid sick pay and the employee had never asked for it when he had previously been sick. The Court of Appeal ruled that the only implied term was that there was no sick pay entitlement.

- *Jones v Associated Tunnelling Company* (1981) IRLR 477 – The EAT accepted that

(continued)

(Continued)

there was an implied term that, for reasons of business efficiency, the employer could ask the employee to work at any place within reasonable travelling distance of his home.

- *Moores v Bude-Stratton Town Council* (2000) IRLR 676 – The employer has the implied duty to take reasonable steps to protect employees from bullying or undue interference in their work. In this the employee had suffered verbal abuse and accusations of dishonesty, which had breached the duty of mutual trust and confidence.
- *Ali v Christian Salvesen Food Services Ltd* (1997) IRLR 17 – A collective agreement set out terms to be followed in an annual hours agreement. There was no agreement on what happened if employees left partway through the year – and the courts refused to fill in the gap in the agreement.
- *Colen v Cebrian Ltd* (2004) IRLR 210 – If a contract was entered into unlawfully or with the intention of acting unlawfully, it will be unenforceable. However, if it was entered into lawfully, the effect of illegal performance does not automatically make the contract unenforceable.
- *Sanders v Parry* (1967) ER 803 – An employee set up in competition with his employer, poaching a major client. This was found to be a breach of fidelity.
- *Judge v Crown Leisure Ltd* (2005) IRLR 823 – An employee talked to his boss at a Christmas party and was promised a significant pay increase. This did not occur. It was ruled that statements made at a party did not amount to a contractual promise. For there to be a legally binding agreement, there must be certainty about the commitment that has been entered into.
- *Henry and others v London General Transport Services Ltd* (2002) IRLR 472 – The employer introduced new working conditions affecting such things as rotas, payment and holidays. The employees signed a petition but continued to work in accordance with the new arrangements 'under protest'. They submitted claims for unlawful deductions from wages two years later. Their claim failed because they had made little protest and had taken so long to register their objections.
- *McKie v Swindon College* (2011) EWHC 469 – A reference was given without checking facts, which resulted in an employee being accused of improper behaviour. There was no evidence to support this allegation. The reference was found to be negligent and damages were awarded against the employer who supplied the reference.

❓ Examples to work through

1 Joan works as a keep-fit instructor. She teaches at a number of adult education classes. Each term she is asked which classes she wants to teach at and they are advertised in the college literature. If there are enough enrolments, the classes go ahead. If there are insufficient enrolments, the class is cancelled. If she is unable to teach one week, she tells the college that she is not available and they arrange for someone else to take the class. Apply a relevant employment test and determine whether she is an employee.

2 You work in a retail store and the general manager has recently dismissed an employee

who worked in your department for gross misconduct – stealing from the shop where you work. However, there was some doubt about his guilt and you are not comfortable with the final decision that was taken. Today you have received a request for a reference from another shop where the employee has applied to work. How should you proceed?

3 For the past three years your organisation has experienced really good trading results and the managing director has given the employees a Christmas bonus as a 'thank you'. This year's trading has been poor and the managing director has indicated that he will not be paying a Christmas bonus. The employees are arguing that the bonus is contractual because it has been regularly paid over the past three years. Advise the managing director on how to proceed.

04
Atypical contracts and the variation of contracts

CHAPTER OBJECTIVES

The objectives of this chapter are:

- to examine specific legislation relating to agency staff, part-time workers, casual workers, zero-hours contracts, temporary workers and the issuing of fixed-term contracts;
- to outline the provisions regarding flexible working;
- to provide an overview of specific situations such as employing asylum seekers and ex-offenders;
- to examine the process of varying a contract of employment.

4.1 Specific categories of employees

In Chapter 3 we looked at the difference between an employee, a worker and a self-employed individual. In this chapter we look further at the different types of contracts that people might be working under in an organisation, looking at the specific legislation that protects each of them.

The traditional employment contract of nine to five, Monday to Friday, is still common, but it does not have the dominance that it once had. Customers demand certain services 24 hours a day every day of the week; more parents are returning to work and wanting hours to fit around childcare; and more employees are looking to fit working hours around their other interests to try to achieve some sort of work–life balance. This change in working patterns has also led to an increase in the use of atypical workers.

 Task

Is there a need for a wide variety of types of worker (temporary, part-time, casual, agency, etc) in your organisation (or one with which you are familiar)? Find out how the organisation manages this variety.

 Explore further

In this section we address the legal issues relating to a certain number of atypical contracts. However, there are many more types of contracts being used by organisations (eg annual hours contracts). Compile a list of as many of these atypical contracts as you can. Then consider what legislation is relevant to both the employees and employers in specific relation to these contracts. Do you think there is a need for further legislation in some areas?

Useful sources of information about changing contracts include the Labour Force Survey and Labour Market Trends.

4.1.1 Agency workers

The employment status of agency workers has been the subject of a number of cases in recent years. There is now a clear ruling from case law, which concludes that it will be rare for agency workers to be employees. However, there is still some concern that the situation of agency workers needs more clarity. Indeed, judges have commented that there will be no clarity without statute addressing this issue. Although statute might be useful, we have seen how it is difficult to have one definition that suits all situations relating to employment status. Similar problems could occur if there was an attempt to define an agency worker in law. So, for now we have to rely on case law, which we will explore in this section.

Workers provided for an organisation by an employment agency do not have a clear employment relationship. They could argue that they are the employees of the employment agency, but the agency is likely to argue that they have no control over the daily work that the agency worker does. Alternatively, they could argue that they are the employees of the organisation where they are placed. However, the organisation is likely to argue that they do not have to provide work personally, because the agency could provide any individual to do the work. To determine if such employment relationships exist, the tests we examined in Chapter 3 are used.

One of the early cases addressing the issue of employment status was:

- *McMeechan v Secretary of State for Employment* (1997) ICR 549
  In this case McMeechan was a catering assistant who undertook a number of assignments from an employment agency. When the agency entered insolvency, McMeechan claimed entitlement to unpaid wages and redundancy payments from the National Insurance Fund (state funds for employees made redundant – see Chapter 9 – when the employer cannot meet the statutory payments). In favour of his being an employee was that the agency had control over him, because they could terminate his contract and could discipline him. There were also factors consistent with an employment relationship – for example, the agency deducted tax and NI contributions from McMeechan's pay. However, there was a document stating that McMeechan would work as a 'self-employed worker and not under a contract of service'.

  This case finally went to the Court of Appeal, which found on the basis of the evidence outlined that there was an employment relationship, because there was evidence of control, there was evidence of mutuality and there was nothing inconsistent with a contract of employment.

It is important to note that the test of mutuality was key to determining the relationship in this case. A case where the multiple test was more evident is:

- *Montgomery v Johnson Underwood Ltd* (2001) IRLR 269
  Montgomery was placed in an organisation as a receptionist/telephonist by Johnson Underwood (an employment agency). She worked there for two years and then the organisation asked the agency to terminate the contract. She took a claim for unfair dismissal against both the organisation where she worked and the employment agency. This case went through two stages of appeal and it was eventually concluded by the Court of Appeal that Montgomery was not an employee of either organisation. Crucially, they found that Johnson Underwood exercised 'little or no control, direction or supervision' over Montgomery. On the basis of that conclusion one of the three conditions of an employment relationship was not met, so Montgomery could not be an employee. Although they did exercise control over her work, there were no mutual obligations between her and the organisation, as the contract was between the agency and the organisation. In addition, there were factors inconsistent with an employment relationship – primarily that Montgomery was paid by Johnson Underwood.

Although these two cases give examples of how tests that are widely used to determine employment relationships can be applied, they are not robust in helping to determine whether an employment relationship has developed with the agency itself or with the 'end user' (the organisation in which the employee was placed).

An important ruling came in the following case:

- *Dacas v Brook Street Bureau (UK) Ltd and another* (2004) IRLR 190
  Dacas was placed by Brook Street Bureau as a cleaner for a local authority hostel. This was the only work she was assigned to by the bureau. She worked in this role for six years when she was dismissed following an incident in which she allegedly swore at a visitor to the hostel. Dacas claimed unfair dismissal

and took the approach that she had either been an employee of the hostel or of Brook Street Bureau. The Employment Tribunal had to decide whether she was an employee and, if she was, who the employer was. The Employment Tribunal first considered whether she was an employee of Wandsworth Council (who ran the hostel). They concluded there was not an employment relationship here because there was no direct contract between Dacas and the council.

They then considered whether she was employed by Brook Street Bureau. They concluded that, although a contract existed between Dacas and the bureau, they could not be her employers because they had no direct control over her daily work. They concluded, therefore, that she could not bring a claim of unfair dismissal because she had no employer–employee relationship.

The applicant appealed to the Employment Appeal Tribunal (EAT) (only against the decision that she was not an employee of Brook Street Bureau), which overturned the decision of the Employment Tribunal. They determined that Brook Street Bureau exercised control over Dacas because they paid her wages, had the right to exercise disciplinary action and had the right to terminate her contract. They also agreed that mutuality of obligations had been shown. In this case all the other evidence pointed to an employment relationship and therefore that was what existed. So Dacas was an employee of Brook Street Bureau. Brook Street Bureau then appealed to the Court of Appeal, which overturned the EAT's finding and ruled that Dacas was not an employee of the bureau.

In making the judgment, the Court of Appeal made it clear that the Employment Tribunal should always investigate whether an implied contract of employment has arisen between the employee and the end user (in this case, Wandsworth Council). Importantly, the Court of Appeal stated that in such agency situations the Employment Tribunal must find that someone is the employer, and it will usually be the end user. It was also noted that one year's service (which was sufficient to accrue unfair dismissal rights at the time – now if an employee starts work on or after 6 April 2012 they need two years' service) was sufficient to mean that an implied contract of employment had arisen. (In this case it was not possible to make a finding that Wandsworth Council was the employer because Dacas had not appealed against the earlier decision regarding this employment relationship.)

This ruling took on considerable importance because of the suggestion that it is not acceptable to conclude that there was no employment relationship. Here the Court of Appeal was clearly saying that there must be an employer – and suggesting that the most likely conclusion was that the employer was the end user.

In 2006 a further – somewhat complex – case went to the Court of Appeal, where the Dacas principle (that the end user is likely to be the employer) was applied:

- *Cable and Wireless plc v Muscat* (2006) EWCA Civ 220
  Muscat's original employers (EI) asked him to change from an employee to a contractor. To achieve this EI made him redundant and he set up his own company to provide EI with services. Then EI were taken over by Cable and Wireless. They insisted that Muscat supply his services through an agency that they already used – and would not do business directly with Muscat's company. Muscat continued to work through his company, through the agency, for a further eight months until Cable and Wireless decided they no longer required his services.

Applying the Dacas principle, the Court of Appeal determined that Muscat was an employee of the end user – in this case Cable and Wireless.

However, soon after the ruling in this case came an EAT ruling that set out some very useful principles about the employment status of agency workers:

- *James v London Borough of Greenwich* (2008) IRLR 302
  James was an agency worker who worked for the council for five years. Her argument was that an implied contract with the council had arisen. However, the EAT concluded that there was no implied contract because there was no mutuality of obligation in the employment relationship. The EAT went on to give guidelines on when it is appropriate to apply a contract between a worker and end user:
  - If the end user cannot insist on an agency supplying a particular worker, it is not appropriate to imply a contract of employment.
  - It is likely to be a rare situation where there is an employment relationship between the end user and the worker if the arrangements with the agency are genuine and accurately represent the relationship between the parties.
  - If an employment relationship is to be inferred, there must have been some words or conduct before the relationship started that suggested that the worker is working because of mutual obligations between the worker and the end user, and not because of arrangements with the agency.
  - The length of time that the relationship has been in place does not justify the implication of a contract of employment.

This case was referred to the Court of Appeal. In giving their judgment they supported the findings of the EAT, and supported the principles set out in the EAT's judgment. In addressing all employment status issues relating to agency workers, these principles should now be applied.

So, we now have a situation where it will be unusual for an agency worker to be an employee of the employment agency or of the employer where the agency worker is based. In all cases since the James judgment, this approach has been adopted – namely that the agency worker is the employee of no one.

As we have noted, the courts have commented that the situation with agency workers can only be resolved through having clear guidance through statute. Although there is no sign of any statute addressing the employment status of agency workers, there are two important pieces of legislation to note:

The Conduct of Employment Agencies and Employment Businesses Regulations 2003

These aim to improve the relationship between the hirer, agency and agency worker by setting out rules regarding the communication of information between them and the terms of agreements.

Agency Workers Regulations 2010

Maybe of more note is the Agency Workers Regulations 2010. These regulations were introduced as a result of the EU Directive and relate to the terms and conditions of agency workers. From October 2011 agency workers have been entitled to the same terms and conditions as employees in the organisation who are doing similar work. However, this parity is only applicable after the agency worker has worked for 12 continuous weeks for the organisation. The agreement covers terms and conditions such as pay, overtime, rest periods, breaks and holiday entitlement, but does not include any entitlements to sick pay or pension.

It is important to note that the EU Directive does not contain the provision that parity only applies after 12 continuous weeks of service. The 12 continuous weeks was negotiated by the UK Government, the TUC and the Confederation of British Industry (CBI), due to concerns about the effect that the legislation would have on UK businesses. The UK is one of the largest users of agency workers in the EU.

When calculating the 12-week continuous period, breaks between assignments (or during an assignment) will not break the continuity if they are for less than six weeks or the reason for the break is sickness, injury, childbirth, maternity, adoption, shared parental or paternity leave. Agency workers are also entitled to use facilities such as a crèche and have access to training opportunities. This applies from the first day of their placement. Agency workers do not have priority over other workers – so if, for example, there is a waiting list for a car park space, the agency worker can be added to the waiting list but does not go any further up the list than permanent employees. The organisation is required to make the agency workers aware of any employment opportunities that arise.

If an agency worker does not receive these rights he/she can claim compensation at the Employment Tribunal. This will be for a 'just and equitable' amount and will take into account any loss suffered by the agency worker. The agency and/or the organisation where the worker was placed can be liable for the compensation, depending on the extent to which they are responsible for the breach of the regulations.

The agency worker has the right to request information about terms and conditions of employment in the organisation. First the request for information is made to the agency and then to the organisation. This request can be made to determine if the agency worker is suffering from a detriment.

The regulations do not address employment status.

 Explore further

Clarification of the status of agency workers has partly been driven by European legislation. Find out how other member states treat agency workers in relation to their agency status. A good starting point is the websites of the European Commission (www.ec.europa.eu) or the European Parliament (www.europarl.europa.eu).

4.1.2 Part-time workers

In the past, part-time workers were treated less favourably than full-time workers. This is demonstrated in the case of *R v Secretary of State ex parte Equal Opportunities Commission* (1995) 1 AC 1. In this case the ruling that part-time workers needed five years' continuous service to take a claim of unfair dismissal, compared with two years' service for full-time employees, was indirect discrimination against women. This was because significantly more women than men tend to work part-time. On the basis of this challenge, the qualification period for part-time workers was brought into line with that for full-time workers. This case was one of the first suggestions that treating part-time workers less favourably was not acceptable.

In 1997 the issue of part-time workers was addressed by the EU putting in place a directive dealing with the issue of all employment rights for part-time employees. This directive covered a wide range of contractual issues. Most of the directive was brought into place as UK law in the Part-time Workers (Prevention of Less Favourable Treatment) Regulations 2000 (amended in 2002), which we will refer to as PTW Regulations.

Defining a part-time worker

The first stage in considering part-time workers is to determine who they are. First, we have the definition of 'worker', which is the same as that already defined from Section 230 (3) of the ERA 1996 – namely, that 'A worker is an individual who either works under a contract of employment or works under any other contract where that individual agrees to personally perform work or services for another party.'

Having determined that the definition of a worker is the same whether they may be part-time or full-time, the next step is to determine what 'part-time' means. The legislation simply states that a part-time worker is one whose normal hours of work, averaged over a period of up to one year, are less than the normal hours of comparable full-time workers. The comparator is key to these regulations because they give the right to make a claim of less favourable treatment on the grounds of working part-time. To show that a part-time worker has been treated less favourably, he/she must be able to point to a full-time worker and show that his/her own treatment has been different and that it has been less preferable.

The importance of a comparator

A worker might state that he/she does not think the rules regarding access to a pension scheme are fair. If the rules are also applied to full-time workers, the issue is not the part-time employment. However, if the full-time workers had different pension rules that were seen as preferential and he/she was able to identify a comparator who was full-time, the worker could take a claim of less favourable treatment under the PTW Regulations. The comparator should be someone who is employed at the same time, by the same employer, at the same establishment (or if there are no comparators at that establishment at another establishment of the employer), under the same type of contract and doing the same or broadly similar work (given reference to levels of qualification, skill and experience).

There are straightforward examples. In a call centre there might be a core of staff answering calls who all work a basic week of 35 hours. In addition, there are staff who take the same calls at the same call centre who only work for 15 hours each week – they are clearly classified as part-time.

The more difficult examples are when there is not a clear comparator. For example, the person claiming to be part-time is a cleaner working in a factory where there are no other cleaners and no other people doing similar work. In this situation the strict definitions do not allow the cleaner to take any claim under the PTW Regulations because there is no comparator. This might seem unfair, but the regulations are focused on different treatment for full-time and part-time working, and any difference that is identified must be clearly attributable to the part-time status. If that clear distinction cannot be shown, there can be no claim.

There are exceptions to the rules on comparators:

- If a full-time worker reduces his/her hours and becomes part-time, he/she can use the previous terms and conditions of employment as a full-time worker as the comparator.

- In the same way, a worker returning to work after an absence of less than 12 months, who returns to reduced hours, can use his/her previous full-time employment as the comparator.

Treatment of a part-time worker

The regulations give the part-time worker the right not to be treated less favourably by the employer because of the part-time status. This covers contractual issues (eg rate of pay, overtime payments, sickness and maternity pay arrangements, and any other benefits). It also gives the right for the part-time worker not to be subjected to any detriment because of the part-time status. This covers issues such as the possibility of promotion and the access to training. In addition, there must be equal rights to have access to schemes such as pensions and share options and access to statutory leave rights (eg maternity, paternity and parental leave). A worker cannot be selected for redundancy only because of part-time status.

If a worker considers that he/she is being treated less favourably because of part-time status, he/she may ask his/her employer for a written statement explaining the reasons for the treatment. This written statement can be produced as evidence at any subsequent Employment Tribunal hearing.

If the worker is not satisfied with the response from the employer, he/she can take a claim to the Employment Tribunal on the grounds of less favourable treatment or of victimisation. If the worker does take such a claim, the employer has to identify the ground for the less favourable treatment or detriment. The employer is 'vicariously liable' for the actions of its managers, supervisors and other employees. In other words, the employer is responsible for any actions that have been taken by its employees, even if those actions contravene company policy, unless the employer can clearly show that it has taken steps to stop such a situation occurring. (We examine vicarious liability in more detail in Chapter 7.)

If the worker wins the case at the Employment Tribunal, the possible remedies are that the Employment Tribunal can order all or one of the following:

- a declaration of the rights of the worker in respect of the complaint;
- payment of compensation by the employer to the applicant;
- recommended action to be taken by the employer to deal with the issue that has been brought to the tribunal – failure to comply may result in increased compensation being ordered.

- *Matthews and others v Kent and Medway Towns Fire Authority and others* (2006) UKHL 8

  The issue of similarity of work was addressed in this case. The fire service operates with full-time fire officers and part-time (retained) officers. The part-time officers usually have other jobs, but are on call for a set number of hours to respond to peaks in demand.

  The claimants brought a case arguing that the retained firefighters were unfairly being denied pension, sick pay and additional payment rights that full-time firefighters enjoyed. Initially, their claim was rejected by the Employment Tribunal on the basis that the work that they did was sufficiently different from the full-time firefighters for the Part-time Regulations not to apply.

  The case eventually went on to the House of Lords, where the claim from the retained firefighters was allowed. It concluded that the tribunal had focused too much on the differences. However, when deciding claims under the Part-time Regulations, it is most important to focus on the similarities in the core duties. Because these were broadly the same between the full-time and retained firefighters, the claim was upheld.

 Task

Does your organisation (or one with which you are familiar) employ part-time staff? If so, find out if there are any terms and conditions that are specific to part-time employees. Do you see any potential difficulties with the ways in which part-time employees are treated?

4.1.3 Casual workers

We have already examined the status of casual workers in looking at the case of *Carmichael v National Power* (2000) IRLR 43 (see Chapter 3).

If a worker is 'casual' in the sense that there is no obligation on the employer to provide work, and no obligation on the employee to carry out any work, it is unlikely that an employer–employee relationship exists. In this situation the casual worker is not entitled to the same benefits as an employee.

Zero-hours contracts

The use of zero-hours contracts is an issue that has hit the headlines again and again in recent times. There are concerns that employers are using zero-hours contracts in a way that gives no security of income or employment for individuals. However, there are also reports that individuals like the flexibility that zero-hours contracts bring.

Zero-hours contracts are used in different ways by different organisations. Some organisations use them to add flexibility to the workforce, having a bank of individuals that they can call on to work if they have an increased need. This is particularly common amongst seasonal industries, for example a retail organisation that needs increased labour over the Christmas trading period. Other organisations use zero-hours contracts for the majority of their employees, simply allocating shifts on a weekly or monthly basis, with no guarantee of the amount of work offered. When concerns are raised about the use of zero-hours contracts it is the latter use that is most typically criticised.

Most commonly, a zero-hours contract is an arrangement where the employer is not obliged to provide any work, and the individual is not obliged to do any work that is offered – clearly that does not pass the mutual obligations test and hence the individual would not be an employee.

However, some organisations will insist that the individual does do any work that is offered, and if work is regularly offered it is likely that the requirement of the mutual obligations test will be met and an employment relationship will develop.

As a result of the Small Business Enterprise and Employment Act 2015 it is unlawful to include exclusivity clauses in a zero-hours contract. These are clauses that restrict an individual from working for another employer whilst in a zero-hours agreement.

In addition, the Exclusivity Terms in Zero-Hour Contracts (Redress) Regulations 2015 make a dismissal of a zero-hour employee automatically unfair if the principle reason is that the individual worked for another employer – there is no qualifying period to bring such a claim. In addition, it is unlawful to submit a zero-hour worker to a detriment if they breach a clause saying that they are not allowed to work for another employer.

 Explore further

The CIPD has carried out research into the use of zero-hour contracts, and this was published as 'Employer/employee views of zero-hour contracts'. The full report can be accessed at

https://www.cipd.co.uk/knowledge/fundamentals/emp-law/terms-conditions/zero-hours-views-report

---

4.1.4 *Temporary workers*

Temporary workers have exactly the same rights as other workers, presuming that they have acquired the relevant statutory period of employment (eg two years' service to take a claim of unfair dismissal, one year if employment started before 6 April 2012). A temporary worker is usually on a fixed-term contract (see section 4.1.5) or is an agency worker (which we have already examined) or is a casual worker (which we have also examined).

4.1.5 *Fixed-term contracts*

There are situations when an employer wants to employ someone, but for a fixed period of time only. For example, there might be a special project to complete, but once that project is completed it is anticipated that there will be no further work for the employees involved. In this situation an employer can issue a fixed-term contract, which clearly states when the employment will end. The following case shows how this can also be abused:

- *Booth v United States of America* (1999) IRLR 16
  This case centred on three employees who worked at a USAF airbase. They were employed on a series of fixed-term contracts. At the end of each contract there was a short break in service after which a new contract of employment was issued. Upon the issuing of each contract they returned to the same job with the same tools and equipment. However, the breaks in employment meant they never amassed sufficient continuity of service to claim statutory rights (such as the right to take a claim of unfair dismissal). The EAT ruled that they had been unable to show evidence of continuity of service. The employer's actions were lawful, if undesirable, and if this loophole was to be addressed it needed to be done through legislation.

Treatment of a fixed-term worker

The Fixed-Term Employees (Prevention of Less Favourable Treatment) Regulations 2002 introduced new legislation relating to fixed-term contracts. The employee on a fixed-term contract should not receive less favourable treatment when compared to a permanent employee who is employed by the same employer, is engaged in the same or broadly similar work, and is based at the same establishment. If there is no such employee at the same establishment, a comparison may be made by an employee of the employer working at a different establishment. A comparator must be an actual employee, not a hypothetical employee.

Less favourable treatment includes contractual terms (including pay and benefits), opportunities to receive training and secure permanent employment and qualifying periods for benefits. In addition, the legislation limits the issuing of fixed-term contracts to a maximum of four years. If fixed-term contracts are issued beyond that period of time, the contract will automatically become permanent.

Termination of a fixed-term contract

It is also important to note that the termination of a fixed-term contract is a dismissal and should be handled as such. However, the Acas Code of Practice: Disciplinary and Grievance Procedures does not apply to the termination of fixed-term contracts (see Chapter 8). If a contract has a specified end date and the employer wants to terminate the contract prior to that date, there must be some potentially fair reason (eg redundancy or poor conduct of the employee), unless there is a clause in the contract allowing for it to be terminated early.

However, non-renewal of the fixed-term contract does not constitute less favourable treatment, as shown in the following case:

- *Webley v Department for Work and Pensions* (2004) EWCA Civ 1745
  Webley was employed on a number of short fixed-term contracts. Her last contract was not renewed and this resulted in her having an employment length of just less than one year – meaning she could not bring a claim of unfair dismissal. She claimed that the non-renewal of the contract was less favourable treatment, in comparison to a full-time employee.

The Court of Appeal rejected her claim, stating that if she was right there could be no fixed-term contracts – because any non-renewal would result in unfair treatment. The law clearly allows for fixed-term contracts and so the law clearly allows that they can be terminated at the end of the contract.

4.2 Flexible working

The demographics of the workplace have changed greatly over recent years. In particular, there are more women working and more mothers returning to work after childbirth. In addition, there are more parents raising children alone and needing to work because they are the only source of income in the family. On average, people are living longer, and this also means that there are more people who have caring responsibilities towards elderly relatives.

It is these changing demographics of the workplace that have prompted the government to consider a number of aspects of legislation to address the needs of family life. As well as the changing statistics there is also the issue of work–life balance and the amount of time that families have to spend together. The government wants to encourage people to work – and wants to encourage women to return to the workplace to use their skills. However, family life is important, and an appropriate balance must be struck between work and outside commitments.

In response to these needs, the government introduced legislation giving a statutory right to request flexible working. Initially, the law introduced in 2003 was just to request flexible working if the employee had a child aged under six years. In April 2007 the government extended the legislation to cover carers of adults. There was a further extension in April 2009 to include parents of children aged under 17 years (18 years if the child was disabled).

However, all that was changed on 30 June 2014 when the Flexible Working Regulations 2014 were introduced. We now have a situation where all employees who have at least 26 weeks' continuous service can request flexible working, if they have not made a similar request in the last 12 months.

It is important to note that it does not matter why the employee is requesting flexible working. It could be for caring responsibilities, it could be to pursue the dream of being a world-class athlete – the reason is not relevant.

In requesting flexible working, employees can request changes to:

- the hours they work;
- the times they work;
- the place they are required to work.

An employee must write to his/her employer requesting a change to flexible working. In making this written request the employee must set out:

- the date of the application;
- the nature of the change being sought, and when the employee wants this to take effect;
- the effect that they think the change will have on the employer, and how this effect could be addressed;

- that the request is a statutory request;
- whether they have previously made a similar request, and if so when.

4.2.1 Process for managing the request

Once the employer has received the request, they must arrange a meeting with the employee to discuss it. The employee has the right to be accompanied to this meeting by a fellow worker or a trade union representative. The final decision on the request must be made within three months of receiving the application.

If the request is granted, the changes that have been agreed must be specified in writing and a date for the start of the changes must be confirmed. This will be a change of contract (see later in this chapter) and will be considered a permanent change. In other words, the employee has no right to expect a change back to the previous terms and conditions of employment at some future date.

The legislation sets out a number of grounds on which the employer can turn down the request.

They are:

- the burden of additional costs;
- a detrimental effect on the ability to meet customer demand;
- an inability to reorganise work among existing staff;
- an inability to recruit additional staff;
- a detrimental impact on quality;
- a detrimental impact on performance;
- insufficiency of work during the periods the employee proposes to work;
- planned structural changes;
- any other ground the Secretary of State may specify by regulations.

- *Commotion Ltd v Rutty* (2006) ICR 290
  In this case Rutty was granted a residence order to care for her two-year-old granddaughter and made an informal request to work a three-day week. This was refused, so she went ahead and made a formal request in line with the Flexible Working Regulations. Her request (and her appeal) was turned down because the employer wanted all employees working uniform hours and believed that the change would result in a detrimental impact on teamworking. Rutty resigned.
  The Employment Tribunal, upheld by the EAT, found that the employer had not given reasonable grounds for the refusal – as set out in section 4.2.1. The concerns that they had expressed had not been substantiated.

4.2.2 Refusal of a request

If the employee is refused his/her request, he/she may appeal against the decision. If a request for an appeal is received a meeting must be convened. Again, the employee has the right to be accompanied. The decision of the appeal should be communicated to the employee in writing.

If the employee's request is still turned down, he/she can refer the issue to an Employment Tribunal. The Employment Tribunal has a limited role to play. It cannot challenge the validity of the employer's decision and it cannot make its own judgment on whether the request should have been granted. Its role is simply to consider whether the employer has given the request serious consideration, whether the reason for refusal was one permitted by the legislation, whether the facts used to assess the request were correct and whether the employer acted reasonably in the way it addressed the request.

If the Employment Tribunal finds that the employer has erred in the way it has handled the request, it can either award compensation to the employee (at a maximum of eight weeks' pay – the statutory definition of a maximum week's pay, currently [as of April 2018] £508, applies) or it can make an order that the request is reconsidered.

It is possible for employees to bring other claims associated with the way they consider the application has been handled. These might include discrimination on grounds such as sex or disability (we look at these claims later). It is important, therefore, that the employer is careful to ensure a consistent approach to all requests.

- *XC Trains Ltd v CD* (2016) UKEAT/0331/15

  A female train driver, who was also a single mother with three young children, asked for a change to her shifts so that she did not have to work Saturdays, and was not rostered to work shifts starting very early, or ending very late. This was refused because the employer said that it would not be possible to cover all the shifts.

  The Employment Tribunal found that this was indirect sex discrimination because the employer should have thought creatively about how to cover the shifts. The EAT allowed the appeal, and remitted the case to another tribunal to consider. There was a need to balance the needs of the employee against the needs of the employer.

- *Seville v Flybe plc* (2016)

  An Air Stewardess had worked 22 days a month prior to having her baby, with her shifts being given to her the month before she worked them. She made a flexible working request, asking to move to 11 days a month, with fixed shifts, so that she could arrange childcare. This request was refused and she successfully claimed sex discrimination.

 Explore further

Acas has issued a Code of Practice to be followed when handling requests for flexible working. This can be accessed at http://www. acas.org.uk/media/pdf/f/e/Code-of-Practice-on-handling-in-a-reasonable-manner-requests-to-work-flexibly.pdf

Task

How does your organisation – or an organisation with which you are familiar – deal with requests relating to flexible working? Do you think the organisation follows a correct procedure?

4.3 Varying a contract of employment

There will be situations where an employer wants to make a change to a contract of employment. This might happen because of a need to change hours of work to meet with the hours being worked by a competitor, due to a restructuring or due to a change in products or services. Clearly, employers must be able to make changes to ensure that the organisation survives and thrives, but this does not mean that the contract of employment can simply be changed without the employee being consulted.

This is because a contract of employment is a legal agreement between two parties and for that reason an employer cannot unilaterally vary that contract. If the employer, unilaterally, does make a change to the contract, the employee has two options:

- to resign and make a claim of constructive dismissal (see Chapter 8);
- to continue working, but try to seek damages for any loss that has been suffered.

To try to ensure a smooth process, the employer should always start by consulting with the employees affected. If the changes affect 20–99 employees the consultation should be with representatives, and should be for a minimum of 30 days. If the changes affect 100+ employees the consultation should be for a minimum of 45 days. If fewer than 20 employees are affected there is no requirement to consult with representatives but there should be consultation with the individuals affected, regardless of the numbers affected.

Hopefully, agreement to the changes will be reached through consultation. However, if there is no agreement and the employee works in accordance with the proposed changes, without making protest, and continues to work in accordance with the new terms for a significant period of time, it can be interpreted that the employee has accepted the changes to the contract by his/her actions.

If the employee does not agree to the proposed changes and does not work in accordance with the changes, it can be very difficult for the employer to proceed. The options open to the employer include:

- Terminate the contract of employment for the potentially fair reason of 'some other substantial reason', and offer new contracts under the new terms. This option runs a strong risk of claims for unfair dismissal from the employee (see Chapter 8). It could only be defended if the employer could demonstrate that there was a strong business reason that justified the actions and had tried first to seek agreements to the changes.

Negotiate the proposed new terms with the employee representative body and try to seek agreement. If there is a reasonable period ('reasonable' will be the time required for all the issues raised by the employee representatives to be seriously considered and addressed) of negotiation and no agreement can be reached, the employer can give notice that the variation will go ahead, if it can be justified for business reasons. This option will be particularly strong if the majority of employees affected have already agreed to the change. However, there is the danger that an employee might resign and claim constructive dismissal (see Chapter 8).

- *Hepworth Heating Ltd v Akers and others* (2003) EAT 846/02
  Of the employees at Hepworth Heating 280 were entitled to be paid in cash. Hepworth Heating proposed moving all the employees to be paid by direct transfer to a bank account. This had security and cost benefits for the employer. Some of the employees objected on the grounds of inconvenience and security issues surrounding the use of cashpoints. Negotiation took place and was unsuccessful. The employer then wrote to the employees telling them that the change would go ahead and giving notice of dismissal if the employees refused to accept the change. A number of employees returned the required forms but wrote 'under duress' against their signatures. They carried on working after the cashless pay was introduced.

  The EAT ruled that there had been no 'duress' and so by continuing to work the employees had agreed to the variation in the terms and conditions of their employment.

- *Cartwright and others v Tetrad Ltd* (2015) UKEAT/0262/14
  The employer was experiencing financial difficulties and imposed a 5 per cent pay deduction on all employees without their agreement. This took place on 10 May, and there was no objection until 23 October. This was seen to be an implied variation of contract, because the employees worked in accordance with the change from May until October without objecting.

  The employer could have reserved the right to make a contractual change by including a mobility or flexibility clause in the contract. However, that does not mean that the employer can make any change that it wants. A mobility or flexibility clause must be applied reasonably.

- *United Bank v Akhtar* (1989) IRLR 507
  There was a mobility clause within the contract of employment allowing for relocation of the employee anywhere in the UK. The employer gave six days' notice that the employee was to move to Birmingham from Leeds. He was unable to comply, resigned and claimed constructive dismissal. The employee won the case because it was ruled that there was an overriding duty on the employer not to act in such a way as to breach the mutual trust and confidence in the employment relationship – giving such short notice had breached that trust and confidence

4.4 Employing migrant workers and ex-offenders

4.4.1 Migrant workers

Employers have had a responsibility to check the entitlement to work in the United Kingdom of all new employees since 27 January 1997 (under section 8 of the Asylum and Immigration Act 1996), in order to establish a defence against conviction, or an excuse against payment of a civil penalty, for employing an illegal migrant worker. The law was revised by the Immigration Act 2014, which has increased the maximum penalty for illegally employing a migrant worker to £20,000.

The work permit scheme, along with more than 80 other routes of entry into the UK, was replaced by a points-based immigration system during 2008. This does not affect nationals of the states of the European Economic Area, who have the right to seek work in the UK and to accept offers of employment. They are also allowed to live in the UK while looking for suitable work. Citizens of independent Commonwealth countries who have the 'right of abode' in the UK are also allowed to come into the UK and accept offers of employment. These individuals have British citizenship that may be acquired by birth, adoption, descent, registration or naturalisation.

The current system has five tiers, representing different types of worker. Workers require sponsorship from an organisation (apart from Tier 1) in order to enter the UK to work. Employers can register as sponsors with the Home Office. When an individual for a job has been identified a form is submitted to the Home Office, which will then be scored. Points are awarded for a number of factors, including age, aptitude and experience. There are a minimum number of points required, depending on the category under which entry is being sought. There are five such categories:

- Tier 1 – highly skilled.
- Tier 2 – skilled.
- Tier 3 – low skilled (this tier is currently suspended).
- Tier 4 – students (this is still open, but greatly curbed).
- Tier 5 – temporary workers (including working holidaymakers).

 Explore further

To further explore the right to work in the UK go to www.gov.uk and read the guides that are available there, for both the employer and the employee.

4.4.2 Ex-offenders

The primary legislation relevant here is the Rehabilitation of Offenders Act 1974. The Act focuses on the issue of 'spent' convictions. A conviction becomes 'spent' when a set period of time has passed from the date of conviction. The Legal Aid

Table 4.1 Time that must pass before a conviction is spent

Punishment	Period of Time Before Spent (Over 18 Years Old)	Period of Time Before Spent (Under 18 Years Old)
Absolute discharge	No time required	No time required
Fines, community service orders	One year	Six months
Imprisonment for less than six months	Two years	18 months
Imprisonment between six and 30 months	Four years	Two years
Imprisonment longer than 30 months	Seven years	42 months

Sentencing and Punishment of Offenders Act 2012 reduced the set periods of time, and became effective on 10 March 2014. An ex-offender does not have to disclose any information relating to a spent conviction when seeking employment, unless they are working in occupations such as doctors, nurses, social workers, teachers, becoming registered day-care providers or carrying out any other work with children.

The current time periods for a conviction to be spent are outlined in Table 4.1. The Rehabilitation of Offenders Act 1974 makes it unlawful for an employer to question a prospective employee about a spent conviction, and if such questioning arises, the prospective employee can deny the conviction ever occurred. It is also unlawful to deny employment on the grounds of a spent conviction.

 Task

Find out whether your organisation, or one with which you are familiar, has a policy for dealing with asylum seekers, ex-offenders and those seeking work from overseas. If it does, read it through and see if it meets the requirements outlined in this chapter. If it does not have a policy, make an attempt at writing one!

4.5 Vetting and barring

Following the tragic murders of Jessica Chapman and Holly Wells in 2002, the Bichard Inquiry was set up to review the way in which records of people who should be barred from working with children and vulnerable adults are handled. In particular, concern was expressed that a number of different bodies held different lists and the information was not shared. As a result the Safeguarding Vulnerable Groups

Act 2006 was introduced. This made it unlawful for someone who is identified as being barred from working with vulnerable groups to carry out work in a 'regulated activity' (one requiring contact with children and vulnerable adults), and employers were required to make checks relating to this. As part of the Act, the Independent Safeguarding Authority (ISA) was set up. This body was responsible for overseeing a central list of those who were barred. There was a plan for all those working with children and vulnerable adults to be registered with the ISA, with a phased process starting in July 2010. However, there were concerns about this process, in particular that it would require people who only had occasional or supervised contact with children and vulnerable adults to register.

The Coalition Government of 2010–15 put a halt to the registration of individuals with ISA while it reviewed the system. A new scaled-back scheme was then introduced as part of the Protection from Freedoms Act 2012, which was mostly implemented on 10 September 2012. As part of the changes the Independent Safeguarding Authority merged with the Criminal Records Bureau on 1 December 2012 to form the Disclosure and Barring Service.

There are a number of key points to note:

- It is a criminal offence for a barred person to work, or volunteer, in regulated activity.
- It is a criminal offence for an employer to knowingly employ (either on a paid or voluntary basis) a barred person in regulated activity.
- Where a person is removed from regulated activity by an employer because the person has caused harm to a child or vulnerable adult, the Disclosure and Barring Service must be notified.

4.5.1 Regulated activity

The definition of 'regulated activity' was revised in the Protection from Freedoms Act 2012.

The definition of regulated activity relating to children comprises:

1 Unsupervised activities: teaching, training, caring for or supervising children; driving a vehicle solely for children; providing advice/guidance on well-being.
2 Work for a limited range of establishments where there is opportunity for contact (for example children's homes, schools, childcare premises). This does not include supervised contact by volunteers.

Work in these two categories is only a regulated activity if it is done regularly.
Regulated activity also covers:

3 Relevant personal care, for example washing, dressing, health care supervised by a professional.
4 Registered child minding and foster caring.

Regulated activity in relation to adults does not refer to 'vulnerable adults' as it did previously. The focus is on the type of care that the adult requires, rather than the setting within which the adult receives that help. There is no requirement for an activity to be carried out a certain number of times before it is categorised as a regulated activity.

4.5.2 *Disclosure and Barring Service Check*

If an individual is working in a regulated activity they must have a Disclosure and Barring Service Check. If an employer considers that an individual will be engaged in a regulated activity then an enhanced disclosure is required. In addition, the employer will ask for a check against the 'barred list'. The employer is responsible for identifying those who need a check, and ensuring that this takes place. This includes volunteers, although there is no charge for a DBS check for a volunteer.

An individual cannot apply for a DBS check themselves; the employer asking for the check must arrange for this. In Scotland individuals can apply to Disclosure Scotland for a basic check, which gives details of unspent convictions, but cannot apply for their own enhanced check. This means, therefore, that the employer will need to arrange the DBS check for any self-employed individuals doing relevant work for them.

- *R (T and others) v Greater Manchester Police* [2013] EWCA Civ 25
  The claimants successfully argued that disclosing historic and minor convictions was a breach of their human rights. As a result, the government altered the DBS rules such that an adult conviction will be removed from a DBS certificate after 11 years if it is the person's only conviction and did not result in a custodial sentence. If the individual was under 18 years when the offence occurred it will be removed after five and a half years. There are some offences that will never be removed.

Penalties

The Vetting and Barring Scheme gives a variety of criminal offences to ensure compliance:

- For individuals it is a criminal offence to work, or volunteer, in regulated activity whilst barred. Potential penalties include up to five years' imprisonment or an unlimited fine.
- For employers and personnel suppliers it is a criminal offence to:
  - knowingly allow someone to work in a regulated activity while barred – potential penalties include up to five years' imprisonment or an unlimited fine, and managers and directors can be liable as well as the company itself;
  - allow someone to work in regulated activity without carrying out the required checks.

The potential penalty is a fine of up to £5,000.

From 17 June 2013 DBS checks have been available online. This means that an employer can check an existing DBS check for an applicant, rather than the applicant needing to apply again. The employer will be able to see the existing check as well as anything that has been added to it since the check was carried out. The applicant has to pay an annual fee to subscribe to the service.

KEY LEARNING POINTS

1 Agency workers are unlikely to be the employees of the agency or the organisation where they are placed.

2 Part-time workers have the right to be treated the same as full-time workers. To exercise this right they must be able to identify a full-time comparator in the organisation.

3 The Flexible Working Regulations 2014 allow all employees with at least 26 weeks' continuous service to request flexible working.

4 The employer has a duty to check that all prospective employees have the right to work in the UK.

5 Ex-offenders are not required to reveal any details about 'spent' convictions, unless they work in certain professions.

6 An employer cannot unilaterally vary a contract of employment. If a change is needed, negotiation must take place. If that negotiation is unsuccessful, the employer can impose the change, but must be able to show it is for sound business reasons.

7 If an employee objects to a variation of the contract, he/she can resign and claim constructive dismissal. Alternatively, he/she can continue working and try to seek damages for any losses the change has brought.

Case summaries

- *Bunce v Postworth Ltd t/a Skyblue* (2005) IRLR 557 CA – Bunce worked on a number of short assignments through Skyblue (an agency), most of them jobs for Carillion Rail. He could not expect continuous work and there was no mutuality of obligation. Bunce argued that there was an 'umbrella' contract and that additional contracts were implied each time he took a new assignment. The Court of Appeal dismissed the claim.

- *Melhuish v Redbridge Citizen's Advice Bureau* (2005) EAT 1030/04 – Melhuish worked as a volunteer for the CAB and wanted to make a claim of unfair dismissal – an option only open to employees. It was ruled that he was not an employee because the very nature of being a volunteer was that he did not have to attend work and was not paid – so there were no obligations on either side of the relationship.

- *Holt v Bannatyne Fitness* [2016] In this case an employee had previously made a flexible working request to just work Monday to Friday due to childcare issues. This had been granted, but new management wanted her to work at weekends. She refused, and was eventually made redundant. This

(continued)

(Continued)

was found to be unfair dismissal and sex discrimination.
- *Gower and Donnelly v Post Office Ltd* [2017] ET3200588/2017
  A group of employees were told they were to move from weekly to monthly pay. Two employees objected, although they did accept a loan to help them with the change. They successfully argued that there was an unlawful deduction from wages each Friday

when they were not paid, and there was a breach of contract.
- *Bateman v Asda Stores Ltd* [2010] UKEAT/0221/09
  Terms of employment were being harmonised, and following consultation most employees agreed. It then used a statement in the staff handbook, allowing the employer to make changes to the contracts. This was not a breach of contract; the clause allowed reasonable changes to be made.

 Examples to work through

1 Stephen is a graphic designer and he was employed to work with your full-time product development team on a one-year fixed-term contract. The project he was working on has finished after just 10 months and there is no other work for him to do. Can you terminate his contract early? If you can, how should it be done? If you cannot, what other options are available to you?

2 For the past 10 years your organisation has had cleaners supplied by a local employment agency. Most of the cleaners have worked a relatively short period before moving on to other work – and some cleaners have just come for occasional days. However, one cleaner – Daisy – has regularly worked at your organisation for 12 years. You have been made

aware that she has had some sort of argument with the agency and is no longer working for them. However, today she has turned up to carry out her cleaning duties, claiming that she really worked for your organisation anyway. What should you do?

3 You have a small shop that has traditionally opened 9 am to 5 pm Monday to Saturday. However, due to competition from larger stores you have decided that the only way to survive is to extend the opening hours to 8 am to 7 pm. Your existing staff will then be required to work shifts to cover the extra hours and you will employ one additional person. However, your staff are not happy with the change and are refusing to work the proposed shifts. What should you do?

05
Individual protection rights

CHAPTER OBJECTIVES

The objectives of this chapter are:
- to examine the provisions of the Working Time Regulations;
- to consider various provisions relating to the payment of wages;
- to outline the National Minimum Wage Act 1998;
- to consider issues relating to payment during sickness;
- to explore maternity, paternity and shared parental leave;
- to examine regulations relating to parental leave;
- to outline the legislation relating to adoption leave;
- to review situations when the employee is allowed time off work.

5.1 The Working Time Regulations 1998

5.1.1 Who is covered

The Working Time Regulations are the implementation of the Working Time Directive and of provisions of the Young Workers Directive. Their basis relates to health and safety – that employees are healthier, and less likely to have accidents, if they have at least minimum levels of holidays, rest periods and reasonable working hours.

The original regulations did not apply to doctors in training, the armed forces and the police. They also did not apply to the activities of air, road, sea, inland waterway and lake transport, sea fishing and other workers at sea. There were also special cases that were excluded – jobs in domestic service, managing executives, family workers and workers officiating at religious services in churches and religious communities.

The transport categories were largely excluded because workers in these sectors are covered by specific regulations relating to their work. However, this did cause some difficulty, because it is largely 'mobile' workers (eg drivers, fishermen, pilots) rather than 'non-mobile' workers (eg clerical/administration) who are covered by the specific legislation. Thus – as shown in the following case of *Bowden and others v Tuffnel Parcels Express Ltd* (2001) – clerical workers are covered by the legislation that seems to be most appropriate to their situation:

- *Bowden and others v Tuffnel Parcels Express Ltd* (2001) IRLR 838
  Bowden and two colleagues were part-time clerical workers in Tuffnel Parcels Express, which was a business operating in the road transport sector. They were not entitled to paid holidays under their contracts of employment. When the Working Time Regulations 1998 came into force, they asked their employer to give them the minimum holiday entitlement, as defined by those regulations. They were refused, because the road transport sector was specifically excluded from the regulations. The issue was eventually referred to the European Court of Justice (ECJ) to determine if 'non-mobile' workers within the sector were covered by the regulations. The ECJ ruled that the whole sector had been excluded and for that reason the clerical staff were also not covered.

However, these exclusions were amended by the Working Time (Amendment) Regulations 2003. In summary, the impact of these amendments is to apply the regulations to non-mobile workers within the transport sector. If mobile workers within the transport sector are not covered by their own specific legislation, these amendments apply.

5.1.2 Who is a 'worker' under the Working Time Regulations 1998?

The regulations state that a worker includes anyone who has entered into or works under (or where the employment has ceased, worked under): 1) a contract of employment, or 2) any other contract, whether express or implied and (if it is express) whether oral or in writing, whereby the individual undertakes to do or perform personally any work or services for another party.

In essence, the definition of a worker, therefore, covers those employed under a contract of employment and potentially many casual and freelance workers. It excludes self-employed people who are genuinely pursuing their own business activity.

This definition is midway between the definition we had in Chapter 2 of a person employed under a contract for services and a contract of service. In *Torith Ltd v Flynn* (2002) EAT 0017/02, the EAT concluded that the regulations have created a 'hybrid' category of a protected worker.

- *Torith Ltd v Flynn* (2002) EAT 0017/02
  Flynn worked for Torith as a joiner on one of its building sites. He claimed holiday pay under the Working Time Regulations 1998. Torith were

responsible for deducting tax and National Insurance contributions from his pay, although Flynn was still required to submit an annual tax return as a self-employed person. Flynn received limited supervision in his work. He was supplied with materials and power tools, but supplied his own hand tools. He worked exclusively for Torith and was expected to work the normal site hours of 39 per week. He was not entitled to holiday or sick pay, and if he did take a holiday, was not guaranteed any work on his return. Subject to Torith's approval, he could provide a substitute to carry out his work.

The EAT ruled that Flynn was covered by the Working Time Regulations 1998. Flynn fell into this category of a 'hybrid' worker because he clearly was not pursuing a business activity on his own account.

5.1.3 *What is work?*

Work is defined in Regulation 2 as:

- a period when the worker is working, at the employer's disposal and carrying out activities or duties in accordance with usual practice;
- a period when the worker is receiving relevant training;
- any other period that is to be treated as working time within the regulations.

Although this might seem straightforward, it has been the subject of considerable debate in case law – mainly relating to time spent on call.

- *Landeshauptstadt Kiel v Jaeger* (2003) ECR 1–8389/IRLR 804
  In this case a doctor claimed that the time he spent on call where he had to remain at the hospital constituted work. It was agreed that although he was allowed to rest during this period if there was no work requiring his attention, it was classed as work because it was time when the employee was 'at the employer's disposal'.

- *MacCartney v Oversley House Management* (2006) IRLR 514
  MacCartney was a manager of a sheltered housing complex and was on 24-hour call. She had a house on the premises where she lived. She worked for four days per week and during those days she was required to be on or within three miles of (and in mobile phone contact with) the premises.

  She claimed that the working arrangements meant that she was not receiving the rest periods as set out in the regulations. The EAT ruled that she was not getting the required rest periods because any time that she was on call counted as work for the purposes of the regulations.

- *Truslove and another v Scottish Ambulance Service* (2014) UKEATS/0053/13
  Two paramedics were occasionally required to work night shifts away from their usual ambulance station. On these occasions they had to remain within three miles of the station because they had to respond within three minutes to any call they received. They successfully argued that they were working throughout their time at this station, and hence were not receiving the rests that they were entitled to.

5.1.4 *The requirements of the Working Time Regulations 1998*

Annual leave

From 6 April 2009 a worker has been entitled to 5.6 weeks' (28 days') paid leave, which includes the eight public holidays that exist in the UK. This is in excess of the four weeks' minimum that is set out in the European Working Time Directive.

If there is no defined start date for the calculation of holidays (eg many organisations calculate holidays from January to December each year), the leave year runs from the date that employment commenced. The entitlement is only to the holiday entitlement that has been accrued – one-twelfth of the 5.6 weeks being accrued each month.

The workers are entitled to be paid a sum equivalent to a week's pay for each week of leave. If the worker receives a variable amount of pay then the week's pay is an average of the pay received over the past 12 weeks.

- *Bear Scotland Ltd and others v Fulton and others* (2014) and *Hertel (UK) Ltd v Woods and others* (2014) and *Amec Group Ltd v Law and others* (2014) UKEATS/0047/13
  In this case the question of what should be included when calculating the payment during annual leave was addressed. The EAT ruled that workers should be paid a sum of money that reflects overtime worked, whether or not it was guaranteed overtime. In addition, the EAT found that allowances (in this case they related to travel) that were specifically related to the work the employee was doing formed part of remuneration. It was concluded, therefore, that these allowances should also be taken into account when determining the amount to be paid during annual leave.

- *Lock v British Gas Trading Ltd* (2014) IRLR 648 ECJ
  Lock was a salesman who received commission on top of his base pay. Whilst he was on holiday he did not earn commission, and hence his earnings dropped. He argued that his holiday pay should include some element of commission. This case was referred to the Court of Justice of the European Union, which decided that commission should be included when calculating the amount of holiday pay.

Other notable cases relating to annual leave are:

- *Stringer v HMRC* (2009) IRLR 214
  This case was a long-running case – formerly known as the *Commissioners for the Inland Revenue v Ainsworth* (2005). The case questioned whether someone on long-term sick leave continues to accrue entitlement to holidays. The Court of Justice of the European Union ruled that statutory holiday entitlement does continue to accrue. An employee is entitled to take that holiday when he/she returns to work or to receive pay in lieu of the entitlement if the employment is terminated. This only applies to the four weeks' leave that is the minimum allowed under the European Working Time Directive, not the full 5.6 weeks that is allowed under UK legislation.

- *Pereda v Madrid Movilidad SA* (2009) IRLR 959
  In this case the Court of Justice of the European Union was asked to rule on whether an employee should be entitled to rearrange annual leave if he/she

is unwell and unable to take pre-arranged holiday. The case centred on an employee who was injured just prior to a holiday that he had booked and asked to rearrange it, and was refused. The Court of Justice ruled that annual leave and sickness leave are for two different things and cannot take place at the same time. Hence, an employee who is sick during annual leave is entitled to take that time as sick leave and to take annual leave at a later time. If it is not possible for the annual leave to be rearranged within the holiday year it can be carried forward to the next holiday year.

- *King v Sash Windows Ltd* (2017) C214/16
  An employee worked for the organisation for 13 years, as a sales representative. He was told that he was self-employed and therefore he was not entitled to paid annual leave. He took very little leave because he received no money whilst on leave. He challenged his employment status, and it was found that he was a worker and therefore covered by the Working Time Regulations 1998.

  The Court of Justice of the European Union ruled that he was entitled to back pay for the untaken leave for the full 13 years of his employment, because not being paid meant that he had been deterred from taking his leave.

Some employers have operated a system called 'rolled up' holiday pay whereby the money that would be paid for holiday pay is 'rolled' into weekly pay and then the employee receives no payment while on holiday leave. There have been a series of rulings on whether this is lawful practice, culminating with a European Court of Justice ruling in April 2006:

- *Federatie Nederlandse Vakbeweging v Staat der Nederlanden* (2006) IRLR 561
  In this case the ECJ ruled that it is unlawful to allow employers to replace the minimum paid holiday entitlement with a pay-in-lieu system. The reasoning was that such a system might encourage employees not to take their full holiday entitlement. Remember that the Working Time Regulations are based on health and safety – and having adequate rest is a key part of that.

Maximum working week

The number of hours worked, including overtime, must not exceed an average of 48 hours per week over a 17-week reference period. It is therefore not correct to state that a worker cannot work more than 48 hours in any week. He/she can, as long as he/she works less than 48 hours in another week – to give an average of no more than 48 over the 17-week period.

This part of the regulations is a good example of why the UK Government was reluctant to introduce restrictions on working time. The weekly working hours in the UK are some of the longest in Europe, and hence the 48-hour limit was more difficult for the UK to comply with than most other European countries. So, the UK negotiated the introduction of an opt-out. A worker can opt out of the restriction on the working week. Any agreement to opt out must be in writing and either relate to a specific period of time or apply indefinitely. Within the agreement there must be the right for the worker to give seven days' notice (or a greater period of notice, agreed between the two parties – but this must not be more than three months) to terminate the agreement. The employer is also required to keep up-to-date records of all the workers who have signed such an agreement.

The opt-out has caused some concern at European level. There is the accusation that it has become customary for employees to automatically sign an opt-out and that the idea of choosing to opt out is not what happens in reality. Indeed, a number of employers do put the opt-out in an individual's contract of employment. Although an employee could score through this, saying that they do not agree to the opt-out, it is reasonably unlikely that most would. So, it is seen that the employee is not really choosing to opt out. Various reviews have taken place of the opt-out at a European level, but at present there are no plans to remove the opt-out provisions.

- *Barber and others v RJB Mining (UK) Ltd* (1999) IRLR 308
  Barber and his colleagues were pit deputies working in a coal mine in Yorkshire. They were contracted to work 42 hours per week, but also worked substantial overtime. RJB approached them, asking them to sign an opt-out agreement from the maximum working week regulations. Due to ongoing pay negotiations, the workers were advised by their union not to sign the proposed agreement.
  The pit deputies had already worked more than the 48-hour maximum during the 17-week reference period and therefore sought a declaration that they did not need to work again until the average fell below the 48-hour maximum. This declaration was granted by the High Court.

Detriment for not signing the opt-out

An employee must not suffer a detriment for not signing the opt-out, but does not have additional rights either:

- *Clamp v Aerial Systems* (2004) All ER D259
  The employee signed an opt-out and worked an average of 60 hours a week. His wife became ill and hence he withdrew his agreement to opt out. His employer accepted his decision and said that his salary would drop on a pro-rata basis from 60 hours a week to 48 hours a week. He claimed that this amounted to a detriment for withdrawing from the opt-out but was unsuccessful. This was a reasonable step in response to an employee working fewer hours.

Night work

The protection given to night workers is:

- if the work involves any special hazards or physical or mental strain, a maximum eight hours' work in any 24-hour period;
- an entitlement to a free health assessment before starting night work, and at regular intervals thereafter;
- an entitlement to adequate rest periods if the nature of the work is likely to cause health problems.

If the health assessment shows problems that might be connected with night work, the employer should make every attempt to move the worker to work that is not night work.

In the regulations 'night work' is defined as a period that is not less than seven hours in length and includes the normal hours of 11 pm to 6 am (unless the employer and employees agree a different period, but it must be seven hours long and include midnight to 5 am). A 'night worker' is a worker who normally works at least three hours of working time during this period of 'night work'.

So an employee who normally works a shift from 5 pm to 1 am is not a 'night worker' because only two hours fall in the period defined as 'night work'. However, an employee who works from 10 pm to 6 am is a 'night worker' because seven hours fall in the period defined as 'night work'.

It is not necessary for the worker to work these night hours each week. It is required that the hours are a regular feature of the pattern of work.

- *R v Attorney General for Northern Ireland* (1999) IRLR 315
  The employee changed to a shift system that involved working a night shift of 9 pm to 7 am one week in every three. Clearly, the shift was classified as 'night work' because there were at least three hours worked between 11 pm and 6 am. Although the shift was only worked one week in three, it was judged to be a regular feature of the employee's work and he was therefore judged to be a 'night worker'.

 Explore further

Find out how the restrictions imposed on night-time working have affected shifts in various industries. Have a look at the TUC website (www.tuc.org.uk) to see if there is a general policy on how to address negotiations relating to night-time working.

Rest breaks

All adult workers are entitled to at least 11 consecutive hours' rest in every 24-hour period. Young workers (those aged under 18) are entitled to a consecutive rest period of not less than 12 hours in every 24-hour period.

A worker is entitled to at least 24 hours' uninterrupted rest in every seven-day period. The weekly rest period can be averaged over a period of 14 days (eg 12 hours in one seven-day period and 36 hours in the following seven-day period). If a worker's daily work lasts for more than six hours, the worker is entitled to a rest period. The length of time allowed for the break can be agreed in a collective agreement, but it must be for at least 20 minutes and the worker must be entitled to spend that period of time away from the workstation. Young workers are entitled to a break of at least 30 minutes if their working time is for more than four and a half hours.

- *MacCartney v Oversley House Management* (2006) IRLR 514
  MacCartney worked as a resident manager at a development of homes for the elderly. She was required to work for four days per week, providing 24-hour cover. During this time she had to remain on site. She would have to deal with 3–4 emergency calls and 10–11 non-emergency calls per month. She claimed that she was being denied rest periods. The EAT held that an employee who is required to remain at their place of work is working, and hence she was not receiving appropriate rest periods.

- *Commission of the European Communities v United Kingdom* (2006) ECJ 7/9/06 (C 484/04)

  In 2006 the trade union Amicus, supported by the European Commission, brought a challenge against the Department of Trade and Industry (DTI) – now the Department for Business, Innovation and Skills (BIS) – guidelines on rest breaks issued by the UK Government. The DTI guidelines read that 'Employers must make sure that workers can take their rest, but are not required to make sure they do take their rest.' This was challenged on the basis that rests should be obligatory and that the employer should be responsible for ensuring that they are taken. The challenge was upheld by the European Court of Justice (ECJ), which agreed that the guidelines did not give the assurance that the minimum requirements of the regulations would be met. However, in making their judgment, the ECJ did comment that there was a limit to the level of 'policing' that the employer was expected to do. As a result of this ruling the guidelines were reviewed.

 Task

Find out how your organisation calculates payment when an employee takes annual leave.

Does this fit with recent case law?

Protection of young people

Young people aged under 13 years are not allowed to work, unless they are in specific professions such as modelling or acting. They will then require a performance licence, which is issued by the local council.

- 13–14 year olds:
  - can work a maximum of 25 hours a week;
  - can work a maximum of five hours on weekdays and Saturdays;
  - can work a maximum of two hours on Sundays.
- 15–16 year olds:
  - can work a maximum of 35 hours a week;
  - can work a maximum of eight hours on weekdays and Saturdays;
  - can work a maximum of two hours on Sundays.
- Young people aged under 18 years must receive the following rest:
  - a rest period of at least 12 hours in every 24-hour period;
  - a rest period of at least 30 minutes after working for 4.5 hours;
  - a rest period of at least 48 hours in every seven-day period.

Young people must not work more than eight hours a day, or more than 40 hours a week.

Young people must not work between the hours of 10.00 pm and 6.00 am unless they have had a health assessment prior to starting work and then regularly thereafter.

5.2 Payment of wages

As we noted in Chapter 3, one of the obligations on the employer is to pay wages. There are also further, more detailed rights of the employee with regard to wages.

5.2.1 *The right to an itemised pay statement*

In accordance with the Employment Rights Act 1996 (section 8), employees have the right to receive a written pay statement with (or before) each payment of wages or salary. This statement must show the gross and net payments, the nature of any deductions and the purpose of those deductions.

- *City Facilities Management (UK) Ltd v Beckett* (2014) UKEAT/0527/13
  Beckett was a cleaner who was entitled to a London Weighting Allowance (LWA) when working inside the M25. His place of work varied; however, he was never sure whether he was receiving the LWA because it was not itemised on his pay statement. He claimed unlawful deduction from wages, because it was not clear whether he was receiving the LWA or not. To try to clarify this the Employment Tribunal looked at 'salary change' forms that were used to inform payroll what to pay an employee and noted that there was an 11 per cent LWA. It ordered the employer to pay Beckett an additional 11 per cent, but the EAT ruled that this was not reasonable because the salary change forms were not contractual.

If an employee does not receive a pay statement, he/she can apply to the Employment Tribunal, which can declare the particulars that should have been included. If any unnotified deductions have been made during the 13 weeks prior to the application to the tribunal being made, the tribunal can instruct the employer to refund those deductions.

From April 2019 an employer will be required to include the number of hours worked on a pay statement if the amount the employee is paid depends on the hours worked. If there are different rates for different types of work the hours spent on each time of work will have to be specified.

 Task

Look at your last pay statement. What does it include? Does it show all that is listed in section 5.2?

5.2.2 *Authorised deductions*

As we noted in Chapter 2, unlawful deductions from wages is one of the most common claims brought before an Employment Tribunal. The only lawful deductions that can be made are:

- those required or authorised by statute (eg PAYE and National Insurance contributions);
- those required or authorised by a provision in the contract of employment, of which the employee has been made aware (eg a payment relating to the use of company tools and equipment);
- those agreed by the employee in writing (eg a contribution to a club or society run by the organisation).

An agreement to a deduction must be made in writing and it must be made clear that the deduction is to be made from wages – and that the employee agrees to this.

- *Potter v Hunt Contracts* (1991) IRLR 108
  Potter took an HGV driving course that was paid for by the agency he worked for. The agency placed him with Hunt Contracts, who decided to take him on as a permanent employee. As part of the deal with the agency they refunded the cost of the HGV training course. An agreement was drawn up with Potter that he would repay Hunt Contracts for the £545 cost of the course at the amount of £22 per month. One month later his employment was terminated and the outstanding money (£523) was deducted from his outstanding wages. Because this was less than £523 he received nothing in his final pay.
  The EAT ruled that the agreement between Potter and Hunt Contracts did not make it clear that the deduction was to be made from Potter's wages – it was therefore an unlawful deduction.
- *Ridge v HM Land Registry* (2014) UKEAT/0098/10
  Ridge had been absent due to illness and no longer had any entitlement to sick pay. He continued to be absent for occasional days, and was not entitled to any pay on those days. However, sometimes payroll were not informed of his absence until after they had paid him, and then they simply deducted the amount from his next payment. The deductions were not explained on his pay statement. This was ruled not to be an unlawful deduction from wages, but the employer should have itemised the deductions on the statement and the reasons for them.

If an employee thinks that money has been taken from wages by the employer unlawfully he/she can take a claim to the Employment Tribunal. However, the Deduction from Wages (Limitation) Regulations 2014 took effect on 1 July 2015 and do two things:

- They limit claims for unlawful deductions from wages to two years from the date of a claim being made to the Employment Tribunal. This limitation does not apply to claims for unpaid Statutory Maternity Pay, Statutory Paternity Pay and guarantee payments.
- They specifically state that the right to paid holiday is not incorporated as a term in employment contracts.

5.2.3 Definition of wages

Wages are any sum payable to a worker in connection with work done during employment.

- *Delaney v Staples* (1992) IRLR 191
  Delaney was dismissed from employment with Staples and claimed that she was owed commission, holiday pay and pay in lieu of notice (money relating to the wages she would have earned if she had worked her notice period). It was ruled that the commission and holiday pay had been earned, and so failure to pay them equated to unlawful deductions.

  However, the pay in lieu of notice was ruled not to be wages because it was not money relating to work done. On this basis it was not possible for the non-payment of pay in lieu of notice to be an unlawful deduction from wages. However, it was ruled that pay in lieu of notice actually equates to damages to compensate the employee for being dismissed without contractual notice (wrongful dismissal – see Chapter 9). Nonetheless, it was noted that if an employee had been given the correct notice but had not been required to attend work (known as 'garden leave'), then that money would constitute 'wages' because a contract of employment still exists.

 Explore further

As we saw in Chapter 2, unlawful deductions of wages is one of the most common types of claims that come before the Employment Tribunals. Do you think that the reason for this is a lack of clarity in current legislation? If so, what area of legislation needs clarification? Can you think of any other reasons for this type of claim being relatively common?

5.2.4 Guarantee payments

Sections 28 to 35 of the Employment Rights Act 1996 state that an employee with one month's continuous service is entitled to a guarantee payment if he/she is not provided with work throughout a day when he/she would normally expect to work, if the reason for the lack of work is:

- a decrease in demand for the employer's business, or for the type of work that the employee carries out;
- any other event affecting the employer's normal business (eg a power cut).

The employee loses the right to a guarantee payment if:

- the failure to provide work is related to industrial action;
- the employee refuses the offer of suitable alternative work;
- the employee does not comply with a reasonable attendance requirement, so that the employer can keep workers together in the event that work can continue (eg vital supplies can be delivered).

- *Purdy v Willowbrook International Ltd* (1977) IRLR 388
  Purdy worked as a trimmer in Willowbrook's coach factory. There was a reduction in trimming work and Purdy was asked to move to the finishing shop – work with which he was familiar. The pay would have been similar to that which

he earned as a trimmer and definitely in excess of any guarantee payment. Purdy refused to move. Subsequently, the trimmers (including Purdy) were moved to a three-day week. Purdy claimed a guarantee payment for the two days of no work, but it was ruled that he was not entitled to the payments because he had refused the opportunity of suitable alternative work.

- *Meadows v Faithful Overalls Ltd* (1977) IRLR 330
Meadows worked at a clothing factory. On the day in question, when he arrived for work, the heating system was inoperable and the employer was waiting for a delivery of oil to fuel the heating. The employees were asked to wait in the canteen where hot tea was provided. The oil supplier informed the employer there would be a delay in the delivery, and Meadows stated he would only wait until 9.45 am. At 9.45 am he went home and the oil delivery arrived just after 10.00 am. Meadows claimed a guarantee payment.

   It was ruled that the request to wait was a reasonable request and, by refusing to do so, Meadows had no entitlement to a guarantee payment.

The guarantee payment is for the amount of hours normally worked on the day in question, calculated at the hourly rate. The guarantee payment is paid for a maximum of five days in a three-month period. In 2018 this was subject to a daily maximum of £28 (the amount is reviewed in April each year).

5.3 The National Minimum Wage Act 1998

The National Minimum Wage (NMW) Act gives the right for workers to receive a minimum hourly rate of pay. In the Act a worker is described as someone working under a contract of employment or any other contract under which the individual undertakes to perform personally any work or services for another party.

Those who are not covered by the Act include:

- a worker who is on a scheme to provide training or temporary work, or a scheme designed to help him/her find work;
- a worker who is taking part in work experience as part of a first degree course, or as part of a teacher training course;
- a homeless person who is given shelter and other benefits in return for work.

The NMW was added to in April 2016 with the introduction of the National Living Wage (NLW). This is paid to those aged 25 years and above. We have, therefore, five levels of payment.

From 1 April 2018 these are:

- £7.83 per hour for those aged 25+ years;
- £7.38 per hour for those aged 21 to 24 years;
- £5.90 per hour for those aged 18 to 20 years;
- £4.20 per hour for those aged 16 to 17 years;
- £3.70 for apprentices aged under 19 years, or apprentices aged over 19 years but in the first year of their apprenticeship.

These rates are reviewed each October (current rates can be found at www.lowpay.gov.uk).

Clearly, the rates of pay that are set by the NMW relate to age – and it was therefore expected that the introduction of legislation making age discrimination unlawful from 1 October 2006 might impact on the NMW rates. However, it did not. The government justified this by arguing that removing the three bands of payment might make employers less inclined to employ those in the younger age bracket.

As we will discuss in Chapter 7, a decision to offer rates above the NMW, but using the same age bands, would have to be justified – as would, for example, paying 16-year-olds a different rate from 17-year-olds. If there was no justification, this could potentially be age discrimination.

 Explore further

The Low Pay Commission (https://www.gov.uk/government/organisations/low-pay-commission) is an independent body that advises the government about the NMW and the NLW. Go to their website and explore the issues that they address.

5.3.1 National Living Wage

It should be noted that there is also a 'Living Wage', which is different to the National Living Wage. This is an hourly amount that is higher than the NMW/NLW and paid voluntarily by employers. The Living Wage Foundation argues that the NMW/NLW is too low, and hence employers should consider paying the Living Wage instead. There is no legal requirement to pay the Living Wage.

5.3.2 What counts as work for payment of the NMW/NLW?

An employee's pay does not always consist solely of a basic rate. There are often bonuses and other items that make up the total pay. In addition, when calculating an hourly rate, a crucial part of the calculation is the number of hours worked. As we saw when looking at the Working Time Regulations 1998, it is not always clear when an employee is actually 'working'.

A number of cases have addressed the issue of what should be taken into account when calculating the hourly rate of pay:

- *British Nursing Association v Inland Revenue* (2002) IRLR 480
  The BNA provides a 24-hour service supplying nurses to nursing homes and similar establishments. During the day the bookings are made through the head office. During the night (8 pm to 9 am) trained nurses work from home, taking calls and placing nurses accordingly. Between calls the nurses can spend their time as they wish. The Employment Tribunal was asked to determine

what hours the nurses were working at night, for the purposes of calculating their wages in accordance with the NMW. The tribunal found (and was supported by the Court of Appeal) that the nurses were working for each hour of their shift. Although they were not taking phone calls all the time, they were required to be available. In addition, they noted that the process during the night was no different from the process carried out during the day. The nurses had therefore to be paid at least the NMW for each hour of their night shift.

- *Esparon t/a Middle West Residential Care Home v Slavikovska* (2014) UKEAT/0217/12
  Slavikovska worked as a care worker and had to be on her employer's premises for a set number of shifts. She was allowed to sleep on these shifts, but had to be available if there was an emergency. Her employer argued that she was not working whilst asleep, but she successfully argued that she was working because she had to remain on the employer's premises.

5.3.3 Who is a worker?

In determining whether the worker is working for the purposes of entitlement to the NMW it is important to consider the restrictions placed upon the worker when he/she is not actually carrying out a task determined by the employer (does he/she have to be available?). If the worker has restrictions placed on him/her by the employer he/she is likely to be working.

All aspects of the nature of the work must also be examined to see if it can be properly described as 'work'. In determining if someone is being paid at least the NMW the current level of gross pay (ie the payment before tax and National Insurance is deducted) must be considered. Added to that can be the cost of accommodation provided to the employee (a formula to account for this is described in the regulations). From 1 October 2009 employers have not been allowed to include tips, gratuities or cover charges as part of the National Minimum Wage.

- *Aviation and Airport Services v Bellfield and others* (2001) EAT 194/00
  Bellfield worked as a customer care agent. She was entitled to an attendance allowance if strict attendance requirements were met. Due to the introduction of the NMW the employer sought to make alterations to the payment structure. In determining that Bellfield was being paid the NMW, the employer relied on the inclusion of the attendance allowance. It was ruled that this could not be included in the calculation because it was not an allowance attributable to the performance (as opposed to being present at work) of the worker in carrying out her work.

- *Leisure Employment Services v HMRC* (2007) EWCA Civ 92
  The employer (which owned the Butlins and Haven camps) supplied employees with accommodation. In addition, it deducted £3 per week from employees for the cost of gas and electricity. The result of this deduction was that the hourly rate paid was below the NMW. The employer argued that the weekly £3 actually formed part of the employees' wages, but the Court of Appeal did not allow that argument.

5.3.4 Failure to pay the NMW

Employers are required to keep records of payments for a minimum of three years. If a worker believes he/she is not being paid the correct amount under the NMW Regulations, he/she can ask to see these records. If the employer refuses to let the employee see the records, the employee can make a complaint to the Employment Tribunal. In addition, if the employee believes he/she has not been paid the NMW, he/she can make an application to the Employment Tribunal for the situation to be assessed. The possible fine was increased in May 2015 by the Small Business Enterprise and Employment Act 2015 and is now a maximum of £20,000 per employee. In addition, employers who do not pay the NMW are 'named and shamed' by the government.

 Task

List the reasons for and against the introduction of the NMW. Do you think that the reasons for and against have been substantiated by evidence gained since the NMW was introduced? Has the financial level of the NMW been sufficient to have a real impact?

 Explore further

The rate at which the NMW and NLW are paid has been raised significantly since they were first introduced. However, many employee groups still believe that they are set too low to be of any real benefit to the employee. Go to the website of the Living Wage Foundation (www.livingwage.org.uk) to find out more about these arguments.

5.4 Payment and sickness

5.4.1 Statutory Sick Pay

There is no legal requirement on an employer to have a sick-pay scheme. However, all employers are required to pay Statutory Sick Pay (SSP) when an employee qualifies for such payments, and an employer cannot contract out of doing so.

Employees who have been continuously sick for four or more calendar days in a row and have average earnings at least equal to the lower earnings limit (the amount at which National Insurance contributions are payable) are entitled to receive SSP. Any day for which SSP is claimed must be a day on which the employee would ordinarily work. SSP is paid for a maximum of 28 weeks in any 12-month period.

5.4.2 *Suspension on medical grounds*

If an employee is suspended from work on medical grounds (eg the employer cannot provide any work for the employee due to health and safety requirements), the employee is entitled to the normal rate of pay for the first 26 weeks of the suspension. Employees who have worked for less than one month, or who have a fixed-term contract of less than three months, are excluded from this entitlement. In addition, an employee is not entitled to the payment if he/she has refused suitable alternative work or has not co-operated with the employer in being available for suitable work. If the employee is incapable of working due to illness, the terms relating to suspension on medical grounds do not apply.

5.5 Maternity protection

Maternity protection is an area of employment law that has changed greatly over recent years. Maternity protection covers a woman through the periods of antenatal care, care at work during her pregnancy and maternity leave.

A pregnant woman is protected against dismissal on the grounds of her pregnancy, discrimination on the grounds of her pregnancy or any other detrimental treatment relating to the pregnancy.

- *Webb v EMO Air Cargo Ltd* (1994) IRLR 482

  Webb was employed to cover another employee who was taking maternity leave. She was taken on six months before the other employee started her leave, so that she could be trained to carry out the duties of the job. Two weeks after her employment started Webb found that she was also pregnant. EMO dismissed Webb because she was not going to be available to them at the crucial time – ie to cover the whole of the period of the other employee's maternity leave. Webb appealed to the Employment Tribunal, who supported the employer's view. It held that if a man had been recruited to cover, and announced he would be on protracted leave, EMO would also have dismissed the man. The European Court of Justice overruled this finding, ruling that any dismissal relating to pregnancy was sex discrimination and that it was not right to make comparisons with a 'hypothetical' man.

 Task

Find out if your organisation, or an organisation with which you are familiar, has a maternity policy. Read it and compare it with the statutory requirements covered in this chapter.

5.5.1 Antenatal care

A pregnant woman has the right to take paid time off for antenatal appointments during working hours. If she is not allowed the time off, she can complain to an Employment Tribunal that can make a declaration that the refusal was unjustified and order the company to pay the woman an amount equal to that which she would have received for the period of time off requested. If she is allowed the time off but the company refuses to pay her, the Employment Tribunal can make a declaration to that effect and order the company to pay her the rightful amount.

The antenatal treatment must be recommended by a doctor, midwife or health visitor. The woman can be asked to show her employer proof of her appointment (eg an appointment card) for second and subsequent appointments.

Since 1 October 2014 the woman's partner in a qualifying relationship has had the right to take unpaid time off to attend up to two antenatal appointments as long as they are not for longer than 6.5 hours. A qualifying relationship is being the pregnant woman's husband or partner, or in a civil partnership with the woman, or being the father of the baby, or being in a surrogacy situation in relation to the baby.

A straightforward case showing the right to paid antenatal appointments is:

* *Gregory v Tudsbury Ltd* (1982) IRLR 267
Gregory took five consecutive Monday afternoons off to attend antenatal care and relaxation classes. She produced a medical certificate signed by a doctor and midwife.
   Her employers allowed her the time off, but refused to pay her for it, although they agreed it was not practical for her to arrange the classes outside working hours. Gregory complained to the Employment Tribunal and her employer was ordered to pay her for the time spent at the antenatal classes.

5.5.2 Risk assessments

When a woman informs her employer that she is pregnant, the employer is required to consider whether it is appropriate to carry out a risk assessment. If her job poses a danger to her or her unborn child, she should be moved to appropriate alternative employment or suspended on full pay on maternity grounds.

* *O'Neill v Buckinghamshire County Council* (2010) IRLR 384
In this case the EAT ruled that the following three preconditions must apply before an employer is required to carry out a maternity risk assessment:
   - the employee notifies the employer in writing that she is pregnant;
   - the work is of a kind that could involve a risk of harm or danger to the health and safety of the expectant mother or her baby;
   - the risk arises from either processes, working conditions or physical, chemical or biological agents in the workplace.

5.5.3 Maternity leave

There are three periods of maternity leave:

* Compulsory maternity leave – no employee may work for her employer for the two weeks (four weeks for factory or workshop workers) immediately following the date of childbirth. This period of two weeks forms part of the period known as ordinary maternity leave.

- Ordinary maternity leave (OML) – all pregnant women are entitled to take 26 weeks' OML, regardless of their length of service.
- Additional maternity leave (AML) – all pregnant women are also entitled to take 26 weeks' AML, which starts immediately after OML finishes – giving a total leave period of 52 weeks.

Entitlement to maternity leave

Maternity leave (OML and AML) can only be taken by employees (those who have entered into, or work under, a contract of employment that is defined as a contract of service). To qualify for maternity leave the woman must inform her employer no later than the fifteenth week before the expected week of childbirth (EWC) – in writing if requested – of the following:

- that she is pregnant;
- her EWC;
- the date on which she wants to start her OML – this cannot be earlier than the beginning of the eleventh week before the EWC.

During maternity leave

Maternity leave is considered to have started on the earliest of:

- the date the employee has notified to her employer as the intended start date of OML;
- the day that follows the start of sickness absence during the four weeks prior to the EWC, if the reason for absence is related to the pregnancy;
- the day that follows the day on which childbirth occurs (OML starts at this point even if the day falls before the beginning of the eleventh week before the EWC).

During maternity leave the employee is:

- entitled to the benefits of all the terms and conditions of employment that would have applied if she had not been absent (apart from any terms concerning 'remuneration');
- bound by any obligations arising under those terms and conditions (unless they are inconsistent with the right to take maternity leave – eg the requirement to attend work).

Statutory and contractual holiday will continue to accrue throughout OML and AML. In addition, continuity of service continues to accrue throughout OML and AML.

Keeping in touch (KIT) days

The Work and Families Act 2006 added in the concept of 'keeping in touch' (KIT) days. During the period of maternity leave the employee is allowed to work for up to 10 KIT days without losing any entitlement to maternity pay. The employee cannot be forced to work any such days and must not suffer any detriment for refusing to work any such days. The purpose of the days is to keep some relationship between the employee and the employer during the period of leave and to give an opportunity for training or any updating that might occur.

5.5.4 *Returning to work*

When returning from OML an employee is entitled to return to exactly the same job she left and is to be treated as if she had never been absent. If there have been any pay increases in her absence, her pay must reflect this. If the employer does not allow the woman to return to her old job, this would count as a dismissal and would be automatically unfair because it would be a dismissal related to pregnancy.

When returning from AML an employee is entitled to return to her old job unless this is not reasonably practicable. In this case an employer must offer a job that is suitable – which will mean the same status and attracting the same terms and conditions of employment. Again, the rate of pay must include any pay increases awarded during her absence. The exceptions to this are:

- When a woman is returning after two or more consecutive periods of statutory leave, and it is not 'reasonably practicable' for the woman to return to the same job.
- Where a redundancy situation has arisen during the period of leave. In this situation a woman is entitled to be offered any suitable alternative work and must be offered this work in preference to any other employees who have been made redundant.

An example of the issues that can arise relating to redundancy can be found in:

- *Philip Hodges & Co v Kell* (1994) IRLR 568
  Kell worked as a secretary for Philip Hodges & Co. During her maternity leave the firm decided there was no longer a requirement for her role as a personal secretary. They did not give her notice at this time. During her leave they also employed another secretary on an ad hoc basis, but made her permanent and full-time before Kell was due to return to work. The Employment Tribunal found that Kell worked as a legal secretary and so was capable of doing the other role that had originally been ad hoc. On that basis, it was unfair to recruit another employee during her maternity leave and make Kell redundant. They found, therefore, that Kell had been unfairly dismissed.

Notification of returning to work

A woman has the automatic right to return to work following her maternity leave and, unless she says otherwise, it will be assumed that she will return. A woman returning to work after having taken her full maternity leave entitlement is not required to give her employer any notice: she can simply turn up on the day after her period of leave has ended. If a woman decides not to return to work, she is required to give the notice set out in her contract of employment. This cannot be less than the statutory minimum of one week. If a woman wants to return to work before the end of her maternity leave (assuming that the period of compulsory leave has passed) and before the date that she originally gave, she must give her employer at least eight weeks' notice of her intention – specifying the date on which she intends to return. If a woman wants to return to work, but on reduced hours, she must make her request to her employer in line with the rules regarding flexible working, which we looked at in Chapter 4.

5.5.5 *Statutory Maternity Pay (SMP)*

SMP is payable by employers, for a period of 39 weeks, to pregnant employees who have worked for that employer for at least 26 continuous weeks at the fifteenth week before the EWC (the 'qualifying week'). The payment of SMP cannot start until the employee has ceased working (ie started a period of maternity leave). The employee must earn at least the lower earnings limit for the payment of primary Class 1 NI contributions (£116 for the 2018/19 tax year) as an average payment over the eight weeks up to and including the qualifying period.

SMP is paid at a rate of 90 per cent of average weekly earnings for the first six weeks, and then at £145.18 per week (from April 2018) for the remaining 33 weeks. The employer can choose to pay more than this amount.

5.6 Statutory paternity leave

Statutory paternity leave was introduced by the Employment Act 2002. To qualify for paternity leave the employee must have worked for that employer for at least 26 continuous weeks at the fifteenth week before the expected week of the birth of the baby. The employee must be the father of the child, or the mother's husband or partner. The employee must expect to have responsibility for the upbringing of the child. (Note: the partner does not have to be male; it can be a female in a same-sex relationship.)

The employee must give 28 days' notice to his/her employer of the intention to take paternity leave. The leave must be taken within 56 days of the birth of the child. The period of paternity leave will be for up to two weeks. The paternity leave will be paid at the lower rate of SMP (ie £145.18 per week [as at April 2018]). During the period of paternity leave the contract of employment continues and the employee has the right to return to his/her job after the leave ends.

Partners of an adopter also have the right to take statutory paternity leave. The requirements in relation to eligibility are the same as for those taking paternity leave following the birth of a child. The 56-day period in which the leave must be taken runs from the day that the child is placed with the adopter.

Additional paternity leave (APL) was introduced for those with babies due to be born (or adopted) on or after 3 April 2011. However, this was removed on 5 April 2015 when shared parental leave was introduced.

5.7 Statutory adoption leave (SAL)

The Employment Act 2002 introduced a new statutory right for employees who adopt a child to take time off to build up a relationship with that child. The provisions mirror maternity leave – but either of the parents can take the leave (though not both). Originally there was a requirement for the adopter to have been continuously employed for at least 26 weeks before taking SAL but this requirement was removed on 5 April 2015.

There is a period of ordinary adoption leave (OAL), which lasts for 26 weeks, and can be taken by an employee who is the 'adopter'. An employee can choose to commence OAL on the day on which the child is placed with him/her for adoption, or at a predetermined date that is no more than 14 days before the child is expected to be placed, and no later than the day of the placement.

An employee is entitled to additional adoption leave (AAL) if the child was placed with the employee for adoption, the employee took OAL in respect of the child and the OAL period did not end prematurely (for example, because of a disruption to the placement of the adopted child). AAL starts the day after OAL ends and is for a period of 26 weeks. An employee taking adoption leave is entitled to Statutory Adoption Pay, which is exactly the same as SMP. During adoption leave the employee's rights and obligations under the contract of employment continue. The employee is entitled to return to his/her old job with the same seniority and benefits that he/she left.

From 5 April 2015 the primary adopter of the couple (the one who will take adoption leave) has been entitled to attend up to five appointments to meet the child, or deal with other issues relating to the adoption, prior to the child being placed for adoption. This is paid time off. The secondary adopter of the couple can attend up to two appointments, with the time off being unpaid.

Since 5 April 2015 parents in a surrogacy arrangement who are entitled to and intend to apply for a Parental Order under the Human Embryology and Fertilisation Act 2008 have been able to take statutory adoption leave and pay, and paternity leave and pay, if each parent meets the normal qualifying conditions.

5.8 Shared parental leave (SPL)

SPL was introduced by the Shared Parental Leave Regulations 2014. It is an alternative to statutory maternity leave (SML) or SAL. Employees can still choose to take SML or SAL in exactly the same way as described in this chapter. However, they can also choose to end their SML or SAL and take SPL instead.

SPL is quite simply sharing the leave with their partner. If the employee has already taken some SML/SAL then the time that has been taken is deducted from the SPL that the employee is entitled to take. In addition, an employee taking maternity leave must take compulsory maternity leave – this cannot be shared as part of SPL.

An employee can give notice of the intention to take SPL before the birth or adoption. Alternatively, the employee can give eight weeks' notice that she/he wants to terminate the SML/SAL and start taking SPL instead.

SPL can be taken as continuous or discontinuous leave. Continuous leave is when one partner takes some leave followed by the other partner taking some leave; this cannot be refused by an employer. Discontinuous leave is where there is any other pattern of leave, for example the two employees taking alternating short periods of leave. An employer can refuse a request to take discontinuous leave and ask the employee to take continuous leave instead.

To be eligible to take SPL the employee must be eligible to take SAL or SML, or be entitled to Statutory Maternity Pay (SMP), Statutory Adoption Pay (SAP) or

Maternity Allowance (MA). Also, to be eligible, the mother or adopter must share responsibility for raising the child with the child's father or her partner.

As well as these requirements there is a 'continuity test' that is applied to determine eligibility:

- One parent of the two who are applying to take SPL must have worked for the same employer for at least 26 weeks by the end of the fifteenth week before the week in which the child is due to be born (referred to as the Expected Week of Confinement – EWC) or the week in which the adopter is notified of having been matched with a child. The parent must still be employed in the first week that SPL is to be taken.
- The other parent must have worked for 26 weeks in the 66 weeks leading up to the date that the baby is due/placed and must have earned above the Maternity Allowance threshold (currently £30 per week) in 13 of those 66 weeks.

Whilst on SPL the employee is entitled to receive Shared Parental Pay (ShPP). This is the same amount as SMP/SAP, but it is an entitlement for the couple not for each member of the couple. If any SMP/SAP has already been taken it is deducted from the ShPP entitlement.

Employees who are taking SPL can take up to 20 SPLIT (shared parental leave in touch) days each. The principle of these is the same as for KIT days.

- *Capita Customer Management Ltd v Ali* (2018) UKEAT/0161/17
  Ali's wife returned to work early from her maternity leave, and he took shared parental leave. In his organisation women received full pay for the first 14 weeks of maternity leave. However, he was told that shared parental leave was all paid at the statutory rate. The Employment Tribunal agreed that this was direct sex discrimination, but the EAT overturned this decision. The purpose of maternity leave is to recognise the health and well-being of a woman in pregnancy and after childbirth. The situation for a man taking shared parental leave is not the same, and therefore does not have to be paid in the same way.

 Explore further

To explore the details of shared parental leave read the Acas good practice guide, which can be accessed at http://www.acas.org.uk/media/ pdf/9/f/Shared-Parental-Leave-a-good-practice-guide-for-employers-and-employees.pdf

5.9 Parental leave

The Maternity and Parental Leave Regulations 1999 laid down a minimum framework of parental leave rights. Employers and employees have to adhere to the minimum rights, but can work out their own agreement to operate parental leave. The minimum framework is:

- It applies to employees with at least one year's continuous service with their employer who have responsibility for a child.
- Up to 18 weeks' leave may be taken for each child.
- The leave has to be for the purpose of caring for the child.
- The right to take leave applies during the child's first 18 years of life.
- The employee remains employed while on leave, so the contract of employment continues.
- The employee has the right to return to the same job, or to another suitable job, after the period of leave ends.

The 18 weeks' leave is a total allowance, and under the statutory scheme leave must be taken in blocks of at least one week. An employee cannot take more than four weeks' leave in respect of any individual child during a particular year. Parental leave is unpaid. If the period of intended leave is two weeks or less, then at least four weeks' notice must be given. For longer periods at least twice the length of leave requested must be given in notice (ie six weeks' notice for three weeks' leave).

- *Rodway v South Central Trains* (2005) IRLR 583
  Rodway was separated from his partner. She asked him to look after their two-year-old son on a particular day. He requested annual leave but was refused, and so he requested a day's parental leave, which was also refused on the grounds that his job could not be covered. He took the day off and was disciplined. He claimed that he had suffered a detriment for taking parental leave. This was rejected by the Court of Appeal because parental leave has to be taken in blocks of at least one week.

5.10 Time off for dependants

The Employment Rights Act 1996 gives a right to enable an employee to take a reasonable amount of time off during working hours to take action that is necessary to:

- provide assistance when a dependant falls ill, gives birth or is injured or assaulted;
- make arrangements for the care of a dependant who is ill or injured;
- take actions in connection with the death of a dependant;
- deal with disruption to or cancellation of arrangements for the care of a dependant;
- deal with an incident involving a child at school.

A dependant is the employee's wife, husband, child, parent or someone living in the same house as the employee who is not a lodger, tenant, boarder or employee. The right is not paid, but if the employer has allowed employees paid time off in the past to deal with such issues then it must continue to do so. An employee must make the employer aware of the reason for the absence as soon as is reasonably practical, but there is no requirement to give notice.

- *Qua v John Ford Morrison Solicitors* (2003) IRLR 184
  Qua had a child with medical problems. She was dismissed after taking 17 days off during a 10-month period to deal with the child's problems. She claimed that the dismissal was unfair because of her right to take time off to care for dependants. However, the EAT stated that the right was to take time off to deal with an immediate crisis, not to deal with ongoing medical care.

 Task

Find out if there have been any requests for paternity, adoption, parental or dependant leave in your organisation, or an organisation with which you are familiar. How have these requests been addressed? Does the employer feel that the requests have been disruptive to the efficiency of the organisation?

5.11 Time off for public duties

Section 50 of the Employment Rights Act 1996 gives employees the right to take time off for certain public duties. They are not entitled to payment from their employer when taking this time off. Duties include meetings of, or work in relation to, membership of:

- a local authority;
- a statutory tribunal;
- a health authority, NHS trust or health board;
- a relevant education body;
- a police authority;
- the Service Authority of the National Crime Squad or the National Criminal Intelligence Service;
- a board of prison visitors or a prison-visiting committee;
- the Environment Agency.

In Chapter 10 we also note the right to time off for trade union duties, and in Chapter 9 we note the right to time off to seek employment when faced with impending redundancy.

5.12 Time off for training

From 6 April 2010 employees with at least 26 weeks' continuous service with an employer have been allowed to request time off for training. This applies only to employees working in an organisation with at least 250 employees. The right applies to employees only.

Employees are entitled to request time off for training that leads to a qualification, or for training that helps them to develop their skill in their job, workplace or business. The training must help to improve the business performance or the employee's performance in that business.

There is no requirement to pay employees during any time that they take off for training or pay for the course, although employers can if they want to. There is no limit to the length of the training that is requested.

An employee must set out the details of the request for training in writing. The employee can only make one request for training in any 12-month period. If the employee has previously made a request for training, this must be detailed when making a further request. If an employer receives a written request it must either accept the request or arrange a meeting to discuss the request with the employee. This must take place within 28 days of receiving the request. The employee must then be informed of the decision relating to the request within 14 days of the meeting.

The employer can grant the request, agree to part of the request, agree to a different approach to the training or refuse the request. An acceptance of the request must be in writing, confirming the details relating to the training. A refusal must also be in writing, citing one of the following reasons:

- The training would not improve the employee's effectiveness in their business.
- The training would not improve the performance of their business.
- The absence would incur additional costs.
- The time off would cause a detrimental effect on the ability of the employer to meet customer demand.
- The employee's work cannot be reorganised among existing staff.
- Additional staff cannot be recruited to cover the employee's work.
- The time off would cause a detrimental impact on quality.
- The time off would cause a detrimental impact on business performance.
- There is insufficient work available during the periods the employee proposes to work.
- The request conflicts with planned structural changes.

If the employee is dissatisfied with the decision, he/she may appeal. An appeal must be in writing and sent to the employer within 14 days of receiving the decision in relation to the request. The employer must then arrange a meeting to hear the appeal within 14 days of receiving the appeal letter and must inform the employee of the decision, in writing, within 14 days of the appeal meeting.

If the employee does not attend the training, stops attending the training or changes the agreed plans in any way, he/she must inform the employer immediately. Failure to do so could lead to disciplinary action.

KEY LEARNING POINTS

1   The Working Time Regulations set minimum standards relating to the working week, annual leave, night work and rest periods.
2   An employee is entitled to receive an itemised pay statement.
3   Deductions from wages are only lawful if they are determined by statute, are agreed within the contract of employment, or if they are agreed between the employer and employee in writing.
4   Pay in lieu of notice is not classed as wages.
5   Guarantee payments are paid to those who have at least one month's continuous employment and are not offered work on a day when they would normally be expected to work.
6   The National Minimum/Living Wage is paid at five levels, dependent on age.
7   The employer has to pay Statutory Sick Pay when the employee qualifies for such payment.
8   Maternity leave falls into three categories: compulsory leave, ordinary leave and additional leave.
9   A dismissal relating to pregnancy is automatically unfair.
10 Paternity leave is allowed up to a period of two weeks.
11 Adoption leave mirrors maternity leave, but can only be claimed by one person in relation to each child (known as the 'adopter').
12 Shared parental leave can be taken as an alternative to statutory maternity or adoption leave.
13 Parental leave up to a maximum of 18 weeks can be taken in the first 18 years of the child's life.
14 Time off to care for dependants can be taken, with as much notice as possible being given.
15 Time off is allowed for a range of public duties.

 Case summaries

- *Hoyland v Asda Stores Ltd* (2006) IRLR 468 – This case established that an employee was entitled to a bonus based on sales performance of the whole team and her own performance. She was absent due to maternity leave and her bonus was reduced pro rata to reflect the days she had worked. She claimed this was unfair. The Court of Session upheld that no reduction should be made for the two weeks of compulsory maternity leave – but she was not entitled to the bonus for the remainder of the maternity leave, because 'remuneration' is not a term and condition of employment that continues during OML and AML.

(Continued)

(Continued)

- *Royal Bank of Scotland v Harrison* (2009) IRLR 28 – Harrison was told her childminder would be unavailable for one day. She asked if she could take the day off, but two days before the day in question the leave was refused. At this stage she could make no other arrangements so she took the day off and received a disciplinary warning. She claimed that she had suffered a detriment for taking time off to care for dependants. The EAT upheld her claim.
- *Byrne Brothers (Formwork Ltd) v Baird and others* (2002) IRLR 96 – This case examined the issue of who is a 'worker' as defined by the Working Time Regulations. The claimants were self-employed builders, but the EAT found that they were workers for the requirements of the Working Time Regulations – if you are researching this area, this is an important judgment to read.
- *Flowers and others v East of England Ambulance Trust* (2017) ET 3400310/2015 – The employees successfully argued that payment they received for covering shifts and also for 'shift overrun' (when they were on a call when their shift ended and had to continue working) should be included when calculating their average payment to determine holiday pay.
- *Royal Mencap Society v Tomlinson-Blake* (2017) UKEAT/0290/16 – Employees were required to be on company premises, but could go to sleep and were only required to work if something occurred that needed their input. They were working whilst asleep because they were not allowed to leave the premises.

❓ Examples to work through

1 You employ a security officer who works at night – from 10 pm to 6 am. He is required to patrol the site at the beginning and end of his shift, and apart from that his only duties are to answer any emergency calls that are received. He is allowed to sleep on the premises and a bed is provided. You pay him for the hours that he patrols and for emergency call-outs. However, he is not paid for any time he is resting. He argues that he should be paid for the full shift. Who is correct?

2 One of your male employees received a telephone call at work telling him that his wife had gone into premature labour (five weeks early). He immediately left work and went to the hospital. The baby has been safely delivered and today he has called you and said he wants to take the remainder of the week off as paternity leave. Is he allowed to?

3 You operate a courier business and one of your drivers has had a minor accident in your vehicle – this is his third accident in six months. You have decided to deduct the excess from the insurance claim from his wages, given the number of accidents he has had. Is this allowed? Justify your answer.

4 You work for a retail organisation that currently has opening hours of Monday to

(Continued)

(Continued)

Saturday, 9 am to 6 pm, and does not open on Sundays. However, due to competition from similar organisations, the management have decided that it will now open from 9 am to 8 pm on Monday to Saturday and 10 am to 4 pm on Sundays. There are 150 full-time employees in the organisation and the managing director has decided that the best way to manage the change in hours is to ask all employees to work shift patterns covering the opening hours. The managing director does not want to ask for volunteers, asking some to work late and some to work on Sundays, as he thinks that this will be divisive. He thinks that it is better if everyone works similar work patterns. There are also 30 part-time employees in the organisation and it has been decided that their working hours will not change because they are employed to work specifically at the busiest times of the day.

You are the HR manager and you have been asked to talk to the employees about the proposed changes that will need to take place to their working hours and to seek their agreement. You have never handled a similar situation before and decide to start by consulting with employees in small groups. This has a varied response, with some groups of employees being quite interested in the ideas and some being very resistant. After two weeks you have the following issues to address:

– Out of the 150 employees in the organisation, 90 have agreed to the proposed changes in the shift patterns. The other 60 have not agreed. You now need to decide how to deal with these 60 employees.

– You have three employees who are aged 17 years and you have been asked if they can work the shift patterns that have been suggested.

– To encourage employees to accept the changes there will be an opportunity to apply to attend a training course that will lead to a professional management qualification. The company will pay the cost of the training course, but if an employee leaves within two years of completing the qualification they will be required to pay a percentage of the cost back to the employer. Employees are saying that this will not be allowed, because it would be an unlawful deduction from wages.

– Matilda is pregnant, and says that she cannot work long shifts because she is struggling with extreme tiredness and some blood-pressure issues. She is told that all employees must work the shifts – it is not optional.

How should you address each of these situations?

06
Forms of discrimination

CHAPTER OBJECTIVES

The objectives of this chapter are:

- to explore the concept of discrimination;
- to analyse the difference between indirect and direct discrimination;
- to understand the concepts of associative and perceptive discrimination;
- to explore the concept of occupational requirements (ORs);
- to outline the concept of 'positive action';
- to consider issues relating to harassment, victimisation and vicarious liability;
- to explore the law relating to equal pay.

6.1 Introduction

Legislation relating to discrimination has developed considerably over recent years. The first piece of legislation specifically focusing on issues of discrimination was the Equal Pay Act 1970.

This legislation was followed by two major pieces of legislation: the Sex Discrimination Act 1975 and the Race Relations Act 1976. No new areas of discrimination law were introduced until nearly 20 years later, when the Disability Discrimination Act 1995 was introduced. In 1999 transsexuals were added to the categories of employees who may not legally be discriminated against, by the Sex Discrimination (Gender Reassignment) Regulations 1999.

In December 2003 two additional pieces of legislation were introduced: the Employment Equality (Sexual Orientation) Regulations 2003 and Employment Equality (Religion and Belief) Regulations 2003. In October 2006, the Employment Equality (Age) Regulations 2006 were introduced.

However, all of this legislation has now been repealed and has been replaced by the Equality Act 2010, which was introduced in October 2010. This Act replaced the nine major pieces of discrimination legislation and more than 100 smaller pieces of legislation that were in place. The Act has harmonised areas of discrimination law that were different for different areas of discrimination and it has made discrimination legislation more straightforward.

In the Act there are nine protected characteristics – these are grounds on which discrimination can occur. We will look at each of these nine in Chapter 7. In the Act there are six main types of discrimination (there is also discrimination arising from disability, which is clearly specific to disability) – that is the focus of this chapter. In this chapter we also look at the specific area of equal pay.

Although the Equality Act 2010 has brought together all areas of discrimination legislation, there are some statutes that are still in place that protect individuals in specific situations against less favourable treatment. There is legislation protecting part-time workers and those working on fixed-term contracts from less favourable treatment (as we saw in Chapter 4), and protection for trade union members (and non-members) against less favourable treatment (see Chapter 10). However, it should be noted that these areas are not covered by the six types of discrimination that we are looking at in this chapter; the protection is limited to less favourable treatment.

In looking at discrimination law it is important to remember that the remit of the legislation is broader than for many other areas of law. Not only employees but potential employees, past employees, trainees, the self-employed, the armed forces and the police are covered. So, for example, someone who applies for a job and does not get it could bring a claim for discrimination, arguing that the recruitment process was discriminatory.

 Task

During your studies ensure that you are aware of new case law as it is reported. Discrimination law is a rapidly moving area of legislation – you must always keep up to date. Useful websites include www.cipd.co.uk (Chartered Institute of Personnel and Development) and www.equalityhumanrights.org.uk (Equality and Human Rights Commission).

6.2 Forms of discrimination

As already noted, there are six types of discrimination. These are:

- direct;
- associative;

- perceptive;
- indirect;
- harassment;
- victimisation.

We will look at each of these in turn.

6.2.1 Direct discrimination

This is where an employee is treated less favourably than someone else on the grounds of a protected characteristic. It is important to note that the issue is being treated less favourably, and therefore there has to be reference to a real or hypothetical comparator who has been treated preferentially to the individual making the complaint. Direct discrimination cannot be justified (apart from in certain situations in age discrimination – see Chapter 7) – and the argument that there was good reason for treating groups differently is not relevant (unless there is an occupational requirement – see section 6.2.4). In addition, direct discrimination cannot be justified by the argument that there is no detriment to the employee:

- *Moyhing v Barts and London NHS Trust* (2006) IRLR 860
  Moyhing was a male student nurse who was required to carry out an ECG on a female Asian patient. Because this involved intimate contact he was told that a female chaperone must be present. There was no similar policy for female nurses carrying out an ECG on male patients. He argued therefore that the requirement for a chaperone was direct discrimination on the grounds of his sex. The Employment Tribunal agreed that there was different treatment, but found that there was no detriment to Moyhing. However, Moyhing successfully appealed to the EAT. The EAT argued that there is no justification to direct discrimination, and assessing there was no detriment did not allow the conclusion that discrimination was justifiable.

Direct discrimination is also not justifiable when the acts have been committed with the very best intentions of the employer:

- *Amnesty International v Ahmed* (2009) IRLR 884
  Ahmed is of Northern Sudanese ethnic origin. She was employed by Amnesty International as a campaigner on issues related to Sudan. A vacancy occurred for the position of researcher for the Sudanese region and Ahmed applied. She was shortlisted for the post, but Amnesty International decided not to appoint her, primarily because they had concerns that she would be at risk of ill treatment or violence if she travelled to Sudan or Eastern Chad (which would be part of the role), due to her ethnic origin. Amnesty International argued that they would have been in breach of the Health and Safety at Work Regulations 1974 if they had appointed Ahmed to a role that put her in danger. The EAT found that Amnesty International had made a decision about Ahmed's appointment to the role of researcher on the basis of her ethnic origin. Even though there was a good motive for this decision, it was direct discrimination.

Comparator

If an employee can show that their treatment is unfavourable, they must be able to point to a comparator of the opposite gender/a different race, etc, and show that this comparator (who is the same as the employee in all other ways) is being treated differently. This comparator can be real or can be hypothetical.

It is accepted that a pregnant woman does not need to be able to cite a comparator. In Chapter 5 we looked at the case of *Webb v EMO Air Cargo Ltd* (1994) IRLR 482. In this case Webb was dismissed because she found she was pregnant and she had only been recruited to cover another employee's maternity leave. The European Court of Justice ruled that any dismissal relating to pregnancy had to be sex discrimination (because only women become pregnant). It ruled that it was not acceptable to make a comparison to a hypothetical man who had announced that he would need to take protracted leave when covering another employee's leave.

In some situations, it is appropriate to point to a hypothetical comparator:

- *Balamoody v United Kingdom Central Council for Nursing, Midwifery and Health Visiting* (2002) IRLR 288, CA
  Balamoody was of Mauritian nationality and was a state-registered nurse who owned a nursing home. He was found guilty of mispractice under the council regulations and his name was removed from the register. However, he claimed that a matron of white ethnic origin was guilty of the offences and therefore applied for his name to be restored to the register. This was refused and an investigation into the matron found her not guilty of any offences.

  Balamoody then took up a claim of race discrimination. The Employment Tribunal (supported by the EAT) held that there was no comparator because no one else had been found guilty of any offences. However, the Court of Appeal ruled that a hypothetical comparator should have been used because there was the possibility that the conclusion that the matron was not guilty of any offences was a result of race discrimination. If an employee can show that there has been less favourable treatment, the next step is to show that the reason for the treatment related to the employee's sex/ race, etc. This is known as the causation question.

For a claim of direct discrimination to be successful the claimant must be able to show that she/he was treated less favourably because of a protected characteristic. There might be unpleasant decisions, or aggressive management behaviour, but it will only be direct discrimination if it can be shown to relate to a protected characteristic:

- *Bradford Hospitals NHS Trust v Al-Shabib* (2002) EAT 709/01
  Al-Shabib, a man of Iraqi origin, decided to join the staff gym. After signing an agreement to abide by the rules of the gym, Al-Shabib allowed his wife and child to use the gym, which was in breach of one of the rules. The gym manager reprimanded him. Following an investigation, during which Al-Shabib was not interviewed, it was decided to withdraw his gym membership. Al-Shabib brought a claim to the Employment Tribunal that he had been subjected to direct race discrimination. The EAT dismissed his claim, ruling that there was no evidence that the treatment of Al-Shabib had been related to his race in any way. Indeed, other employees who had broken the rules in a similar way had also had their membership withdrawn, and they were from a variety of races.

- *Kettle Produce v Ward* (2006) EAT 0016/06
  A male manager entered the ladies' toilets and shouted at the female toilet cleaner, who was on her break. He accused her of 'skiving'. She brought a claim of sex discrimination. The EAT rejected her claim on the basis that she was not able to demonstrate that the treatment was related to her gender. Indeed, there was no evidence that she would have been treated any other way if the manager had been female and had been managing a male employee.

6.2.2 Associative discrimination

Associative discrimination applies to all protected characteristics apart from marriage and civil partnership, and pregnancy and maternity.

Associative discrimination is a form of direct discrimination and is treating someone less favourably because they associate with someone of a particular protected characteristic. This is illustrated in the case of *Coleman v Attridge Law* (2008), relating to disability. At the time of this case associative discrimination did not apply to disability claims. However, this case was reviewed by the Court of Justice of the European Union, and as a result of the case the UK was required to introduce associative discrimination as a concept relating to all protected characteristics. This occurred as part of the Equality Act 2010:

- *Coleman v Attridge Law* (2008) ECJ/303/06
  Coleman's son was disabled. She made a number of requests for flexible working patterns, which were refused. She argued that she had been treated less favourably than parents of other non-disabled children, who had been allowed to work flexibly. She also claimed that she had been harassed due to the time that she had taken off to care for her child.

  The ECJ ruled that this was associative discrimination, under the European Employment Framework Directive 2000/78/EC.

Although an employee must not be treated less favourably because of who she/he associates with, this does not mean that the employer has any obligations to the associated person:

- *Hainsworth v Ministry of Defence* (2014) EWCA Civ 763
  Hainsworth was posted to Germany, and had a daughter with Down's syndrome. She identified schooling that would be beneficial for her daughter back in the UK. She asked to be posted back to the UK so that her daughter could take up this schooling, but the request was refused. Her argument that this was associative discrimination failed because there is no requirement for the employer to make adjustments to assist the employee's associate.

6.2.3 Perceptive discrimination

Perceptive discrimination applies to all protected characteristics apart from marriage and civil partnership, and pregnancy and maternity.

Perceptive discrimination is another form of direct discrimination and is treating someone less favourably because it is perceived that they are part of a protected group, even if they are not part of that group. For example, it might be perceived that someone is of a particular sexual orientation due to the friends they have. Treating that individual less favourably because of this, even if he/she was not of the particular sexual orientation, would be perceptive discrimination.

6.2.4 Occupational requirements

As we have already noted, direct discrimination is not justifiable (apart from specific situations relating to age, which we will look at in the next chapter). However, there can be occasions where there is a reason for needing someone of a specific protected characteristic because of the nature of the role. This is known as 'occupational requirements'. Examples of this are:

- The job requires a certain physiology (excluding physical strength) or a certain authenticity in dramatic performances or other entertainment, and a particular gender or race is therefore required.
- The job involves physical contact with people and it would be inappropriate for this contact to be by a person of the opposite sex. For example:
  - *Etam plc v Rowan* (1989) IRLR 150
    Rowan, a man, was refused employment at the women's clothes shop Etam because the job would have involved measuring women who were unsure of their size and this was inappropriate contact. The EAT held that this was a small part of the job and could have been covered by a female colleague.
- The job holder has to live on the premises and there are no facilities for providing separate sleeping and other facilities for each sex.
- The job involves a special level of care and it would be inappropriate for that care to be given by a member of the opposite sex or of a different race/religion.
- The job requires a particular commitment to a religion (eg being a leader in a religious group).
- The job is one of two jobs to be held by a married couple (or those who have a civil partnership).
- The job involves living in a private home and the degree of contact and intimacy involved would be inappropriate with a person of the opposite sex.
- The job involves work outside the UK in countries where laws or customs would mean that the duties cannot be carried out by a woman.
- The job requires authenticity in the provision of food and drink to the public and for that reason specifying a particular race is allowed.

6.2.5 Indirect discrimination

This is where the employer applies to all people a provision, criterion or practice:

- which puts people of a particular protected characteristic at a disadvantage;
- and it is to the disadvantage of a person that he/she cannot comply;
- and it is not a proportionate means of achieving a legitimate aim.

In summary, this is discrimination that has happened indirectly because of a practice imposed by the employer. The intention of the employer is irrelevant and it is not necessary that the employer realises that the actions are discriminatory.

Provision, criterion or practice

There is no formal definition of 'provision, criterion or practice' – rather the law simply states that it must include a 'requirement or condition'. In reality this is likely to cover most employment practices, including informal arrangements. An example of a criterion applied to all religions is:

- *Williams-Drabble v Pathway Care Solutions Ltd* (2005) ET 2601718/05
  Williams-Drabble was a practising Christian. The employees were required to work to a new shift pattern that would include Sundays. This would have meant that Williams-Drabble would be unable to attend the church service at her chosen church. She resigned and successfully claimed indirect discrimination on the grounds of her religion, because the new shift patterns would be more difficult for a practising Christian to comply with and her employer could not justify why she had to work on Sundays.

This does not mean, however, that employees can never be asked to work on their holy day:

- *Mba v London Borough of Merton* (2013) EWCA Civ 1562
  Mba was also a practising Christian who believed that it was wrong to work on a Sunday. She worked in a care home for children that was open all day every day. When she was interviewed she did say that she would not work Sundays, and the employer said they would try to minimise her Sunday working, but could not guarantee she would never have to work on a Sunday. When she was put on the rota to work on a Sunday she raised a grievance, but was told it was part of her job. She was unsuccessful in claiming indirect religious discrimination because the provision, criterion or practice was a proportionate means of achieving a legitimate aim – namely the smooth running of the care home.

Disadvantage to a group of a particular protected characteristic

The disadvantage must be to the group and not just a particular individual. This is illustrated in the following case:

- *Eweida v British Airways* (2010) IRLR 322
  Eweida is a Christian who was employed by BA as one of the check-in staff. She wanted to wear a small cross on a chain – as a symbol of her religion. However, BA had a uniform code that forbade any visual adornment. Eweida claimed that refusing to allow her to wear her cross visibly was discrimination on the grounds of her religion. This argument was rejected by the Court of Appeal. There is no requirement on Christians to wear a cross and no other Christians had asked BA if they could wear one. There was no evidence that any Christians had been deterred from applying for a job at BA due to the dress code. On that basis, it concluded that the uniform code did not disadvantage Christians as a group and hence it was not indirect discrimination.

This ruling contrasts with the findings in the following case:

- *Noah v Desrosiers t/a Wedge* (2008) ET 2201867/07
  Desrosiers ran a 'funky and trendy' hairdressers and advertised for a hairdresser to work in the salon. She wanted the hairdressers working in the

salon to have funky and trendy hairstyles themselves, as a form of advertising to customers. Noah applied for a job – she was a Muslim and wore a hijab that covered her hair. At interview she confirmed that she would wear a hijab at work and hence her hairstyle would not be visible to customers. On that ground, Desrosiers decided not to employ her.

This was seen to be indirect discrimination. The provision, criterion or practice of having a visible hairstyle was such that Muslim women would be disadvantaged because they would not be able to work in the salon. It was ruled that this was not a proportionate means of achieving a legitimate aim and hence it was indirect discrimination.

Disadvantage to an individual

Once it has been identified that the provision, criterion or practice adversely affects a particular group with a protected characteristic the next question is whether the individual bringing the complaint of indirect discrimination has been disadvantaged.

- *British Airways v Starmer* (2005) IRLR 862
  Starmer was a pilot with British Airways, and requested to work part-time (50 per cent of normal hours) following the birth of her child. She was refused on health and safety grounds – British Airways held that pilots who had not flown at least 2,000 hours could not work less than 75 per cent of full-time because they did not have sufficient experience. This was found to be indirect discrimination against women, because they were more likely to take a career break or want to work part-time due to childcare responsibilities. It also was a particular disadvantage to Starmer because she was not able to reduce her hours. The EAT found that BA had not sufficiently justified the requirement to work at least 75 per cent of normal hours and hence this was indirect discrimination.

Proportionate means of achieving a legitimate aim

The final question is whether the provision, criterion or practice can be justified – if it is a proportionate means of achieving a legitimate aim. If it is then there is no indirect discrimination.

- *Azmi v Kirklees Metropolitan Council* (2007) EAT 0009/07
  A female Muslim teaching assistant was dismissed when she refused to remove her veil, which covered her head and face, but not her eyes, when teaching. The council argued that it inhibited her ability to interact and communicate effectively with the children in her care. Azmi took a claim of indirect discrimination on the grounds of religion. The EAT ruled that although the requirement not to wear a veil was a provision, criterion or practice that put her at a disadvantage compared with those who were not of the Muslim religion, it was justified as being a proportionate response to the requirement to give effective education to young children.

- *Ladele v London Borough of Islington* (2010) IRLR 211
  Ladele is a Christian and worked as a registrar for the council, conducting marriage ceremonies. When the Civil Partnership Act 2004 was introduced the work of the registrar extended to include civil partnership ceremonies. Due to her religious beliefs, Ladele believed that civil partnerships were

wrong and refused to conduct the ceremonies. When her employer insisted that she carried out the ceremonies, she took a claim of indirect discrimination on the grounds of her religion.

The Court of Appeal found that promoting equal opportunities was a legitimate aim for the council and a proportionate means of achieving this was for all registrars to be required to carry out civil partnership ceremonies. Hence, Ladele's claim failed.

6.2.6 Victimisation

Victimisation is the term used for the act of penalising employees in some way for exercising their rights under the Equality Act 2010. Victimisation is unlawful if the employer knows, or suspects, that the person being victimised intends to, or has:

- brought proceedings relating to alleged discrimination;
- given evidence or information in relation to a claim of discrimination;
- done anything else in reference to discrimination legislation;
- alleged that a person has committed an act that would be a contravention of discrimination legislation;
- and treats the person less favourably as a result.

These are all known as 'protected acts'.

In determining whether someone has suffered victimisation their treatment must be compared with the treatment of someone who has not carried out a protected act, and it has to be judged whether that treatment was less favourable. It is also important to consider whether the treatment was that of a 'reasonable and honest' employer.

- *St Helens Metropolitan Borough Council v Derbyshire* (2007) UKHL 16
  A claim under the equal pay legislation was brought by 470 female employees involved in school catering. Around two months before the claims were due to be heard the council wrote to all the employees telling them that continuing with the claims would have damaging effects on the council.

  The employees brought claims that the letters from the council amounted to victimisation – that they were a direct result of the employees taking action under discrimination legislation and that sending the letters was not the act of an 'honest and reasonable employer'. The House of Lords agreed that the letters were not an act of a reasonable employer and therefore ruled that victimisation had taken place.

Post-employment victimisation

Victimisation can also occur after the employment relationship ends. This was determined by the case of *Coote v Granada Hospitality Ltd* (1998), which was referred to the Court of Justice of the European Union for a ruling.

- *Coote v Granada Hospitality Ltd* (1998) IRLR 656
  Coote was employed by Granada from December 1992 to September 1993. In 1993 she brought a claim of sex discrimination against the employer, which was settled. She left the organisation in September 1993 and was unable to

find alternative employment. She believed it was because Granada had refused to supply her with a reference. She challenged this decision in the Employment Tribunal, which ruled that it could not be classified as victimisation because the employment had ended (although the issue at the centre of the argument was a protected act). The case was eventually referred to the ECJ, which ruled that the employer should be required to give a reference once the relationship had ended, and failure to do so had resulted in victimisation.

There was some debate about whether post-employment victimisation was covered by the Equality Act 2010. After two contrasting rulings in the Employment Appeal Tribunal the Court of Appeal confirmed that it is covered.

 Task

Find out if your organisation, or an organisation with which you are familiar, has a policy relating to victimisation. What training do managers have in this policy?

6.2.7 Harassment

Within the Equality Act 2010, harassment is defined as:

> Unwanted conduct related to a relevant protected characteristic, which has the purpose or effect of violating an individual's dignity or creating an intimidating, hostile, degrading, humiliating or offensive environment for that individual.

Harassment applies to all protected characteristics except for pregnancy and maternity, and marriage and civil partnership. It is important to note that the definition given refers to behaviour that creates an offensive environment. Hence, it is possible for someone to complain of behaviour that is not specifically directed at them, but creates an environment that they find offensive. For example, a heterosexual might find office banter directed at a homosexual employee offensive. The heterosexual employee could take a claim of harassment on the grounds of sexual orientation, even if the homosexual employee was not offended by what was being said.

The Equality Act 2010 originally included third-party harassment. This was when discrimination comes from someone who is not an employee of the company (eg a customer), it had occurred on at least two previous occasions and the employer had not taken reasonable steps to prevent it. However, the government was concerned that this was an unworkable concept and it was removed on 1 October 2013.

A series of events

Harassment can relate to a series of events that add up to an unbearable situation:

- *Strathclyde Regional Council v Porcelli* (1986) IRLR 134
  Porcelli was employed as a laboratory technician working in a school. Two male colleagues subjected her to a series of degrading treatment that included

making suggestive remarks, deliberately brushing against her, removing her personal belongings, storing equipment where she could not reach it and withholding information from her. They were eventually successful in their aim of forcing her to leave. The tribunal found that this was direct sex discrimination and harassment because the male employees would not have acted in the same way to a fellow male colleague.

One event

Harassment can also relate to one single incident, provided that it is deemed to be sufficiently serious:

- *Bracebridge Engineering Ltd v Darby* (1990) IRLR 3
  Darby had been criticised on a number of occasions for leaving work early. On one occasion two male supervisors stopped her as she went to wash her hands, thinking that she was attempting to leave early. She denied this, but they carried her forcefully into a darkened room where they made lewd remarks to her and sexually assaulted her. She immediately complained to a superior, but the general manager decided that no action should be taken against the supervisors. She resigned and claimed sexual discrimination and harassment. The employer argued that harassment had to relate to a series of acts and not one incident. However, the EAT found that a single incident, if sufficiently serious, can constitute harassment.

Determining whether acts amount to harassment

In determining whether something is harassment it is important to see the situation from the view of the claimant:

- *Richmond Pharmacology v Dhaliwal* (2009) IRLR 336
  Dhaliwal was of Indian origin. She had a conversation with the medical director in which he said, 'We will probably bump into each other in future – unless you are married off in India.' Dhaliwal claimed that this was racial harassment and the EAT agreed.

However, just because the claimant takes offence it does not automatically mean that the treatment will be harassment:

- *Quality Solicitors CMHT v Tunstall* (2014) UKEAT/0105/14
  Tunstall overheard a colleague talking about her to a client and saying 'She is Polish, but she is very nice.' The colleague said that he actually said: 'She is Polish, and she is very nice.' Tunstall took a claim of harassment arguing that, regardless of the actual words spoken, the implication was that Polish people are not usually very nice. Her claim was unsuccessful, with the EAT not agreeing that this one comment was sufficient to amount to harassment.

Even if the harasser does not mean to create an intimidating environment, it will still be harassment if that is the result of the behaviour. A further case illustrates the issue of considering the situation from the view of the claimant, and the issue of an 'intimidating, hostile, degrading, humiliating or offensive environment':

- *Moonsar v Fiveways Express Transport Ltd* (2004) IRLR 9
  Moonsar worked in an open-plan office with a group of men. On three occasions she was aware that they were downloading and viewing pornography on a computer in the office. She did not see any of the pornography and was not asked to become involved in the activity.

  After being made redundant she took claims of race and sex discrimination. Her sex discrimination claim related to the instances of the pornography – claiming that the events created an environment that amounted to sexual harassment. The EAT upheld her claim.

It should also be noted that employees who resign from employment as a result of harassment could potentially bring an additional claim of constructive dismissal. We explore this in more detail in Chapter 8.

Protection from Harassment Act 1997

The Protection from Harassment Act 1997 makes harassment, of whatever nature, a criminal offence. In this Act harassment is defined as pursuing a course of conduct that the harasser knows, or ought to know, amounts to harassment or conduct that causes fear of violence in another person. Conduct includes speech. Note also that 'course of conduct' suggests that the conduct has occurred on more than one occasion. Injunctions can be brought, under this Act, against those causing or likely to cause harassment. The Act also allows for the person who has been harassed to seek damages for financial loss and anxiety caused by the harassment. The Act is rarely used in employment situations.

 Task

Find out what policy your organisation, or an organisation with which you are familiar, has for dealing with alleged incidents of harassment. Do you think the policy addresses all the potential issues sufficiently?

6.3 Burden of proof

If the employee can present facts that suggest that discrimination might have occurred, the respondent has the responsibility to show non-discriminatory reasons for the act that is being complained of.

- *Barton v Investec Henderson Crosthwaite Securities Ltd* (2003) IRLR 332
  The female employee was concerned that her remuneration package was inferior to a male colleague's. In particular, she was awarded a significantly smaller bonus than her male colleague. The employer held that this was the result of the male colleague in question having been headhunted by a competitor and the need to improve his remuneration package to keep him. The EAT ruled that once the claimant has shown a potentially discriminatory

action, the burden of proof moves to the employer to prove that the acts are not discrimination. In this case it was not possible to argue that there was no discrimination.

- *Igen v Wong* (2005) ICR 931
  The employee does have to present some level of reasonable suspicion before the burden of proof moves to the employer. Igen was female and had recently returned from maternity leave when she was selected for redundancy. This was not enough evidence to suggest that discrimination had occurred. In giving its judgment on this case, the Court of Appeal said that a two-stage process should be followed when the courts consider a discrimination claim:
  - The claimant must prove facts from which the tribunal could conclude, in the absence of an adequate explanation from the respondent, that the respondent had discriminated against the claimant.
  - The burden of proof then moves to the respondent and the respondent must prove that it did not discriminate – that there was some other good reason for the action that is the focus of the complaint.

6.4 Discrimination questionnaires

To help with the process of proving discrimination there used to be a statutory questionnaire procedure. This allowed someone who thought that they had been discriminated against to ask questions of the employer to gather more facts. The employer did not have to reply, but if it did not the Employment Tribunal could draw an inference from this. This procedure was removed on 6 April 2014.

However, a potential claimant might still ask questions and Acas has issued a guidance booklet titled *Asking and Responding to Questions of Discrimination in the Workplace*, giving guidance on any questions that an individual might ask in relation to discrimination. The guidance booklet certainly suggests that the employer should still answer questions, and refusing to do so might give a negative impression at any subsequent Employment Tribunal hearing.

 Explore further

To understand the Acas guidance on managing questions relating to discrimination read the guidance booklet, which is available at http:// | www.acas.org.uk/media/pdf/m/p/Asking-and-responding-to-questions-of-discrimination-in-the-workplace.pdf

---

6.5 Vicarious liability

Vicarious liability means that the employer is held liable for wrongs committed by employees in the course of their employment.

An example to explain this is embodied in the following case:

- *Jones v Tower Boot Company* (1996) IRLR 168
Jones, a 16-year-old of mixed-race origin, started work at Tower Boot Company. He was immediately subjected to a campaign of physical and verbal assaults from two of his colleagues. This included his being burned with a hot screwdriver and having metal bolts thrown at his head. He resigned after one month and brought a claim of racial discrimination. The Court of Appeal found that the employees had been acting within the course of their employment and so Tower Boot Company was vicariously liable for the actions of the employees, even though they were not aware of what was happening.

Course of employment

The employer is responsible for all actions of employees, and those working on its behalf in the 'course of their employment'.

This has been interpreted broadly by the courts:

- *Cox v Ministry of Justice* (2016) UKSC10
A prisoner, working in the prison kitchens, accidentally dropped a heavy bag on the Catering Manager causing her an injury. The employer argued that it was not liable because the prisoner was not an employee. This argument was unsuccessful, because the prisoner was doing work on behalf of the employer.

- *Mohamud v Morrisons Supermarket plc* (2016) UKSC11
A customer went into a supermarket garage kiosk to ask if he could print some documents from a memory stick. The employee racially abused him, then followed him out to the forecourt and attacked him. The employer argued that it was not liable because the employee's actions were too distant from the duties of his job, but the Supreme Court ruled that this was in the course of employment.

- *Various Claimants v Barclays Bank plc (Dr Bates (deceased) and Barclays Group Litigation)* (2017) EWHC 1929
A group of women have claimed that they were sexually assaulted by a doctor who carried out medicals on them prior to them starting employment. These claims relate to assaults that happened many years ago, and the doctor has since died. The employer argued it was not liable because the doctor was not an employee, but was contracted to carry out the work. It has lost the argument – the doctor was working for the employer, following the employer's requirements and hence the employer was liable for what happened.

6.6 Remedies for discrimination

If it is found by an Employment Tribunal that there has been an act of discrimination, the following can be awarded:

- A declaration of the rights of the parties.
- An order of compensation that is not subject to a maximum. The compensation should address any loss or damage that has occurred and can include a sum relating to injured feelings.
- A recommendation of actions that the employer should take.

Prior to the Equality Act 2010, the recommendation had to relate specifically to the case that was under consideration. However, the Equality Act 2010 broadened the remit such that recommendations could address discrimination more generally. The Deregulation Act 2015 returned the remit of recommendations to the pre-Equality Act 2010 approach with effect from 1 October 2015.

As noted, the compensation can include an amount for injury to feelings. This is clearly a rather subjective assessment, and guidelines were laid down for the range of compensation that should be offered in the following case:

- *Vento v Chief Constable of West Yorkshire Police* (2003) IRLR 102
  In this case, in which the Court of Appeal was asked to consider whether an award that had been made for sex discrimination was excessive, the following guidelines were set out:
    - Top band: sums in this range may be awarded in the most serious cases, such as where there has been a lengthy campaign of discriminatory harassment on the grounds of sex or race. Only in exceptional cases should more than the top band be given.
    - Middle band: this should be used for serious cases, but which are less serious than those in the top band.
    - Lowest band: awards in this range are appropriate for less serious cases, such as where the act of discrimination is an isolated or one-off occurrence. In general, awards of less than £500 are to be avoided altogether because, if there is injury to feelings, such a small sum would not be appropriate.

The monetary ranges that reflected each band were increased in the case of *Da'Bell v NSPCC* (2010) IRLR 19, and were then increased again for all claims brought on or after 6 April 2018. The current bands are:

- Exceptional cases: £42,900+
- Top band: £25,700 to £42,900
- Middle band: £8,600 to £25,700
- Lowest band: £900 to £8,600

 Explore further

Go to the website of the Equality and Human Rights Commission (www.equalityhumanrights.com) to find out more about discrimination.

Take time to browse through the wide range of materials that are available here.

6.7 Positive action

In certain situations it might be lawful to positively encourage, for example, members of an underrepresented group of employees to apply for a job. Note, however, that there is no such thing as 'positive discrimination'; what we are referring to is 'positive action'. Acceptable actions could be advertising a job in an area where people from an underrepresented ethnic minority are likely to live, or guaranteeing an interview for all disabled applicants (if disabled individuals are underrepresented in the organisation).

The Equality Act 2010 introduced the ability to go further than just encourage people from a particular characteristic to apply for a job. If there are two or more people applying for a job or promotion who are judged to be equal in every way, the employer is allowed to consider whether one of these people has a protected characteristic that is underrepresented at that level within the organisation. If this is the case, the employer can decide to appoint the person from the underrepresented group. Note, however, that this only applies when the individuals have been assessed to be equal in every way. It has to be applied on a case-by-case basis; the employer is not allowed to have a general policy giving preference to an underrepresented group.

 Task

Find out if your organisation, or an organisation with which you are familiar, has a policy relating to discrimination in the workplace. Read the policy, if it exists, and consider whether it meets the legal requirements. If there is no policy, try drafting one.

6.8 Equal pay

As we noted at the start of this chapter, legislation making it unlawful to discriminate between men and women in relation to their terms and conditions of employment was introduced in 1970. This legislation is now part of the Equality Act 2010. Although the term 'equal pay' suggests a focus only on pay, it does actually address all terms and conditions of the contract of employment. It is important to emphasise that 'equal pay' is looking at comparisons between men and women. It is not relevant in addressing grievances of men complaining against their conditions in comparison to other male colleagues, or of women complaining against their conditions in comparison to other female colleagues.

This issue of identifying a comparator can be complicated by the employee not knowing exactly what others are paid. The Equality Act 2010 helps to address this by making it unlawful to include a pay secrecy clause in the contract of employment if this restricts an individual from disclosing their pay in a potential discrimination claim. A comparator in an equal pay case must work for the same employer, but could work at a different location. It is possible to make a comparison with a predecessor in the job role.

When bringing a claim of equal pay the claim can be because terms and conditions of employment of a woman are less favourable than those of a man (and vice versa) if they are employed on:

- like work;
- work rated as equivalent;
- work of equal value.

It is important to note that the terms and conditions of employment are considered individually in claims of equal pay. Hence, an employer cannot argue that a female employee, for example, has a lower salary than a man, but better holiday allowances – and hence overall the package is equal. The requirement is for there to be equality in each individual term of the contract.

6.8.1 *Like work*

This is defined as 'work of the same or a broadly similar nature'. Generally, the Employment Tribunals take quite a broad view of this concept. They are not looking for identical work but an overall similarity in the work that is done. It is important that the total work is looked at and not too much emphasis is placed on small tasks that rarely occur. It is also important that the focus is on what actually happens regularly in the job, rather than a narrow focus on what the contract suggests will happen.

The comparison focuses on the jobs in question and not on the individuals carrying out the jobs.

The need to take this broad approach is shown in the following case:

- *Capper Pass v Lawton* (1977) ICR 83
  Lawton was employed as a cook working a 40-hour week and being in sole charge of preparing daily lunches for 10 to 20 directors and their guests. She brought an equal pay claim, comparing her job with that of two male assistant chefs. They worked a basic 40-hour week with five and a half hours of regular weekly overtime and they worked one weekend in three. They prepared 350 meals each day in two sittings of breakfast, lunch and tea. The tribunal held that the cook and assistant chefs did 'like work' and thus the equal pay claim was upheld. In supporting this decision the EAT emphasised that a broad consideration of the skill and experiences required to do the job and a general consideration of the type of work required was essential. Although there were clearly differences between the jobs, these were largely trivial.

  If there are genuine differences between the jobs, and they are compensated for separately, it does not mean that basic terms and conditions should also vary:

- *Dugdale and others v Kraft Foods Ltd* (1977) ICR 48
  Women quality controllers, working with a food-processing company, were paid at a lower rate than the male quality inspectors. The men and women all worked shifts, but only the men were expected to work nights and Sundays. The men were paid an additional shift allowance for Sundays and nights. The Employment Tribunal found that the differences in shifts were 'differences of practical importance' and so this was not a case of like work. However, the

EAT overturned this finding, stating that the work of the men and women was broadly similar. They found that the hours when the work was carried out should be discounted, especially because the men were compensated for the different shift patterns.

However, if there are genuine differences in the work being carried out, the differences cannot be separated from the main duties and ignored in making a claim of like work.

6.8.2 Work rated as equivalent

This can only be used where an analytical, non-discriminatory job evaluation scheme is in place. An analytical scheme is one that breaks down jobs into component parts whereas a non-analytical scheme simply compares whole jobs and does not consider the individual tasks and components that make up the job. There are many ways in which a job evaluation scheme can become discriminatory. Main pitfalls include relying too heavily on subjective judgments rather than objective data, and basing schemes on existing internal benchmark jobs that could perpetuate existing discrimination.

If the points allocated in a job evaluation scheme are directly related to a job grade within the company, the employee should receive the terms and conditions of employment relating to the grade in which he/she is placed:

- *Springboard Sunderland Trust v Robson* (1992) IRLR 261
  Mrs R was a team leader and she compared her terms and conditions to those of Mr R, an induction officer. Following a job evaluation process carried out by the employer, Mrs R's job was evaluated at 410 points and Mr R's job at 428 points. The company grading scheme stated that jobs with between 360 and 409 points were grade three and jobs with between 410 and 439 points were grade four. However, the company continued to treat Mrs R as a grade three. The tribunal found – supported by the EAT – that Mrs R had to be treated as a grade four, in accordance with the job evaluation scheme, and that Mrs R and Mr R were therefore carrying out work 'rated as equivalent'.

 Task

Find out if your organisation, or an organisation with which you are familiar, has a job evaluation scheme. Is it analytical and non-discriminatory? Could it be used to defend a claim for equal pay?

6.8.3 Work of equal value

This category of equal pay claims adds the opportunity to make a claim when there is no like work or work formally rated as equivalent. It is a complicated and lengthy process to prove a case of equal value. An Employment Tribunal often appoints an independent expert to investigate the claim.

- *Asda Stores Ltd v Brierley and others* (2016) EWCA Civ 566
  Female employees, working as sales assistants in Asda stores, claim that their work is of equal value to predominantly male employees working in the warehouse who are paid considerably more than them. The case was referred to the Court of Appeal to determine whether it could be heard in the Employment Tribunal. It ruled that it could, so we now await the ruling on whether this is work of equal value.

One of the difficulties that the tribunal has in determining whether there is a situation of work of equal value is in deciding how to make this judgment:

- *William Ball Ltd v Wood and others* (2002) EAT 89/01
  Nine female employees (one supervisor and eight cleaner/packers) claimed work of equal value in comparison with work being carried out by picker/packers. The female employees appointed their own expert who carried out a system called 'value check' to determine if the jobs were of equal value. He concluded that they were. This was presented to the tribunal and the employers brought no alternative evidence. The tribunal worked through the 'value check' system after hearing all the evidence and altered any scores that they disagreed with, based on what they had heard. They concluded that the jobs were of equal value. The EAT supported their finding, concluding that they had acted fairly on the only constructive approach available to them.

6.8.4 *What defence can the employer give?*

In some cases it might be possible for the employer to argue that there is a reason for the differences in the terms and conditions of employment. This is known as a 'material factor' defence. If there is a significant and relevant factor, other than sex, that is the reason for the difference, the claim of equal pay will fail. The tribunal must be convinced that the reason given is genuine and not an excuse. There have been a number of cases relating to this point, covering a wide range of different factors.

Different negotiating groups

- *Enderby v Frenchay Health Authority* (1993) IRLR 591
  Enderby, an NHS senior speech therapist, claimed she was employed on work of equal value to that of male principal grade pharmacists and clinical psychologists also employed in the NHS. The NHS claimed that the differences related to the fact that the two groups of employees were represented by different negotiating groups. The case was referred to the ECJ. They ruled that there was a clear difference in pay between the groups, which gave a prima facie case of sex discrimination. They ruled that it was insufficient to rely on the defence that the pay rates were arrived at through separate negotiations. Justification for the actual differences in pay had to be given.

Explore further

The case of *Enderby v Frenchay Health Authority* (1993) is an interesting one and somewhat complicated to follow because of the number of stages of appeal involved. Students wanting to explore this issue further are recommended to read the whole judgment in the case – particularly the ruling of the ECJ. It is particularly interesting to note the reasons that each stage of the court process gives for reaching its conclusions.

Collective bargaining

Returning to the case of *William Ball Ltd v Wood and others* (2002), part of the defence of the employer was that the rates of pay had been agreed through a process of collective bargaining. The relevant collective agreement categorised workers in the furniture-making industry. It was noted that the agreement predated any equal pay legislation and the tribunal concluded that it was 'tainted' because, for historical reasons, it maintained higher pay rates for picker/packers, a job traditionally reserved for men. For this reason, the collective bargaining process (resulting in the collective agreement) was not allowed as a material defence.

Experience

- *Cadman v Health and Safety Executive* (2006) IRLR 969
  Cadman worked as a health and safety inspector. She was paid less than two male colleagues doing the same job. This was justified by the employer because she had less service, and thus less experience, than her male colleagues.

  The case eventually went to the Court of Justice of the European Union (CJEU), where it ruled that an employer does not have to justify differing payments reflecting differing levels of experience, unless there is evidence that suggests that such differences are not being applied fairly. In addition, there is no requirement that the employer demonstrates that the differing levels of service and experience do result in an employee's having different capability in doing a job. The case was remitted to an Employment Tribunal to consider whether there was any evidence that suggested the differences were not being applied fairly.

Red circling

Red circling is where one or more employees have their pay protected either for a specific period of time or for the full duration of the remaining period of employment. For example, an employee might need to move to a lighter job for medical reasons and the employer could decide not to reduce his/her pay accordingly. Alternatively, following a restructuring, there might be a group of employees who are demoted, but again the decision is made not to reduce the pay accordingly. There have been a number of cases examining whether this is a fair defence for a difference in terms and conditions. An interesting ruling is in:

- *Audit Commission v Haq and others* (2010) UKEAT/0123/10
Nine female inspection and information officers, working within the commission's Housing Inspectorate, made an equal pay claim. They compared themselves with colleagues, who were mostly male, who had been transferred from the Housing Corporation in 2004. They had been employed on different pay scales, had more senior job titles and their pay was subject to pay protection. In 2007 the posts were merged, with 11 posts being filled from the existing 15 employees. Two of the posts went to male employees who had previously worked for the Housing Corporation and who, because of their pay protection, were on higher salaries than the females appointed to the posts. The female employees made a claim under equal pay legislation.

  The Employment Tribunal supported the women's claims, agreeing that the difference in pay was unlawful. However, the EAT disagreed. Although the merger of the two groups of employees did result in the female employees being paid less than the male colleagues, there was no reason that the men were disproportionately advantaged by the pay protection policy. The pay protection scheme had a legitimate aim and was a proportionate means of achieving that aim. There was nothing discriminatory in the approach that had been used and hence the claims of equal pay were dismissed.

However, note also the following case:

- *Bury Metropolitan Borough Council v Hamilton and others* (2011) UKEAT/0413–5/09
This case related to equal pay claims from female employees at Bury Metropolitan Council and Sunderland. The predominantly female group of employees (carers, for example) had compared themselves against a predominantly male group of employees (maintenance workers, for example). There was a bonus in place that related to predominantly male jobs, which was not applicable to the predominantly female jobs. It was accepted that this bonus had been linked to productivity when it was first introduced, but the link between productivity and the bonus had been lost over time. Hence, it meant that non-payment of the bonus to the female claimants could not be justified. However, the EAT did not support the Employment Tribunal's view that the payment was a 'sham'. Rather, the relevance of the bonus had disappeared over time.

  The EAT also addressed the issue of pay protection – amounts of money that had been given to the predominantly male employees when the bonus had been removed, to 'cushion' the drop in pay due to no longer receiving the bonus. The EAT ruled that these arrangements were unlawful. It did not find that the argument that paying similar payments to the women was unaffordable was an acceptable defence.

Location

- *Navy, Army and Air Force Institutes v Varley* (1976) IRLR 408
Nottingham office staff worked a 37-hour week, whereas London staff worked a 36.5-hour week. Varley, a female clerk in Nottingham, claimed that her hours should be brought in line with a male clerk's in London. This claim was not allowed because it was held that the difference was due to location and not to sex.

6.8.5 *Enforcement of claims*

A claim relating to equal pay can be brought to the tribunal at any time during the period of employment when the comparator is also working, or within six months of leaving employment. The remedy is arrears of pay or damages limited to a maximum of two years before the proceedings were instigated. No payment for injury to feelings is awarded – because this legislation is based on the law of contract (and hence compensates for any contractual payments that have not been paid) and not on the law of tort (as in the case of other discrimination legislation).

 Task

Find out if your organisation, or one with which you are familiar, has significant differences in pay relating to any of the material defences outlined in section 6.8.4. Do you think they are defences that would be accepted by the courts?

6.9   Equal pay audits

The Enterprise and Regulatory Reform Act 2013 introduced legislation relating to pay audits, which was implemented on 1 October 2014. If an organisation loses an equal pay claim they will be ordered to carry out a pay audit in the organisation unless:

- an audit has been carried out in the past three years;
- the organisation has a transparent pay scheme;
- the organisation has a good reason for not carrying out a pay audit, and the tribunal accepts this reason.

The Employment Tribunal will set the timeframe in which this audit must be carried out, and can order the organisation to publish the results on their website, and for this to remain for up to three years.

6.10   Gender pay reporting

There is a significant gap between the earnings of men and women in the UK. The specific figure varies from survey to survey, but it is widely accepted that the gap is a problem. To help address this the government has introduced gender pay reporting.

    The Equality Act 2010 (Gender Pay Gap Information) Regulations 2017 sets out that any organisation in the voluntary or private sector with at least 250 employees must report annually on their gender pay gap. The Equality Act 2010 (Specific

Duties and Public Authorities) Regulations 2017 extend this requirement to the public sector (excluding the armed forces, government departments and those parts of the public sector listed in Schedule 19 of the Equality Act 2010).

In calculating whether an organisation has 250 employees it should be noted that an 'employee' includes employees, workers, agency workers and any self-employed individuals who have to provide work personally to the organisation. For this calculation part-time workers count as one person. So, if there are two people job sharing they will count as two people.

Organisations in the private sector are required to calculate a 'snap shot' of their pay data on 5 April each year, and the public sector is required to calculate their 'snap shot' on 31 March each year. A report then has to be made within 12 months. The first calculations were in 2017, with the first reports being made in 2018.

When calculating the amount that an individual is paid the following should be included:

- basic pay;
- allowances;
- pay for piecework;
- pay for leave;
- shift premium pay.

The following are not included:

- overtime pay;
- termination payments (including redundancy);
- pay in lieu of leave;
- remuneration that is not provided in money.

The organisation must report:

- the mean pay for men and women and the gap between the two;
- the median pay for men and women and the gap between the two;
- the proportion of men and women in each quartile when they are arranged in order of pay;
- the mean bonus payment for men and women and the gap between the two;
- the median bonus payment for men and women and the gap between the two;
- the proportion of men and women receiving a bonus.

Bonus data is calculated over the 12-month period leading up to the 'snap shot' data.

The report must be accompanied by a signed statement from senior management that the information is correct. There is no requirement to have a commentary explaining the data, but an organisation can include this if they want.

The information must be published on the organisation's website and remain there for at least three years. The information must also be uploaded to a government portal. At present, there is no penalty for not complying with the requirements although there have been suggestions that the government might 'name and shame' non-complying organisations if the lack of compliance does become a problem.

Explore further

Go to the government portal where organisations have uploaded the outcomes of their gender pay reporting analysis (https://gender-pay-gap.ser-vice.gov.uk). Look at a range of results to understand the differences that have been reported.

 KEY LEARNING POINTS

1 Discrimination legislation has grown rapidly over the past 30 years. All discrimination legislation is now contained within the Equality Act 2010.

2 Direct discrimination is where an individual is treated less favourably on the grounds of a protected characteristic.

3 Associative discrimination is where an individual is treated less favourably because he/she associates with individuals of a particular protected characteristic.

4 Perceptive discrimination is where an individual is treated less favourably because he/she is perceived as having a particular protected characteristic.

5 Indirect discrimination is where an employer applies a criterion that adversely affects a considerably larger proportion of one group than another and it is to that group's detriment that it cannot apply, and the criterion cannot be justified.

6 There are occasions when the employment of someone of a particular protected characteristic is essential because of the nature of the job – this is known as an occupational requirement.

7 Individuals are protected against victimisation for carrying out a 'protected act' as defined under discrimination legislation.

8 Harassment is unwanted conduct related to a relevant protected characteristic, which has the purpose or effect of violating an individual's dignity or creating an intimidating, hostile, degrading, humiliating or offensive environment for that individual.

9 'Vicarious liability' means that the employer is held liable for wrongs committed by an employee during the course of his/her employment.

10 Equal pay claims focus on a comparator carrying out like work, work rated as equivalent or work of equal value.

11 An employer can defend the difference in pay between a man and a woman doing equal work if it can prove a material defence other than sex.

12 Gender pay reporting is required if an organisation has at least 250 employees.

Case summaries

- *Betsi Cadwaladr v Hughes* (2014) UKEAT/ 0179/13 – An employee was unable to work in her previous role due to illness and was initially given meaningful work. However, over time the work became menial and this was found to violate her dignity, and hence meet the definition of harassment.
- *Canniffe v East Riding of Yorkshire Council* (2000) IRLR 555 – Canniffe was sexually harassed and assaulted by a work colleague. Before this event it was known that the colleague had carried out inappropriate conduct towards her. The employer argued that it had a discrimination policy that included harassment and it had brought these to the attention of the employees involved. For that reason, the employer argued, it was not liable for the events. However, the EAT ruled that just having a policy was not enough when there was further action that could have been (and should have been) taken.
- *Chief Constable of Lincolnshire Police v Stubbs* (1999) IRLR 81 – The claimant was sexually harassed by a colleague who was on secondment to another part of the police force. One incident of harassment occurred at a social function. The EAT ruled that the employer was still liable because seconded officers did remain employees of their home force throughout the secondment. Also, the social function was work-related and so the employer was liable.
- *Christie and others v John E Haith Ltd* (2003) IRLR 670 – The claimants worked packing birdseed. They were women and packed bags up to 12 kilogrammes in weight, for £4.32 per hour. The men packed bags up to 30 kilogrammes in weight and were paid £4.58 per hour. The men also loaded and unloaded delivery trolleys. The women submitted an equal pay claim – but the employer argued that the men's work was more arduous and unpleasant and there was therefore a genuine material defence for the differences. This was upheld.
- *London Underground v Edwards* (1998) IRLR 364 – A new roster of shift patterns was put in place that Edwards was unable to comply with because of her childcare arrangements. Edwards successfully claimed that the criterion was indirect discrimination in that significantly fewer women than men would be able to work the new shifts because significantly more women than men have childcare responsibilities.

 Examples to work through

1 Susan is a teacher within a large secondary school. She has always trained the school choir after the school day has finished. She has now been asked to start a further choir for the younger children, again rehearsing after school hours. She has refused to do this because she has her own young children and staying late on two days causes her childcare difficulties. The head teacher has stated that she is head of the music department and so these duties are

(Continued)

(Continued)

part of her job. She is threatening to resign and claim indirect sex discrimination. What is your advice to the head teacher?

2 You are the HR manager and a head of department has informed you that he is concerned about the relationship between one of his senior managers(a man) and a young female employee. He is concerned that some of the behaviour he has witnessed amounts to sexual harassment. He has spoken to the senior manager and explained his concerns, which have been dismissed as 'overreacting'. What else might you do to ensure that the organisation is not vicariously liable for any harassment that might occur?

3 Your organisation has three different branches – one in London, one in Swindon and one in Bolton. The wage rates at the London branch are higher than those in Swindon and Bolton. The employees at Swindon are claiming that the 'London allowance' is unfair because the costs of living in Swindon are similar to those of living in London. They are planning to put in an equal pay claim. What should you do to address this issue?

4 An Indian restaurant has advertised for waiters/waitresses and chefs of Indian origin. Is this allowed?

07
Discrimination – the protected characteristics

CHAPTER OBJECTIVES

The objectives of this chapter are:

- to explore the specific protected characteristics within the Equality Act 2010 – sex, marital status and civil partnership, pregnancy and maternity, race, disability, gender reassignment, sexual orientation, religion and belief, age;
- to consider the legislation relating to unfair treatment on the grounds of trade union membership.

7.1 Introduction

In Chapter 6 we focused on different types of discrimination. In this chapter we will look in more detail at the nine protected characteristics within the Equality Act 2010. We will be applying direct, indirect, associative and perceptive discrimination, and harassment and victimisation as we look at the protected characteristics. We will also look at the specific claim of discrimination arising from disability.

7.2 Sex

Discrimination on the basis of the gender of an individual is unlawful. For there to be sex discrimination, the treatment must relate to the gender of the individual:

- *Shamoon v Chief Constable of the Royal Ulster Constabulary* (2003) IRLR 285
  Shamoon was a chief inspector in the Constabulary. One of her duties was to carry out staff appraisals. There were complaints about the manner in which she conducted some appraisals and hence it was decided that she would no longer carry out that duty. However, the two other (male) chief inspectors continued to carry out appraisals. Shamoon claimed that this was sex discrimination. This claim was rejected because her sex was not the reason that she was no longer carrying out appraisals.

It has been held that requiring women to work shift patterns that make it difficult to meet childcare responsibilities can be indirect sex discrimination. However, this does not mean that the woman is also entitled to any benefits associated with such shifts:

- *Blackburn v Chief Constable of West Midlands Police* (2009) IRLR 135
  Blackburn was a front-line police officer – the officers were required to work a 24/7 shift rota, but she was excused from working this because of her childcare responsibilities. Those who worked during night-time (which she did not) received a bonus. Blackburn claimed that not receiving the bonus made her contract unequal to her male comparators and hence was discriminatory. Her claim failed. There is no requirement to pay employees for work that they do not do.

7.3 Marital status and civil partnership

Discrimination against employees on the grounds of their marital status or civil partnership is covered as part of the Equality Act 2010, but there is no similar protection for people who are living together outside marriage. Single people are not covered under this protected characteristic.

- *Chief Constable of Bedfordshire Constabulary v Graham* (2002) IRLR 239
  Graham was an inspector in the Bedfordshire force and married a chief superintendent in the same force. In May 1999 Graham was appointed Area Inspector in the same division that her husband commanded. In June 1999 she was told that her appointment had been rescinded. It was claimed that her appointment was inappropriate in view of the role of her husband in the division. The claims of indirect sex discrimination and direct and indirect discrimination on the grounds of marital status were all upheld. The EAT confirmed that the decision to rescind the job had clearly been on the basis of Graham's marital status.

Those who have entered into a civil partnership are specifically covered by the Equality Act 2010. They are also protected by the Civil Partnership Act 2004. Any benefits that are given to married partners of an employee (eg transport subsidies given to employees and their spouses) must also be applied to an employee and his/her civil partner.

7.4 Pregnancy and maternity

As we discovered in Chapter 6, dismissal on the grounds of pregnancy or any matter relating to pregnancy is automatically unfair. Refer back to the case of *Webb v EMO Air Cargo Ltd* (1994) IRLR 482.

7.5 Race

7.5.1 What is race?

The Equality Act 2010 defines 'race' as being colour, nationality and ethnic or national origins. A series of cases have helped to define what is and is not a racial group. Sikhs, Jews and Gypsies have all been held to be ethnic groups, but Rastafarians have not. In determining that Sikhs were an ethnic group (*Mandla v Dowell Lee* (1983), IRLR 209, 2 AC 548) it was stated that to be an ethnic group the group must regard itself, and be regarded by others, as a distinct community with long-standing cultural traditions and a shared history. Because Rastafarians have been an identifiable group for only around 60 years, they did not meet this definition. However, Rastafarians are now covered by religious discrimination.

- *Dziedziak v Future Electronics Ltd* (2012) UKEAT/0270/11
  An employee who was of Polish nationality was told that she should not use her own language in the workplace. This was seen to be direct discrimination, because other employees who were of other nationalities had not been given the same instruction.

This ruling contrasts with that in *PF Franco v Fyffes Group Ltd* (2012) where an employee who worked with a number of Polish employees claimed that he felt isolated because they spoke Polish in the workplace, which he did not understand. His claim of discrimination was unsuccessful because the employer had told the employees to speak English when others were around, the work did not require a high level of English and speaking Polish between themselves was not a detriment to other employees.

 Explore further

As you are working through the different protected characteristics take time to go back to the Equality and Human Rights Commission website (www.equalityhumanrights.com) that

you looked at when reading through the last chapter. Read about the different protected characteristics as you work through the chapter.

7.6 Disability

7.6.1 Definition of a disabled employee

In the Equality Act 2010 a disabled person is defined as having a 'physical or mental impairment that has a substantial and long-term adverse effect on a person's ability to carry out normal day-to-day activities'. The definition is extended by the following:

- a mental impairment does not have to be one of a list of clinically recognised illnesses to be classed as a disability, rather the impact of the impairment should be considered;

- all people diagnosed with cancers, HIV or multiple sclerosis are classified as disabled from the date of diagnosis.

Disabled individuals are covered by all types of discrimination law. Indirect discrimination was added by the Equality Act 2010, but it will be difficult for a disabled person to bring this claim. This is because the definition of indirect discrimination requires a disadvantage to be experienced by a group with a protected characteristic. Disabled persons vary considerably in the difficulties they experience, and hence it will be difficult to show this group disadvantage.

✳A specific aspect of direct discrimination is the requirement to make reasonable adjustments, as we will explore later in this section. The purpose of making reasonable adjustments is to assist the disabled person to work. If reasonable adjustments are not considered or made it can be argued that there has been less favourable treatment, and hence there has been direct discrimination.

An interesting question that caused a lot of debate was whether obesity could be a disability. This was raised in the case of *Kaltoft v The Municipality of Billund* (2014) EUECJ C-354/13, when a Danish childminder who weighted 25 stone argued that he had been dismissed due to his weight. The case was referred to the Court of Justice of the European Union (CJEU), for them to determine whether obesity could be a disability.

The CJEU ruled that if obesity has reached a point at which it results in physical or psychological limitations then it can be a disability. It is important to note that this ruling does not conclude that obesity will always be a disability. The focus has to be on the impairments caused by the obesity, rather than the obesity itself.

This ruling has been applied in the UK in the case of *Bickerstaff v Butcher* (2015) NIIT/ 92/14. Bickerstaff had a body mass index of 48.5 and was constantly teased by colleagues about his weight. Applying the CJEU guidance the tribunal concluded that Bickerstaff was disabled and hence this amounted to harassment on the grounds of disability.

Physical or mental impairment

In the majority of cases this is a relatively straightforward concept. However, there have been cases brought to the Employment Tribunal for a judgment on less clear illnesses:

- *Millar v Inland Revenue Commissioners* (2006) IRLR 112
  Following a fall at work when Millar hit his head, he developed vision problems primarily, including sensitivity to bright lights. This meant that he could not

drive at night or on sunny days and could use a VDU only for limited periods of time. Despite a number of medical investigations, no cause for his problems could be found, although it was not disputed that the problems existed.

The Court of Session held that he was disabled in accordance with the definitions set out in section 7.6.1. He clearly was restricted in relevant day-to-day activities and reaching the definition of disability does not require reference to cause or to a specific named illness.

Substantial and long-term adverse effect

An illness is deemed to have had a 'long-term effect' if it has lasted, or is likely to last, at least 12 months or (in the case of a terminal illness) is expected to last for the rest of the employee's life. The definition of a 'substantial and adverse effect' is more difficult. Clearly, it is related to the latter part of the definition – the ability to carry out normal day-to-day activities. However, that amounts to a yard-stick, and if the employee is unable to carry out normal duties at work there is also the possibility that a disability exists.

- *Chief Constable of Sussex Police v Millard (2016) UKEAT/0341/14*
  The employee had suffered from anxiety, depression and a panic disorder. The episode that led to him being dismissed had lasted for less than 12 months. The EAT concluded that there was no evidence that the problem would last for at least 12 months, and therefore his claim of disability discrimination failed.

✳ Normal day-to-day activities

These must be normal activities that might occur regularly. The Disability Discrimination Act 1995 contained a list of activities that were considered to be 'normal' and 'day to day'. However, that list is not part of the Equality Act 2010. The definition of normal day-to-day activities needs to be considered taking into consideration the European Equal Treatment Directive Framework. This refers to a disability restricting full engagement in professional life – extending the definition of normal day-to-day activities to include work. This was applied in the following case:

- *Banaszczyk v Booker (2016) UKEAT/0132/15*
  The employee worked in a warehouse and was required to lift items up to 25 kilogrammes in weight. He had a back problem and struggled to meet the targets of 10 items an hour. He was dismissed. He argued that this was disability discrimination, but the employer argued that he could do 'normal day-to-day activities'. Lifting 25-kilogramme items was not something that was normal on a day-to-day basis. Applying the Equal Treatment Directive Framework the EAT concluded that he was not able to fully participate in professional life and therefore he was disabled.

This contrasts with an earlier case:

- *Quinlan v B&Q plc (1998) EAT 1386/97*
  Quinlan underwent open-heart surgery. As a result of the surgery he was unable to lift the heavy loads that were required of him as a general assistant in the garden centre. He was therefore dismissed. The EAT supported the Employment Tribunal's view that he was not suffering from a disability because he was still

able to carry smaller loads that would be typical of day-to-day activities, even though he was not able to carry out the duties required of him at work.

It is also important to note that a recurring illness can be treated as a disability, even if it is not evident at the specific time of events:

- *SCA Packaging Ltd v Boyle* (2009) IRLR 746
  Boyle suffered from hoarseness and problems with her vocal nodes. She controlled her condition by regular exercises, drinking water and not raising her voice. The employer removed a wall between her area of work and the warehouse, which resulted in increased noise and the need for her to raise her voice. She asked to move to another area, but this was refused. The House of Lords ruled that this was disability discrimination because it was likely to result in her situation recurring.

- *Richmond Adult Community College v McDougall* (2008) EWCA Civ 4
  McDougall had been offered a job at the college, but this was withdrawn when it became apparent that she had previously suffered from a mental illness, although she had not had an 'episode' for three years. When the offer was withdrawn she had a relapse. The Court of Appeal ruled that this was not disability discrimination because events subsequent to the actions of the college could not be taken into consideration.

A severe disfigurement is treated as a disability. However, there are certain conditions that do not constitute a disability, which are: an addiction (eg alcohol, nicotine); a tendency to set fires, steal or abuse other people; exhibitionism and voyeurism; hay fever.

Reasonable adjustments

Direct disability discrimination is treating a disabled person less favourably because of the disability. If an individual is disabled the employer is required to make 'reasonable' adjustments to accommodate the needs of a disabled employee. These might include such adjustments as making physical adjustments to the workplace, changing the hours of work or changing the process of work. The duty to make a reasonable adjustment arises in three situations:

1 Where there is a provision, criterion or practice put in place by the employer that puts the disabled person at a substantial disadvantage when compared to a non-disabled person.

2 Where a physical feature puts a disabled person at a substantial disadvantage when compared to a non-disabled person.

3 Where a disabled person would, but for the provision of an auxiliary aid, be put at a substantial disadvantage when compared to a non-disabled person.

 Task

Find out if your organisation, or an organisation with which you are familiar, has had to make any reasonable adjustments due to an individual having a disability.

Do you think that these adjustments were reasonable? Why/why not?

All of these possible modifications have a potential impact on the employer. There is clearly a financial impact in most cases and some adjustments (although highly preferable) might be impossible for logistical reasons. In determining whether the employer has acted reasonably, the Employment Tribunal will take all of these issues into consideration.

- *Archibald v Fife Council* (2004) IRLR 651, HL
  Archibald worked as a road sweeper but became unable to walk and therefore unable to do her job. She applied for over 100 administrative jobs with the council, but was unsuccessful with all the applications. She was eventually dismissed on grounds of capability.

  She took a claim for disability discrimination, stating that she should have been offered an administrative post without having to go through the process of competitive interviewing. The House of Lords supported her claim – stating that there is an obligation on employers to make reasonable adjustments for disabled employees, and giving her a job without the process of competitive interviewing was a reasonable adjustment that should have been made.

- *Wade v Sheffield Hallam University* (2013) UKEAT/0194/12
  In this case an employee who suffered from an allergic condition, which amounted to a disability, relied on the ruling in the Archibald case to argue that a reasonable adjustment would be to allow her to bypass a competitive interview for a role that she had applied for. However, she was unsuccessful because she did not meet the essential criteria for the job. Her case differed from Archibald, because here the employee did not meet the essential criteria.

- *O'Hanlon v Commissioners of HM Revenue and Customs* (2007) IRLR 404
  O'Hanlon was absent from work with clinical depression. After a period of time her entitlement to company sick pay ran out, in accordance with the company procedure. She took a claim that failing to pay her full pay during her period of illness was either direct discrimination or disability-related discrimination (not making a reasonable adjustment in light of her disability).

  The Court of Appeal rejected her claims. The purpose of a reasonable adjustment is to aid the employee to be part of the workforce. Paying additional monies during a period of sickness absence did not help meet the purpose of reasonable adjustments.

- *Cordell v Foreign and Commonwealth Office* (2011) UKEAT/0016/11
  Cordell was profoundly deaf. She was successful in gaining promotion to an overseas job, and asked her employer to provide her with lip-reading services. They refused, and she claimed that this was disability discrimination. Her claim was unsuccessful because the cost of providing the services would have been around five times her annual salary, and that did not amount to a reasonable adjustment.

An interesting question is whether a disciplinary procedure that includes 'triggers' for giving warnings when a certain amount of absence has accrued can be used if the individual is disabled:

- *Commissioners for Her Majesty's Revenue and Customs v Whiteley* (2013) UKEAT/0581/12
  Whiteley was asthmatic and reached the trigger point at which a disciplinary warning for absence would be given. She argued that a reasonable adjustment, given her disability, which meant she was more likely than other

employees to get respiratory infections, would be to allow her a greater number of days of absence before a warning was given. The EAT suggested two approaches to reasonable adjustments – one would be to exclude any days of absence that related to the disability or the other would be to estimate the number of days of absence someone with the particular disability might be expected to have, and reduce the trigger points accordingly.

- *Griffiths v Department for Work and Pensions (2015) EWCA Civ 1265*
  Griffiths received a disciplinary warning due to her level of absence. The company operated a trigger system whereby a warning was automatically given after a set period of absence. The Court of Appeal ruled that there was a requirement to make a reasonable adjustment, but her proposal (to discount the 62 days of absence that she had accrued due to her disability) was not reasonable because it would lead to a perpetual extension of sickness absence.

Knowledge of the disability

The issue of whether an employer cannot be held responsible for making adjustments when it did not know the employee was disabled has been the subject of case law:

- *O'Neill v Symm & Co Ltd* (1998) ICR 481, IRLR 233
  O'Neill worked as an accounts clerk. Three months after starting work with Symn & Co she was dismissed for sickness absence. At her interview she had told them that she had previously suffered from viral pneumonia, but had since recovered. During her period of employment she was diagnosed as suffering from ME – but she did not tell her employers. When she was dismissed she claimed disability discrimination, but it was found that the employer could not have discriminated if it did not know that there was a disability.

However, that decision was overturned in the case of:

- *H J Heinz Co Ltd v Kenrick* (2000) ICR 491
  Kenrick had symptoms of chronic fatigue syndrome (CFS), although he was dismissed prior to any firm diagnosis being given. (He was actually dismissed just two weeks before he was due to see a consultant.) The EAT ruled that even though the employer did not know that he was disabled as defined by the Disability Discrimination Act (DDA), the fact was that he did indeed have a disability. So reasonable adjustments should have been made and the act of dismissal without making these adjustments was discrimination.

The courts will consider what a reasonable employer ought to have known or ought to have reasonably investigated.

Discrimination arising from disability

The Equality Act 2010 has also introduced the concept of 'discrimination arising from disability'. This is defined as an employer treating an individual unfavourably for a reason arising in consequence of the individual's disability. For example, this could be penalising an employee who makes a lot of spelling mistakes due to having dyslexia. Unlike direct disability discrimination, this will be justifiable if it is a proportionate means of achieving a legitimate aim.

Explore further

Acas has written a detailed guide about disability   http://www.acas.org.uk/index.aspx?articleid=1859
discrimination in the workplace. Access this at

7.7 Gender reassignment

It is unlawful to discriminate against an individual who proposes to, starts or has completed a process to change his/her gender. Discrimination is unlawful at any stage of the process of gender reassignment, not just when the process is completed. The Equality Act 2010 extended the protection by stating that there is no requirement for the person to be under medical supervision to be protected. Hence, this would include someone who lives as someone of the opposite gender but does not undergo any medical procedures. Cross-dressers are not protected because they do not intend to live permanently in the opposite gender to their birth gender.

- *A v Chief Constable of West Yorkshire Police* (2002) EWCA Civ 1584
  A was born male, but underwent gender reassignment surgery in May 1996. Since that time she has dressed and presented herself as a woman. In 1997 she applied to join the West Yorkshire Police Force but was told that that the force had decided not to employ transsexuals because they were unable to perform all the necessary duties. In particular, they would not be able to carry out searches of individuals. A brought a claim of discrimination. The Court of Appeal upheld A's claim, stating that the force could sensibly have avoided the problem by exempting her from the requirement to carry out searches.

- *Croft v Consignia plc* (2002) EAT 1160/00, IRLR 851
  Croft started work with Consignia in March 1987 as a man. In April 1998 Croft started the process of gender reassignment by taking feminising hormones. At this stage she announced that she would adopt a female role. The way of announcing this to the workforce was discussed and, in particular, there was discussion about which toilet Croft should use. It was agreed that she would start by using the gender-neutral disabled toilet, but would eventually move to using the female toilet. Croft was concerned about this because she wanted to live fully as a female and that included using the relevant toilets.

  However, the female staff (who had known Croft as a man for many years) were not happy with her using their toilets. Her claim of discrimination was unsuccessful because it was found that Consignia was not refusing to allow her ever to use the female toilet, but was trying to deal with a difficult employment relations issue as well as waiting for medical advice.

7.8 Sexual orientation

Sexual orientation is defined as 'a sexual orientation towards persons of the same sex, persons of the opposite sex, or persons of the same sex and the opposite sex'. The definition thus covers all aspects of sexual orientation. The definition does not include discrimination relating to any particular fetishes (eg sado-masochism) and it cannot be argued that 'orientation' covers orientation towards children (ie paedophilia is not covered by the Act).

The majority of cases that have been heard under this statute have related to harassment on the grounds of sexual orientation:

- *Whitfield v Cleanaway UK Ltd* (2005) ET 3201666/04
  Whitfield was subjected to a series of taunts about his sexuality, including a manager calling him 'Sebastian' after a homosexual character in the television programme *Little Britain*. Eventually he resigned and successfully claimed constructive dismissal and sexual orientation discrimination.

- *Reaney v Hereford Diocesan Board of Finance* (2007) ET 1602844/2006
  Reaney was a homosexual who applied for a job as a youth worker. He was quizzed by the bishop about his sexuality. At the time he was not in a relationship and he assured the bishop that he would not become involved in any sexual relationship if he was appointed to the job. The bishop's concern was not so much the homosexuality, rather that the teachings of the Church see any sexual relationship outside marriage as wrong.

  The bishop was concerned that Reaney could not make a commitment that he would be celibate in the future and he was rejected for the job. Reaney successfully won his case of discrimination. This was because the bishop's refusal to accept that the requirements of the job had been met (ie not engaging in sexual relationships outside marriage) was not reasonable.

- *Thomas Sanderson Blinds v English* (2011) UKEAT/0316/10
  English was heterosexual and was married with children. However, because he had been to boarding school and lived in Brighton, there was general banter and teasing about him being homosexual (based on stereotypical views). The employees involved did not think that he was homosexual, but the banter continued. English's claim of harassment on the grounds of sexual orientation was initially rejected because he was not homosexual. However, it was ruled that the legislation states that discrimination is unlawful on 'the grounds of' sexual orientation. The treatment met with this definition and hence the courts found in English's favour.

The sort of harassment identified in the Whitfield and English cases can be difficult for the employer to control. As we saw in Chapter 6, the employer is vicariously liable for events that occur in the course of employment. A useful outline of what is expected of the employer is set out in the following case:

- *Martin v Parkam Foods Limited* (2007) ET/1800241/2006
  Martin is homosexual. Unacceptable remarks and graffiti appeared in the workplace relating to this. The employer removed his name from the homophobic graffiti, but it was replaced by those involved in the harassment.

The employer then posted notices warning employees not to write graffiti and advising that disciplinary action would be taken against anyone who did. It also reminded managers of the equal opportunity policies, monitored the sexual orientation of potential employees and interviewed some employees to try to determine who was responsible for the graffiti.

However, the Employment Tribunal found that this was not sufficient and Martin's claim succeeded. It ruled that firmer instructions should have been given to employees about the seriousness of homophobic behaviour and that the employer should have apologised to Martin for what had occurred.

7.9 Religion and belief

When legislation was initially introduced relating to religion or belief it was defined as 'any religion, religious belief or similar philosophical belief '. However, in April 2007 the Equality Act 2006 amended the legislation, changing the definition to 'any religion, or religious or philosophical belief ' (ie omitting the word 'similar'). Prior to this change, political beliefs were excluded from the regulations. In a House of Lords debate on this point it was later suggested that a philosophical belief should cover a 'world view or life stance' – and it is possible that it could be argued that this would encompass political beliefs.

- *GMB v Henderson* (2015) UKEAT/0073/14
  Henderson worked for the GMB trade union. He was dismissed for gross misconduct, because he was seen to be unmanageable and had made a number of allegations about collusion between the GMB and the Labour Party. He had also written a letter arranging a day of action, which had caused considerable embarrassment for the Labour Party. It was found that his belief in left-wing democratic socialism was a belief protected under the Equality Act 2010. However, his dismissal was fair and he had not suffered discrimination, because his conduct was unacceptable.

- *Redfearn v UK* (2012) ECHR 1878
  Redfearn was a bus driver transporting children and adults with disabilities. He worked in Bradford where 25 per cent of the employees and 70–80 per cent of the passengers were of Asian ethnic origin. The employer discovered that Redfearn was standing for election as a local councillor, representing the British National Party. The employer was concerned about the health and safety of the passengers, due to the likely reaction to Redfearn's actions and hence dismissed him. Redfearn claimed that this was race discrimination.

  His claim was unsuccessful because his dismissal was not due to his race, but because of his membership of a political party. He eventually took the claim to the European Court of Human Rights (ECHR) arguing that his dismissal was a breach of Article 11 of the European Convention on Human Rights – the right to freedom of assembly. The ECHR ruled that there should be some protection against dismissal for membership of a political party, and hence the Enterprise and Regulatory Reform Act 2013 altered the law such that someone who is dismissed because of political beliefs or affiliation does not need any qualifying service to bring a claim of unfair dismissal.

7.9.1 Defining a belief

It is clear that people who belong to established religions (eg Christians, Jews, Muslims) are covered by the Equality Act 2010. What is less clear is whether those who belong to non-conventional 'religions' such as Druidism, or who have 'beliefs', such as animal rights activists, are covered.

The difficulties over defining 'religion or belief' have resulted in a number of cases:

- *Grainger plc v Nicholson* (2009) UKEAT/0219/09
  Nicholson had been a senior executive with Grainger and claimed that he had been selected for redundancy due to his strong beliefs relating to the environment. He was able to demonstrate that his environmental concerns affected the way he lived his life, for example he did not use aeroplanes and he had carried out extensive work on his home to make it eco-friendly. The tribunal ruled that this was a belief under the regulations – and this decision was upheld at a later EAT hearing.

  The EAT specified that to be covered by the Act a philosophical belief must be genuinely held, must be a belief in a weighty and substantial matter, must not be just an opinion or viewpoint based on present facts (it must be deeper than that) and must be cogent, coherent, serious, important and worthy of respect in a democratic society. This case was then remitted to the Employment Tribunal to determine if the belief was the reason for the redundancy, but the matter was settled out of court.

- *Hashman v Orchard Park Garden Centre* (2011) ET/3105555/09
  Hashman worked at the garden centre and was an ardent animal rights activist. He was made redundant and believed that this was due to his beliefs – particularly given that the owners of the garden centre were members of the local hunt and he had been involved in hunt saboteur activities.

  The issue was referred to a pre-hearing review to determine whether his beliefs were protected by the Act. The judge found that the beliefs were strongly held and influenced the way he lived, hence he was protected by the Act.

- *Maistry v BBC plc* (2011) ET/1313142/10
  Maistry was a journalist working for the BBC. He had worked for the BBC for 14 years and had been a journalist for 30 years. He was dismissed and claimed that his dismissal was a result of the BBC discriminating against his values about being 'straight and up front' and promoting cultural interchange, citizenship and social cohesion. However, the BBC argued that he was dismissed after a lengthy internal capability process. At a pre-hearing review, the Employment Judge found that his belief in the 'higher purpose of journalism' was protected as a philosophical belief because it met the criteria set out in the case of *Grainger v Nicholson*.

7.10 Age

It is unlawful to discriminate on the grounds of age. This includes discrimination against both younger and older individuals. An area that is important to note is that of length of service. For example, requiring an employee to have a certain length of experience before applying for a job will make it more difficult for younger workers to be able to apply for the job. However, in line with other indirect discrimination legislation, it is allowed if it is a proportionate means of achieving a legitimate aim. For example, if it could be shown that the employee would be a danger to the public in a particular job if he/she did not have a certain amount of experience, it is likely that this would make the criteria justifiable.

Care also needs to be taken when requiring qualifications that only younger people are likely to have. For example, requiring a media studies degree is likely to make it more difficult for people aged around 40 years or more because such degrees were not available when most of this age group would have attended university. Requiring a 'media studies degree or similar' will be more appropriate.

Particular care must be taken when carrying out graduate recruitment. It is lawful to have specific graduate recruitment and training programmes – but graduates of any age must be allowed to apply, not just those who are recently leaving university.

When recruiting people to training schemes it is not allowed to set age limits that are not justifiable. This applies to both maximum and minimum age limits. Care needs to be taken that there is no age discrimination in the recruitment process:

- *Cunningham v BMS Sales Ltd* (2007) FEB/EE/2007/017
  In a case ruled in the Republic of Ireland the applicant for a job was asked questions about his age at an early stage of the interview process. This included questions on the application form such as 'number of children', 'age' and 'date of birth'.

  Cunningham provided incorrect answers to the questions, claiming that they were irrelevant and invasive. Despite being suitable for the job he was not offered it. At the equality tribunal it was ruled that age discrimination had occurred in the recruitment process and he received 5,000 euros in compensation.

- *Rainbow v Milton Keynes Council* (2008) ET/1200104/07
  An advertisement was placed for a job that would suit a teacher in their 'first five years of their teaching career'. Rainbow claimed indirect discrimination because she was 61 years old and had over 30 years' experience of teaching. The council tried to argue that the requirement was a proportionate means of reaching a legitimate aim – because teachers with less experience cost less to employ and the aim was cost saving. This argument was rejected.

- *Homer v Chief Constable of West Yorkshire Police* (2012) ICR 987
  Homer retired from the police force after 30 years and moved to be a legal adviser. The requirements for the job were to have a law degree or equivalent, or extensive relevant experience. He did not have a law degree but did have extensive experience. He was given the opportunity to study for a law degree, but he refused this because he would have been over 65 years when he qualified, and he planned to retire at this age. A grading structure was then put in place that paid more to those with a law degree, and he argued that this was indirect age discrimination. His claim was unsuccessful because paying more for those with a law degree was a proportionate means of achieving the aim of having highly qualified staff in senior positions.

7.10.1 Retirement

When legislation relating to age discrimination was introduced in 2006 a default retirement age of 65 years was introduced. Unless an organisation had an earlier retirement age that was justifiable, it was possible to lawfully retire an employee when he/she reached that age, as long as a statutory procedure was followed.

As soon as the age discrimination legislation became law, Heyday (an organisation for people at or near retirement) lodged a claim against the UK Government, claiming that the interpretation of the Equality Directive was wrong and that there should be no mandatory retirement age. This matter was referred to the Court of Justice for the European Union, which ruled that the justification of the retirement age was a matter for national law. The Supreme Court went on to rule that the retirement age was justifiable, but probably not on an ongoing basis.

The government committed to review the default retirement age and as a result of that review it was removed. The removal was phased in, starting in April 2011 and concluding with the full removal in October 2011.

Employers are now no longer able to force an employee to retire unless there is an 'employer justified retirement age' (EJRA). An EJRA applies when an employer can show that a retirement age can be objectively justified. This will be in a situation when the employer can demonstrate that there is a sound reason for not employing individuals over a certain age in certain roles. Examples could be air traffic control or the police force. If there is no EJRA, the decision of retirement rests with the employee. The employer cannot force the employee to retire. As a result of the default retirement age being removed, 'retirement' is no longer one of the potentially fair reasons for dismissal (see Chapter 8).

- *Seldon v Clarkson, Wright and Jakes* (2014) IRLR 865
  Seldon was a partner in the law firm, which had a retirement age of 65 years. He did not want to retire, and took a claim of age discrimination. It was found that there was a legitimate aim in having this retirement age, because it gave the opportunity for partnership vacancies to occur for others, and facilitated planning for partnership roles. This was not age discrimination.

7.10.2 Benefits

It is not unusual for organisations to have benefits that link in some way to length of service. This could include long-service awards or increased sick-pay entitlements as service progresses, or increased holiday allowance. Clearly, there is an obvious link between service-related benefits and age – because older people have more opportunity to have longer service. There is, therefore, the potential that any such benefits could be seen as indirect age discrimination.

To partly address this issue the law specifically allows for service-related benefits when the length of service in question is five years or less. Any benefits relating to longer service could be allowable if they are necessary for fulfilling a business need – such as loyalty or motivation of staff. Any benefit that mirrors the calculations for statutory benefits (eg an enhanced redundancy-pay scheme that mirrors the statutory scheme) is allowable. This is a little vague – because it could be argued that any benefit is introduced to enhance loyalty and motivation and therefore every benefit is allowable! What is allowable within this part of the statute is likely to be determined through case law.

- *MacCulloch v ICI plc* (2008) ICR 1334
  MacCulloch was made redundant. She was 37 years old and had seven years' service, which meant that she received 55 per cent of her salary on her redundancy. However, someone aged 50–57 years who had 10+ years' service was entitled to 175 per cent of salary when made redundant. MacCulloch claimed that this was age discrimination. The EAT found that the scheme rewarded loyalty and hence it could potentially be justified. However, the

extent of the difference in redundancy payment between the two ages was not proportionate and hence could not be justified, and this was discrimination.

7.10.3 Other age-related issues

As we will see in Chapter 8, the process for calculating statutory redundancy pay and the basic award is based on a combination of age and length of service. In the light of that very clear link to potential age discrimination, it was expected that the legislation would introduce a new calculation method for these items – but it did not.

The formula for statutory redundancy and the basic award remains the same. In justifying keeping these bands, the government explained that this approach is still justified because the job market is different for these three groups. (In other words, the government sees it as relatively easy for someone aged up to 21 years to find work and relatively difficult for someone aged 41+ years to find work.)

In addition, the age bands that relate to the National Minimum Wage remain. The government defends this because it does not think that employers would be willing to pay young people more – and also it thinks that the bands, set as they currently are, encourage young people to remain in education.

7.11 Caste

As a result of the Enterprise and Regulatory Reform Act 2013 caste was going to be added to the list of protected characteristics. Caste is a form of social stratification that is common in some religious or racial groups. However, in 2018 the government announced that it was no longer going to add caste. It concluded that this could cause unnecessary tensions, and was not a necessary addition. It also noted that caste could be seen to be part of ethnic origin, as ruled in the following case:

* *Chandok and another v Tirkey* (2014) UKEAT/0190/14
  Interestingly, a case has already come before the courts alleging discrimination on the grounds of caste. Tirkey worked in domestic service for the Chandoks and alleged that she was treated unfavourably because she is of the Adivasi caste, which is known as being a servant caste. The Employment Tribunal and the EAT have both concluded that caste could be part of the definition of ethnic origin, although it might not always be part of this definition.

7.12 Trade union membership

As noted at the start of Chapter 6, nine major pieces of discrimination legislation and more than 100 smaller pieces of legislation were replaced by the Equality Act 2010. However, there are still some areas that relate to unfavourable treatment that are covered in other legislation. For example, in Chapter 4 we saw that it is unlawful to treat someone less favourably because they work on a part-time basis or on a fixed-term contract.

In the same way, it is unlawful to treat someone less favourably because they are, or are not, a member of a trade union. Although this is not part of the Equality Act 2010, we will explore that issue here.

7.12.1 Refusal of employment

It is unlawful (Section 137(1) of the Trade Union and Labour Relations (Consolidation) Act 1992) to refuse employment to people because:

- they are, or are not, members of a trade union;
- they refuse to accept a requirement that they either become a member of a trade union or that they cease to be a member of a trade union, or they refuse to make payments to the trade union if they fail to join.

It is important to note that this legislation makes the concept of the 'closed shop' illegal. This used to exist in many organisations where, upon starting employment, it was a requirement to join the relevant trade union.

   Task

Try to find someone who was at work in the 1970s who is willing to discuss their experiences with you. Ask them about the 'closed shop'. How did it work? What were the advantages and disadvantages associated with it?

'Refusing employment' covers all of the following:

- refusing to consider a job application or enquiry;
- asking the applicant to withdraw an application;
- refusing to offer employment;
- making an offer of employment that includes terms that no reasonable employee would agree to, thereby making it difficult for the person to accept the offer;
- withdrawing an offer of employment after having made it or causing the applicant to refuse the offer;
- including a requirement that goes against that which is listed above (s137(1)).

An example of 'refusing employment' can be found in the following case:

- *Harrison v Kent County Council* (1995) ICR 434
  Harrison was a social worker working for Kent County Council. He was an active trade union member with a reputation for being a 'strong and forthright' negotiator. He resigned from his job for family reasons, but later reapplied to the council. He was refused re-employment on the account of his 'confrontational and antimanagement approach' in his previous post. The Employment Tribunal held that this was a fair refusal because it related to previous activities as a trade union member, rather than specifically to trade union membership. The EAT overturned that view, stating that the trade union membership could not be separated from activities carried out because of that membership. The refusal to re-employ Harrison had therefore been unfair.

7.12.2 Detriment

Section 146(1) of the Trade Union and Labour Relations (Consolidation) Act [TULRCA] 1992 provides for employees not to suffer any detriment by an act (or omission of an act) by the employer if this takes place for the purpose of:

- preventing or deterring him/her from becoming a member of an independent trade union or penalising him/her for doing so;
- preventing or deterring him/her from taking part in the activities of an independent trade union or penalising him/her for doing so;
- compelling him/her to become a member of a trade union.

An example of such a detriment is:

- *British Airways Engine Overhaul Ltd v Francis* (1981) ICR 278
  Francis was a shop steward. She made a statement to the press criticising her trade union for taking so much time to pursue an equal pay complaint by her members. She made this statement during her lunchtime. When the article was published she received a formal warning from British Airways, stating that unauthorised statements to the press were forbidden. Francis challenged the warning in the Employment Tribunal, stating that it was a detriment based on trade union activities. The employer argued that the statement came about after an informal meeting of union members and was too remote from Francis's union duties to be classed as trade union activity. The tribunal found, however, that the statement was linked to trade union activity and the warning was therefore unfair because it was a detriment related to such activity.

7.12.3 Dismissal

Section 152(1) of TULRCA 1992 defines a dismissal as being unfair if the principal reason was that the employee:

- was, or proposed to become, a member of an independent trade union;
- had taken part, or proposed to take part, in the activities of an independent trade union;
- was not a member of a trade union and had refused to become a member.

- *Port of London Authority v Payne and others* (1992) IRLR 447
  The Port of London Authority derecognised the Transport and General Workers' Union (TGWU) and also carried out a redundancy process. Employees were selected for redundancy based on a number of criteria, including attitude. Among those selected for redundancy were 17 shop stewards; they claimed they had been selected on the grounds of their trade union activities and that their dismissal was therefore unfair. The tribunal held, and the EAT supported this view, that the shop stewards had been selected by the employer because there was concern that they would become involved in a campaign by the TGWU to restore negotiation rights. Because this campaign was authorised and run by the TGWU, it was held that it must be classified as trade union activity and the dismissal was therefore unfair.

There is no statutory definition of trade union activity and therefore, in supporting this conclusion, the EAT spelled out the process that must be followed to determine if there has been an unfair dismissal relating to trade union activity:

> An employment tribunal must determine the following: the belief held by the employers that formed the basis of the decision to dismiss; whether that belief was genuinely held; and whether the facts upon which that belief was based, judged objectively, fell within the phrase 'the activities of an independent trade union'.

🔑 KEY LEARNING POINTS

1 There are nine protected characteristics in the Equality Act 2010.
2 Sex discrimination covers discrimination against men or women.
3 Marital status and civil partnership does not include protection for single individuals.
4 Pregnancy and maternity does not require a comparator.
5 Race is defined as ethnic origin, colour or nationality.
6 Disability is a physical or mental impairment that has a substantial adverse long-term effect on the ability to carry out normal day-to-day activities.
7 Gender reassignment applies from the start of the gender change process.
8 Sexual orientation covers heterosexuality, homosexuality and bisexuality.
9 A wide range of beliefs are covered by the religion/belief characteristic.
10 Age covers both older and younger employees.
11 Employees are protected against less favourable treatment on the grounds of trade union membership in recruitment, dismissal and other areas of employment where they might suffer detriments.

Case summaries

- *Department of Work and Pensions v Thompson* (2004) IRLR 348 – A dress code requiring men to wear a collar and tie and women to dress professionally was not necessarily discrimination. If the requirement was for the same level of smartness for men and women, this was not discriminatory.

- *B v A* (2007) IRLR 576 – A PA was dismissed by her employer after her romantic relationship with him broke down. She claimed direct sex discrimination, but her claim was rejected because the dismissal was because of the breakdown of the relationship rather than because of her gender.

- *McClintock v Department of Constitutional Affairs (2008)* IRLR 29 – McClintock was a Christian and a magistrate sitting on the Family Panel. He did not want to place children with same-sex couples for adoption. He was not allowed to be relieved of this duty and he

(continued)

(Continued)

resigned. He stated that he was resigning because he did not think that the adoptions would work; he did not say that it was because of his religious convictions. Hence, this was not religious discrimination.

- *Achbita, Centrum voor Gelijkheid van kansen en voor racismebestrijding v G4S Secure Solutions* (2017) C-157/15 – The organisation had a rule that no employee should wear a political or religious symbol. Achbita was a Muslim and wanted to wear a hijab. She was told she could not, and resigned and claimed direct discrimination. The Court of Justice of the European Union ruled that this was not direct discrimination because all employees were treated the same, but it potentially could be indirect discrimination.

- *Kelly v Covance Laboratories Ltd* [2015] UKEAT/0186/15
  The employee, who was Russian, spent a considerable amount of the working day talking on the phone in Russian. The employer was concerned about what she might be saying and asked her to only speak in English. She unsuccessfully claimed race discrimination and harassment. She had not been treated less favourably by being asked to speak English and it was not a violation of her dignity.

- *G4S Cash Solutions (UK) Ltd v Powell* (2016) UKEAT/0243/15
  The employee was moved to a less skilled job because of his disability. His pay was cut by 10 per cent to reflect the lower level of skill. He successfully argued that a reasonable adjustment would have been keeping his pay at his previous level (although the EAT did say that this would not always be a reasonable adjustment).

- *Metroline Travel Ltd v Stoute* (2015) UKEAT/0302/15
  The employee had type 2 diabetes, which he controlled by diet. He claimed he had been dismissed due to his disability. He was not disabled. His diabetes was under control therefore it did not have an adverse effect on his ability to do normal day-to-day activities.

- *Lisk v Shield Guardian Company and others* [2011] ET3300873/11
  A belief in the importance of wearing a poppy near Remembrance Day was not a protected belief because it did not have cogency, coherence and sufficient importance.

❓ Examples to work through

1 Your organisation works a shift system. One of your employees has informed you that he does not want to work on Fridays because it is the holy day in his religion. Other employees have protested at this request, explaining that they have to work every day of the week on a rota basis and this interferes with their plans. (One employee explains he has to miss football matches every third Saturday – and he is a member of the team.) As a result, 13 employees write to you requesting not to work on certain days because of commitments that they have. How do you proceed?

2 A local church is advertising for a youth worker. One applicant for the job is homosexual and has been refused on the basis that this does not fit with the Christian ethos. He decides to claim discrimination on the grounds of sexual orientation. Do you think he is likely to be successful? Justify your answer.

(Continued)

(Continued)

3 Following an accident one of your workers is no longer able to stand for long periods of time. The employee works as a sales assistant in a busy retail store and has to be available on the shop floor to advise customers. The job involves standing for most of the day. How do you proceed?

4 Your organisation has experienced a lot of conflict with the trade unions over the years. As a result, the managing director has an unwritten rule that it is inappropriate for managers to be trade union members. Is this lawful?

  Case study 7.1

A new managing director was recently appointed in your organisation, which is a call centre handling insurance queries and claims. The organisation has been struggling for some time and the new managing director was appointed with the specific brief of turning around the fortunes of the organisation. She certainly seems to have a track record of introducing change at a great speed and with success.

However, after the first month, you – the HR manager – have a number of employees coming to you with complaints. First there is Mary. She has two children aged four and two years. The children are looked after by Mary's mother when Mary is working. However, Mary's mother suffers from diabetes and is unable to look after the children for more than five hours at a time because she tires very quickly. Mary, who lives near the call centre and hence does not have much travelling time, works from 10 am to 2 pm each day. The managing director has told her that she must extend those hours to 9 am to 3 pm with immediate effect.

Next, there is Raj. Raj suffers from a visual impairment, which means that he needs regular breaks from looking at a VDU screen. As all the call handlers are working at a VDU screen, his needs have been accommodated by allowing him to work for two hours in the call centre, then one hour in the post room, and so on, throughout his shift. The managing director has said that there is no need for him to spend so long in the post room each day and is proposing that he works for two hours in the call centre, followed by a 30-minute unpaid break, and so on, throughout his shift.

Muhammad is a recent recruit to the organisation. He is a Muslim and has asked for permission to attend the local mosque on Friday lunchtimes. Due to the travelling time to the mosque, as well as the time that he will want to spend there, he will be absent for three hours. So, he has asked for permission to take an extended break. The managing director has refused his request.

Valerie is a rather quiet employee. She is a vegetarian and is passionate about animal welfare. Last evening her section of the call centre went out for a meal because one of the team was leaving. During the evening one of the team constantly teased her about being vegetarian, calling her 'my little animal terrorist' throughout the meal. This morning she has brought a complaint that this was harassment, but the managing director has told her to 'grow up and stop being silly'.

Using your knowledge of discrimination legislation, advise the managing director about any problems that might arise from these four situations.

08
Termination of employment

8.1 When does a dismissal occur?

Section 95 of the Employment Rights Act 1996 states that an employee is to be treated as dismissed if:

- The contract under which he/she is employed is terminated by the employer (this can be with or without notice). This is probably the most common form of dismissal. It typically occurs when the employee has not met the required standard of performance, or the conduct of the employee has been unacceptable. This type of dismissal is the focus of most of this chapter.

- The employee is working under a fixed-term contract and the contract is not renewed. For example, an employee is recruited for a 12- month fixed period to cover the maternity leave of an employee. At the end of the 12 months the employee returns from maternity leave, and the fixed-term contract of the employee covering the role ends. It might seem strange to refer to this as a dismissal, but this is the legal term.

- The employee terminates the contract of employment (with or without notice) in circumstances when he/she is entitled to terminate the contract without notice due to the employer's conduct. This is known as constructive dismissal, which we look at later in this chapter.

8.2 Termination without a dismissal

There are circumstances in which a contract of employment can be terminated without a dismissal occurring – resignation of the employee, mutual agreement, frustration – as set out below.

8.2.1 Resignation of the employee

If an employee states that he/she wishes to terminate the contract of employment, it is not a dismissal. However, if the employee considers that he/she has been forced into the resignation by the actions of the employer, there is the potential for a claim of constructive dismissal (see section 8.7).

Most resignations are very clear – the employee resigns calmly and having planned for the future. However, there are occasions where it is not clear whether the employee really meant to resign:

- *Kwik-Fit v Lineham* (1992) ICR 183
  Lineham was a depot manager. One night he entered the depot to use the toilet and in doing so deactivated and then reactivated the alarm. Security officers realised that someone had entered the premises and Lineham explained what had happened. Lineham was given a disciplinary warning for what he had done and had an angry exchange with one of the directors about this. He threw his keys into reception and left. The next day he told the employers that he would take them to the Employment Tribunal for unfair dismissal. They presumed that he had resigned.

  The tribunal found that he had been unfairly dismissed. The resignation had taken place in the heat of the moment and therefore the employer was responsible for checking the employee's true intention. The employer should have done more to investigate and retrieve the situation, and hence this amounted to a dismissal.

  The EAT agreed that this was unfair dismissal. If words are ambiguous, or are uttered in the heat of the moment or under pressure, the employer ought to investigate further before accepting that the employee has resigned. The employer was not entitled to presume that a resignation had occurred.

- *Sothern v Franks Charlesly* (1981) IRLR 278
  The office manager of a law firm attended a partnership meeting and said 'I am resigning'. He later claimed that he did not mean to resign and stated that he did not want to leave. However, the employer argued that he had resigned and hence his employment had terminated. He claimed unfair dismissal.

The Court of Appeal identified three situations in which an employer ought to investigate further before accepting a resignation. They are: when the employee is immature, when the decision is taken in the heat of the moment, and when the employee has resigned in response to 'jostling' by the employer.

In this case the words 'I am resigning' were unambiguous and there was no requirement for the employer to explore any further.

8.2.2 Mutual agreement

If the employer and employee mutually agree to terminate the contract, a dismissal will not be deemed to have taken place. There is the possibility of an employee feeling forced into reaching a mutual agreement and again this could lead to a potential claim for constructive dismissal.

If the employer gives an indication that the employment will terminate at 'some time' but gives no precise details about when, it is unlikely that a dismissal will have taken place.

This was determined in:

- *Morton Sundour Fabrics Ltd v Shaw* (1966) ITR 84

  Shaw worked in the velvet department of the employer. He was told that the velvet department would close at some time in the future, although no precise details of dates were given. The employer offered to put him in contact with another employer. Shaw met this other employer, was offered a job, resigned from Morton Sundour and started with the new employer. He then claimed a redundancy payment from Morton Sundour. They refused to make the payment, claiming that he had resigned and had not been dismissed.

  The Employment Tribunal stated that a redundancy had taken place and instructed Morton Sundour to make the payment. However, the EAT overruled this decision, stating that the employee had only been given a warning about a possible dismissal at some time – but no actual dismissal had taken place.

8.2.3 Frustration

A contract of employment is held to be 'frustrated' when some unforeseen event occurs that prevents one or both of the parties from performing the contract, or results in the performing of the contract being radically different from that which was originally envisaged. Examples of potential frustration include long-term sickness and an employee being sentenced to a term of imprisonment.

One case relating to frustration caused by imprisonment is:

- *Harrington v Kent County Council* (1980) IRLR 353

  Harrington was a primary-school teacher who was convicted of indecency offences and sentenced to 12 months' imprisonment. Kent CC informed Harrington that his contract of employment had ended due to his inability to carry out the duties for which he was employed, for a substantial period of time. When Harrington was released from prison, he wrote to Kent CC and requested his job back – Kent CC refused. He made a claim of unfair dismissal. However, both the Employment Tribunal and the EAT agreed that the contract had been automatically terminated by the prison sentence and therefore no longer existed.

In the case of *Marshall v Harland and Wolff Ltd* (1972), a series of requirements were set out that should be used to determine whether a contract of employment has been frustrated:

- *Marshall v Harland and Wolff Ltd* (1972) WLR 899
  Marshall was a shipyard fitter and had been absent for 18 months due to angina pectoris. He expected to return to work after having an operation. However, the shipyard where he worked closed and so Marshall claimed a redundancy payment. It was argued that his employment had terminated due to frustration and he was therefore not entitled to a redundancy payment. The National Industrial Relations Court (NIRC) ruled that he was entitled to a redundancy payment because there was no certainty that the contract had terminated. It determined that the following should be taken into consideration:
  - the terms of the contract;
  - how long the employment would have lasted if there had been no absence;
  - the nature of the employment;
  - the nature of the illness and the likelihood of recovery;
  - the period of past service to the employer.

Note that this case was decided before the introduction of the Disability Discrimination Act 1995 and, more recently, the Equality Act 2010. However, it still has relevance, because not every absence due to ill health can be linked to a disability.

 Explore further

To obtain a further understanding of frustration of contract read through the judgments in *Marshall v Harland and Wolff Ltd* (1972), *Egg Stores v Leibovici* (1976) ICR 260 and *Four Seasons* *Healthcare Ltd v Maughan* (2004) EAT 0274/04. Having read the judgments, evaluate why the courts are usually reluctant to apply the approach of frustration of contract.

8.3 Eligibility to make a claim of unfair dismissal

Section 94 of the Employment Rights Act 1996 states that an employee has the right not to be unfairly dismissed by his employer. There are cases where a dismissal can be judged to have occurred but the person in question cannot make a claim of unfair dismissal to the Employment Tribunal. These persons/situations include:

- non-employees (this includes those who are workers; as we defined in Chapter 3, only employees can bring a claim of unfair dismissal);
- those with less than two years' continuous service of employment (one year if the employee started work before 6 April 2012) (unless the reason for dismissal was one of those that are automatically unfair and does not require a qualifying period of service – see section 8.8);

- where the employee is employed under an illegal contract;
- persons employed in the police service.

Section 109(1) of the Employment Rights Act 1996 did prohibit any employee who had reached the normal retiring age for an employee holding that position, or was aged 65 years or more, from taking a claim of unfair dismissal. However, that restriction was removed by the Employment Equality (Age) Regulations 2006.

8.4 Potentially fair reasons for dismissal

Section 98 of the Employment Rights Act 1996 lists five potentially fair reasons for dismissal:

- capability or qualifications;
- conduct;
- redundancy;
- statutory ban;
- some other substantial reason.

Note that retirement was added as a potentially fair reason by the Employment Equality (Age) Regulations 2006. However, the default retirement age that was central to the statutory process of retirement has been removed (the removal was phased from April to October 2011). As there is no longer a statutory process of retirement, this is no longer one of the potentially fair reasons for dismissal.

8.4.1 Capability or qualifications

The Employment Rights Act 1996 defines capability as 'skill, aptitude, health or any other physical or mental quality'. Qualifications are defined as 'any degree, diploma or other academic, technical or professional qualification relevant to the position which the employee holds'.

The employer should, at the recruitment stage and in the subsequent period of induction, make sure that the employee understands the requirements of the job. The employer should determine any training needs that exist and act upon them. The employer should also make clear to the employee the likely penalty of failing to meet the required standards. If the employee does not meet the required standards of performance, the employer would be expected to try to assist that employee through further training and education before taking disciplinary action.

If a capability issue relates to ill health, the employer must consider the nature of the illness, the actual and potential length of the absence and the employer's situation (eg the size of the business and the impact that the absence is having on the organisation). It is also important to have due regard to the Equality Act 2010. Further guidance on such situations was given in the following case:

- *BS v Dundee City Council* (2013) CSIH19
  An employee with 35 years of unblemished service was absent for more than a year. He had a number of illnesses and personal problems and his doctor indicated that he might be ready to return to work in one to three months.

The employer dismissed the employee on the basis that the absence had lasted too long, and that there was no definite date for his return. The Inner House of the Court of Session identified a number of factors that should be considered when deciding whether a dismissal on the grounds of long-term sickness is fair:

- Would a reasonable employer have waited longer before dismissing the employee?

- Is the employer able to wait longer, and is it reasonable to expect the employer to do so?

- Has the employee been consulted, and have his/her views been taken into account?

- Have the opinions been balanced against the opinions of a medical practitioner?

- Have reasonable attempts been made to understand the medical condition and the long-term prognosis?

It is also important that the employer takes reasonable steps in understanding the issues and investigating potential solutions:

- *D B Schenker Rail (UK) Ltd v Doolan* (2011) UKEAT/0053/09
Doolan worked as a production manager for the organisation. This was a safety-critical role and one that he found stressful. Towards the end of 2007 the stress was such that he took a period of sickness absence; he felt ready to return to work in early 2008. Before allowing him to return to work the organisation carried out a medical investigation and an occupational psychologist expressed concerns that Doolan would suffer from stress-related issues if he returned. The employer was not convinced that Doolan could return to the role and offered various alternative roles. Doolan refused these and was subsequently dismissed on the grounds of capability.

  The Employment Tribunal found that this was an unfair dismissal, but the EAT overturned this decision. The EAT ruled that the medical investigation had been thorough, there was a reasonable belief that further periods of absence due to stress would occur and, in the circumstances, it was appropriate to dismiss.

If the employer has taken action to try to help the employee improve the standard of performance but capability remains an issue, the dismissal can be potentially fair:

- *Gozdzik and Scopigno v Chlidema Carpet Co Ltd* (1979) EAT 598/78
The two employees were employed as winders. Due to the effects of the recession the employer introduced a new bonus system aimed at improving the productivity of the winders. The two employees did not meet the new standards and were given further training by the employer. They still did not meet the new standards and they were dismissed. Their claim for unfair dismissal failed because the employer had acted reasonably in providing them with additional training before taking the decision to dismiss.

Task

Find out what procedures your organisation, or an organisation with which you are familiar, has for addressing capability issues. (It might be useful to ask the HR department.) Do you think they are adequate in defending potential claims of unfair dismissal?

In assessing cases of dismissal on the grounds of capability, the Employment Tribunal will have due regard to reasonableness. What help and training should a reasonable employer give and what is a reasonable expectation of the employee?

8.4.2 Conduct

Conduct – that is, misconduct – is typically divided into two categories:

- Gross misconduct, which can result in summary dismissal (dismissal without notice): examples of gross misconduct include theft, assault, vandalism and falsification of records.

- Misconduct, which is a less serious offence and is usually dealt with through disciplinary warnings: if the behaviour does not cease, there is the possibility that the employee will be dismissed – examples of this include bad language, poor time-keeping and improper wearing of uniform.

A dismissal for misconduct is potentially fair, but the employer must show that it has acted reasonably in reaching the decision to dismiss. The role of the Employment Tribunal is not to determine whether the employee committed the act of misconduct, but whether the employer investigated the situation thoroughly, had a reasonable belief that the employee committed the act and then took a reasonable course of action. This is referred to as acting within the 'range of reasonable responses'.

This test of reasonableness is set out in the following case, which is relevant to most situations of misconduct:

- *British Home Stores v Burchell* (1980) IRLR 379
  This case demonstrates the need for the employer to have a reasonable belief in the guilt of the employee, based on a reasonable investigation.

  Burchell was dismissed because of irregularities in staff purchases. Evidence was obtained from dockets relating to purchases of Burchell and other staff, and a statement from another employee. Burchell took a claim of unfair dismissal to the Employment Tribunal, which supported her claim, stating that BHS had not clearly established Burchell's guilt. The EAT overturned this decision, stating that the Employment Tribunal had tried to apply tests more fitting to a criminal investigation. This strict standard of proof was not required – what was required was that the employer had a reasonable belief based on a reasonable investigation. The EAT identified three key elements to this process:

  - the fact underlying the belief must be established;
  - the belief must be held on reasonable grounds, after an appropriate investigation;
  - the investigation must be reasonable, in the circumstances.

It is important to note that the level of investigation and belief required in order to proceed with a dismissal is not the same level as that required in a criminal prosecution. The importance of carrying out a fair investigation was emphasised by the Court of Appeal in the following case:

- *Salford NHS Trust v Roldan* (2010) EWCA Civ 522
  Roldan, who had worked for the employer without any problems for four years, was accused by another employee of abusing a patient. Roldan was suspended without the allegations being put to her, and another allegation (that had never been investigated) was also considered in making the decision to dismiss. The first time that Roldan saw the charges in writing was in her dismissal letter.
  The employer only spoke to the employee who accused Roldan of abusing the patient. They did not speak to any other employees or patients who might have witnessed the event. The employer went ahead and dismissed Roldan. The Court of Appeal held that the dismissal was unfair.
  In doing so, it set out three important principles:

  – The more serious the potential consequences of the dismissal, the more thorough should be the investigation. In this case, Roldan faced the possibility of deportation if she was dismissed (she was a Filipino) and hence the potential consequences were severe.

  – If the investigation results in two witnesses saying different things, the employer is not required to decide to believe one and disbelieve the other. If there is no way of resolving the conflict, the employer could give the employee the benefit of the doubt.

  – If the Employment Tribunal has applied the ruling of *British Home Stores v Burchell* to its deliberations and there is evidence to support its conclusion (and the decision is not perverse), its conclusion should not be overturned.

The reasonableness of a dismissal can also relate to the impact of the behaviour:

- *Crisp v Apple Retail* (2011) ET1500258/11
  Crisp worked at one of the Apple stores and posted derogatory comments about the Apple brand and its products on his Facebook page. He had privacy settings, but a friend saw the posts and passed them on, and eventually the store manager became aware of them. Crisp was dismissed. This was found to be a fair dismissal because Apple had a very clear policy on the use of social media sites and was very protective of its brand. The comments were derogatory and could have damaged the brand.

It is important to note that the Employment Tribunal is only required to judge whether the actions of an employer are within the range of reasonable responses. An Employment Tribunal is not required to rehear the facts and to determine guilt – or to decide what it would have done in the circumstances. It has to concentrate solely on reasonableness. This is demonstrated in the following case:

- *Bowater v NW London Hospitals NHS Trust* (2011) IRLR 331
  Bowater, a nurse, was part of a team that struggled to restrain a patient who was fitting. It was alleged that she acted improperly in her approach to the restraint and that she had made a lewd comment about the patient in a public area of the department. She was dismissed for gross misconduct.

The Court of Appeal found that there was no restraint policy and hence Bowater's actions could not be in breach of any agreed approach and her comments could have been interpreted in a way that did not see them as being lewd. Hence, the dismissal was not within the range of reasonable responses and the dismissal was unfair.

 Explore further

Read through the judgments in a variety of unfair dismissal cases (for some ideas of where to find these, look at the end of this chapter under 'Case summaries'). In each one identify the test of reasonableness and how it is being applied. Build up a clear picture of what the courts consider to be reasonable behaviour on the part of both the employer and the employee. Do any clear guidelines stand out? Are there cases that do not fit in with these guidelines? How can any such anomalies be explained?

If an employee is charged with a criminal offence it can be reasonable to proceed with a dismissal, even if that employee will not co-operate with any dismissal hearings. The tests established by *British Home Stores v Burchell* are relevant here. This is demonstrated in:

- *Harris and another v Courage (Eastern) Ltd* (1982) IRLR 509
  Courage believed that Harris and another had stolen some beer, and the police charged them both. Courage also started disciplinary proceedings. On legal advice the two employees did not attend the disciplinary hearings and were not prepared to co-operate with any investigation by Courage. Courage carried out an investigation to the best of its ability – including the taking of witness statements. On the basis of the evidence it had obtained it dismissed the two employees. The claim for unfair dismissal was rejected because Courage had carried out a reasonable investigation and had a reasonable belief that the employees had stolen the beer. It was found that there was no requirement to wait until after a criminal trial. (In the actual criminal trial the employees were acquitted.)

 Task

There are many cases of unfair dismissal that are regularly reported in the personnel press (for example, *People Management*). Read some recent cases and apply the 'Burchell test' to them. Try to develop an understanding of what the Employment Tribunal sees as a 'reasonable response' from an employer.

8.4.3 Redundancy

We explore this issue in detail in Chapter 9.

8.4.4 Statutory ban

This is when it is unlawful to continue working because of a legal restriction or duty. An example of this is an employee who has the job of a driver within an organisation, but who loses his/her driving licence because of motoring offences that he/she committed. Clearly, the employee cannot continue to work in the role of driver while this ban is in place.

Again, the concept of reasonableness is central to the reaction of the employer. The employer should consider the length of time that the restriction is likely to be in place. If, to continue the use of our example, the driver has lost his/her licence for three months, it might be possible to find alternative duties for him/her during this period. If, however, the employee has lost his/her licence for five years, there would be the need to completely redeploy him/her, which might be more difficult.

This issue is illustrated in the case of:

- *Roberts v Toyota (GB) Ltd* (1981) EAT 614/80
  Roberts was an area sales manager and there was an implied term in his contract that he would have a driving licence. He was convicted of driving while over the legal alcohol limit and lost his licence for 12 months. He offered to purchase a company car and provide a driver to drive him during this 12-month period, but the employer went ahead and dismissed him, viewing the option of using a driver as impractical. His claim of unfair dismissal was rejected because there was clear evidence that the requirement to have a driving licence was an implied term of his contract of employment.

8.4.5 Some other substantial reason

This category allows the Employment Tribunal to consider any dismissal that does not fall under one of the other four headings and to consider the reason and its fairness. Examples under this heading are:

Pressure from an external source to dismiss

- *Henderson v Connect (South Tyneside)* (2009) UKEAT/0209/09
  Henderson was a bus driver working for Connect. He worked on a contract that Connect had with South Tyneside Metropolitan Borough Council, driving disabled children. Under the terms of the contract, the council had the right to veto the use of any driver. All drivers had to be Criminal Records Bureau (CRB) checked prior to working on the contract. Henderson underwent a CRB check, which was clear. However, there were subsequently allegations that he had sexually abused children. The allegations were never proven and the police did not prosecute. Henderson protested his innocence. However, a meeting took place between the council, Connect and the police and it was agreed that there was some substance to the allegations.

  As a result, the council operated its right to veto the use of Henderson as a driver on its contract. Connect tried to persuade the council not to do this, but they were unsuccessful. As Connect had no other employment for Henderson, he was dismissed. This was found to be a fair dismissal.

Reorganisation of the business

If an employer has to reorganise the business and can show that it is essential to make alterations to an employee's working pattern, there is a potentially fair reason. Again, the employer must show that all the options have been considered and that the conclusion that dismissal is the solution has been reached after reasonable consideration. This occurred in the following case:

- *Davey v Daybern Co Ltd* (1982) EAT 710/81
  Davey worked in a sweet kiosk. Business was poor and it was decided to reorganise the working hours in order to cut wage costs. The reorganisation meant that Davey would be required to work two evenings, which she was unable to do because of family commitments. A temporary arrangement was put in place, but eventually Davey was dismissed. Her claim of unfair dismissal was unsuccessful because the Employment Tribunal found that the employer had acted fairly. It was able to demonstrate the commercial need for the reorganisation and thus the reason for the dismissal was reasonable under the heading of 'some other substantial reason'.

In the case of *Scott & Co v Richardson* (2005) the EAT emphasised that the Employment Tribunal should not try to 'second-guess' the soundness of a business decision made by an employer:

- *Scott & Co v Richardson* (2005) EAT 0074/04
  Richardson worked as a debt collector. The employer wanted to change the hours of work to include collecting debts in the evening, when more people were at home. Richardson refused to do this unless he received overtime payments, as he had done previously for any evening work. The discussions went on for some seven months and eventually Richardson was dismissed. The Employment Tribunal found that it was unfair dismissal, but the EAT overturned this decision. The EAT stated that the Employment Tribunal was not allowed to second-guess whether the business decision was a good one. If the employer firmly believed that the change was for the good of the business, it did not have to prove the advantages.

Mistaken belief

If an employer has a genuine belief that the reason it has for dismissing an employee is fair, the dismissal could come under the heading of 'some other substantial reason' if it is later shown that the belief was actually mistaken. This categorisation refers back to the need for an employer to carry out a reasonable investigation, which leads to a reasonable belief.

This is demonstrated in:

- *Bouchaala v Trusthouse Forte Hotels Ltd* (1980) ICR 721
  Bouchaala was a Tunisian student who was given limited leave to enter and remain in the UK. Trusthouse Forte employed him as a trainee manager, but was then informed by the Department of Employment that he did not qualify for a work permit and to continue to employ him would be illegal. He was

dismissed. The Department of Employment then informed the employer that Bouchaala had been given indefinite leave to remain in the UK and so a work permit was not required. Bouchaala took up a claim of unfair dismissal. This claim was not supported because the employer had a genuine belief that there was a substantial reason for the dismissal of Bouchaala. Although that belief was later shown to be mistaken, the dismissal, at the time, was still fair.

Breakdown in working relationship

It is important that the employer identifies the reason for dismissal. Sometimes there can be a dispute relating to the reason, as demonstrated in the following case:

- *Ezsias v North Glamorgan NHS Trust* (2011) ICR 1126
  Ezsias was openly critical of his colleagues and regularly raised concerns about the NHS Trust. His colleagues were very frustrated with his actions and some signed a petition saying that they had a complete lack of trust in Ezsias and asking management to address the issues. The management asked a senior HR manager to investigate the issues and he reported that the relationships had irreparably broken down and that Ezsias's behaviour had been a significant part of this occurring. The NHS Trust then wrote to Ezsias, stating that the working relationship had broken down and it had no alternative but to terminate his employment.

  The NHS Trust argued that the dismissal was not on the grounds of conduct, but on the grounds of 'some other substantial reason'. The EAT supported this, finding that the dismissal was fair. It found that it was the breakdown of relationships – not the conduct – that had resulted in the dismissal.

8.5 Disciplinary and grievance procedures

8.5.1 Acas Code of Practice: Disciplinary and Grievance Procedure

A key part of showing that any dismissal has been reasonable is demonstrating that the procedure for carrying out the dismissal has been fair. The Employment Act 2002 introduced a statutory dismissal and disciplinary procedure and a statutory grievance procedure. The main motivation for introducing this procedure was to reduce the number of claims being brought to the Employment Tribunal. It was hoped that having set procedures would result in more disputes being resolved within the organisation. However, the reality was that the number of claims actually increased. This was partly because any dismissal that did not follow the procedure was automatically unfair and hence claims were made relating to non-compliance with the procedure (sometimes on small points) in the hope of winning a claim.

In March 2007 the Gibbons Report (which the government had commissioned to look at various issues relating to dispute resolution) recommended that the statutory procedures were repealed. This happened in April 2009.

Organisations are now required to follow the Acas Code of Practice: Disciplinary and Grievance Procedure. This procedure does not have the same status as statute, but if it is not followed the employer would have to show very good reasons when defending a claim to the Employment Tribunal. It is important to note that, if the procedure is not followed, there will not be an automatically unfair dismissal. If the Employment Tribunal judges that either the employer or employee has not complied with the procedure, it can reduce/decrease the compensatory award by up to 25 per cent.

Note that the Acas Code of Practice: Disciplinary and Grievance Procedures do not apply to redundancy situations or to the termination of a fixed-term contract. The Acas Code of Practice sets out three steps that should be followed when addressing a disciplinary situation:

- Stage 1: the employer must write to the employee setting out the grounds on which it is considering taking disciplinary action. The letter must invite the employee to a meeting to discuss the allegations. If specific documents or evidence are being relied on by the employer a copy should be attached to the letter inviting the employee to the meeting.

- Stage 2: a meeting must be held at which the allegations are formally put to the employee. The meeting must be at a time and location that is reasonable for the employee and must give adequate opportunity for the employee to explain his/her case. After the meeting the employee must be informed of any disciplinary action that is to be taken.

- Stage 3: if disciplinary action is to be taken, the employee has the right to appeal against that decision. Again, the meeting must be held at a reasonable time and location, and the employee must have adequate opportunity to put his/her case. As far as is reasonably practical, the appeal should be heard by a more senior manager than the one who took the decision to dismiss – and someone who was not involved in the original dismissal decision.

It is important to ensure that the employee understands the allegations, so that the employee can prepare an appropriate defence:

- *Celebi v Compass Group* (2010) UK/EAT/0032/10v
  Celebi was asked to attend a disciplinary meeting in relation to the loss of £3,000. It was not made clear to her that she was being accused of the theft of £3,000. The Employment Appeals Tribunal found that the dismissal was not fair because the allegation was not clearly stated. Although the employer had tried to 'soften the blow' by using softer language, this was not an acceptable reason for the lack of clarity.

The Acas Code of Practice also sets out some fundamental principles that should be considered in all dismissal situations:

- The employer and employee should act promptly in addressing any disciplinary issues. There should not be any unreasonable delays in holding meetings, making decisions or confirming decisions.
- There should be consistency in how disciplinary issues are addressed.
- Employers should carry out appropriate investigations to establish the facts of a case.
- Employers should set out the facts as they have investigated them and allow an employee to respond before making any decision on a sanction.

- Employees should be allowed to be accompanied at a disciplinary meeting.
- Employers should allow an employee to appeal against a disciplinary decision.

Suspension is often part of the process followed by the employer. However, the Employment Tribunals have been increasingly critical of employers who suspend an employee automatically, without considering whether it is essential to do so:

- *Agoreyo v London Borough of Lambeth* (2017) EWHC 2019
  The employee was a teacher and was accused of using unnecessary force to control a child. She was suspended pending enquiries, and resigned claiming that this was a breach of contract, and therefore claiming constructive dismissal. She was successful. Suspension is not a neutral act, and by suspending her without considering any alternatives there had been a breach of contract.

8.5.2 *Grievance procedures*

The Acas Code of Practice also sets out three stages that should be followed when addressing a grievance. These are:

- Stage 1: the employee writes to the employer setting out the nature of the grievance.
- Stage 2: the employer arranges a meeting with the employee to discuss the grievance.
  This meeting must take place in a reasonable time period and when the employer has had a chance to investigate the grievance. After considering the situation, the employer must inform the employee of any action that is to be taken in response to the grievance or explain why no action is to be taken.
- Stage 3: the employee has the right to appeal against the response to the grievance.
  Wherever possible a more senior manager must hear the appeal. After this meeting the employee must be informed of what action, if any, is to be taken.
  It is important to note that there is no requirement on an employee to raise a grievance with the employer prior to bringing a claim to the Employment Tribunal.

 Explore further

It is very important to understand the Acas Code of Practice: Disciplinary and Grievance Procedures. Read it in full at: http://www.acas. org.uk/media/pdf/f/m/Acas-Code-of-Practice-1-on-disciplinary-and-grievance-procedures.pdf

8.5.3 *Disciplinary warnings*

Not all disciplinary situations warrant summary dismissal – indeed, most result in action short of this being taken. In these situations disciplinary warnings are given.

The law does not set out what warnings are to be given, but it is expected that organisations will follow the guidelines set out in the Acas Code of Practice. The code suggests that there should be the following levels of warning:

- formal written warning (that remains on the employee's record for six months);
- final written warning (that remains on the employee's record for 12 months);
- dismissal.

It is important to emphasise that these levels of warning, and time periods on record, are not legal requirements. Some organisations will have more levels of warning, or different time periods that warnings are kept on the record. However, in considering the reasonableness of any procedure, the Employment Tribunal will have regard to the Acas Code of Practice.

If, during the period that the warning is still on the employee's record, the employee does not improve, the next level of warning can be given. It is important that any action taken is reasonable – that the employee has a reasonable amount of time to make improvements and that any targets set are reasonable.

- *Airbus UK Ltd v Webb* (2008) EWCA Civ 39
  Five employees were found to be watching TV when they should have been working. One of the employees had previously had a final written warning, which had expired. He was dismissed, due to his poor disciplinary record, but the other employees received a final written warning. Although his warning had expired it was fair to dismiss given his disciplinary history.

8.6 The right to be accompanied

Sections 10 to 15 of the Employment Relations Act 1999 give workers the right to be accompanied by a fellow worker or trade union representative to any disciplinary or grievance hearing that falls within the following definitions:

- the giving of a formal warning to a worker by the employer;
- the taking of some other action to a worker in relation to a disciplinary matter;
- the confirmation of a warning or other action that has been taken.

If the hearing is informal, there is no statutory right to be accompanied. It must also be emphasised that the usual right is to be accompanied by a fellow worker or a trade union representative. However, there might be rare occasions when it is appropriate to have legal representation:

- *R (on the application of G) v The Governors of X School and Y City Council* (2011) UKSC 30
  In this case a music assistant was accused of improper contact with a child at a school where he worked. The nature of the allegations were such that he would not be able to continue in his career if found guilty. He argued that refusal to allow him legal representation at the disciplinary hearing was a breach of Article 6 of the European Convention on Human Rights.

The Supreme Court ruled that there is no right under Article 6 of the ECHR to legal representation at a disciplinary hearing where dismissal could lead to being barred from the profession if the decision on barring is sufficiently independent of the dismissal decision.

The Supreme Court found that any actions of the Independent Safeguarding Authority were independent of the employer's dismissal decision and hence there was no requirement for the school's disciplinary procedures to comply with Article 6. However, it did note that if the dismissal had automatically determined the outcome in subsequent proceedings that impact on an employee's civil rights, the right to legal representation might be engaged.

It is also important to note that the employee can choose their representative, and there is no requirement for the employer to agree with who they choose:

- *Toal and another v GB Oils Ltd* (2013) UKEAT/0569/12
  Two employees raised a grievance and were invited to separate grievance hearings. They both asked to be represented by a particular trade union representative but the request was refused. So, they both attended with a colleague and then a different trade union representative at the appeal. They successfully argued that their rights had been breached by refusing to allow them their chosen representative.

8.7 Constructive dismissal

If the employer's conduct is such that it breaches the contract of employment, and that breach goes to the very root of the contract, the employee can terminate the contract of employment and claim constructive dismissal.

In order to show that there has been a constructive dismissal, the employee must demonstrate that:

- there was a fundamental breach of the contract on the part of the employer;
- the breach of the contract caused him/her to resign;
- there was no significant delay in resigning.

Common examples of the way that constructive dismissal occurs are bullying and situations involving change. It can occur during bullying because the employee argues that the behaviour of the employer, either in doing the bullying or in letting the bullying occur, amounts to a breach of contract. Typically, it will be argued that it is a breach of the implied term of mutual trust and confidence.

In a change situation it can occur if the employer forces a change to happen. For example, if the employer wants to change the hours of work and the employee resists, the employer might decide to force the change. In this case the employee would argue that the fundamental contractual term of hours of work had been breached – and resign in response to this.

As we noted in Chapter 4, in a change situation the employer must consult with the employee. If the employer had made every effort to consult, and could show that there was a strong business reason for making the change, it could be possible to defend the actions and hence the constructive dismissal claim would fail.

The Court of Appeal ruled in *Western Excavating (ECC) Ltd v Sharp* that the employer's conduct that gave rise to the claim of constructive dismissal must involve a breach of contract:

- *Western Excavating (ECC) Ltd v Sharp* (1978) IRLR 27
  Sharp asked for an afternoon off and was refused. Nevertheless, he still took the afternoon off. He was dismissed, but successfully appealed. The appeal reduced the punishment to five days' suspension without payment. However, this led him into financial difficulties so he asked the employer to pay him five days' accrued holiday pay. This was refused because it was against company policy. He then asked for a loan and that was also refused. He then resigned, claiming constructive dismissal. The Employment Tribunal upheld his complaint. This finding was overturned by the Court of Appeal. They found that the Employment Tribunal had focused on whether the conduct of the employer was unreasonable. However, the test in a case of constructive dismissal is whether the contract of employment has been breached. In this case, they found no evidence of a breach of contract and so the complaint was dismissed.

It can be difficult to determine whether the behaviour of the employer has actually breached the employment contract. It is not important to consider what the employer intended to do.

The Employment Tribunal will focus on the actual behaviour of the employer and whether an employee cannot reasonably have been expected to tolerate such behaviour. This is illustrated in the case of:

- *West Sussex County Council v Austin* (2014) UKEAT/0034/14
  Austin was accused of harassing an employee who reported to him. He was suspended. His suspension was never reviewed, he was never told who had made the allegation and he was never told the details of the allegation. He resigned, arguing that the employer had not followed a fair procedure. His claim of constructive dismissal was successful – the employer should have suspended him for a short time whilst carrying out investigations, he should have been told what the allegations were and he should have been given an opportunity to respond to them.

The employee must resign in response to the breach that has occurred:

- *Mruke v Khan* (2014) UKEAT/0241/13
  Mruke was working in domestic service in the UK, did not speak English and was being paid less than the National Minimum Wage. A trafficking charity became aware of her, and she left her employment with their support. After resigning she realised that she had not been paid the National Minimum Wage. She claimed constructive dismissal. Although there was a breach of contract, because her pay had been unlawful, that was not the reason that she resigned because she was not aware of this at the time of resignation, Hence, her claim of constructive dismissal was unsuccessful.

Constructive dismissal can also be the result of a series of actions, rather than one single action:

- *Lewis v Motorworld Garages Ltd* (1986) ICR 157
  Over a period from November 1981 to August 1982 Lewis claimed that he had been subjected to a series of events that, when added together, resulted

in a breach of mutual trust and confidence. These events included demotion, alteration of his pay and constant criticism of his performance (which he claimed was unjustified).

The Court of Appeal accepted that the accumulation of the various situations could result in constructive dismissal, even if the single events on their own were not breaches of contract.

If a breach of contract has occurred, it cannot be 'righted' at a later date:

- *Bournemouth University Higher Education Corporation v Buckland* (2010) WCA Civ 121
  Buckland was a lecturer at the university. A large number of students failed a course that he taught. Buckland and a second marker marked the resits. The course leader remarked the scripts, criticising the original marking. Unknown to Buckland, a further marker was asked to look at the papers.

  When Buckland did find out, he complained and an investigation was ordered. A report into the situation criticised the fact that scripts had been remarked without consulting Buckland. When the report was published, Buckland resigned and claimed constructive dismissal.

  As he had resigned when the report was published it was seen that he had resigned in a timely manner. However, the university argued that the report exonerated Buckland and hence corrected any breach that had occurred. The Court of Appeal rejected this argument, ruling that a breach cannot be corrected once it has taken place – hence Buckland won his claim of constructive dismissal.

The important factor in determining whether constructive dismissal has taken place is whether the actions (or inaction) of the employer have amounted to a breach of the contract. The specific part of the contract that has been breached must be identified.

8.8 Automatically unfair reasons for dismissal

There are situations in which a dismissal is automatically unfair. On the following grounds dismissal is automatically unfair and the one/two-year qualifying period, otherwise required to bring a claim of unfair dismissal, is not necessary:

- the employee's membership (or non-membership) of a trade union;
- the employee's pregnancy or any maternity-related issue;
- the refusal of a retail employee to work on a Sunday;
- activities carried out in the role of health and safety representative;
- asserting a statutory right;
- making a protected disclosure under the Public Interest Disclosure Act 1998 (see Chapter 10);
- asserting the right to be paid in accordance with the National Minimum Wage Act 1998;
- disclosing fraud or corruption.

There are two situations in which a dismissal is automatically unfair, but the one/two-year qualifying period is still required. These are:

- dismissal because of a spent conviction;
- dismissal where there is a transfer of the undertaking (presuming that there is not a valid economic, technical or organisational reason for the dismissal – see Chapter 9).

8.9 Remedies for unfair dismissal

If the Employment Tribunal finds that an employee has been unfairly dismissed, it has to decide on the remedy. As explained in Chapter 2, there are three possible remedies:

- re-engagement;
- reinstatement;
- compensation.

8.9.1 Re-engagement and reinstatement

Although re-engagement and reinstatement are by far the least common remedies, the Employment Tribunal has a duty to explain these options and to ask the employee whether he/she wants the tribunal to make such an order. In reality, the employee rarely wants such an order, either because he/she has already obtained alternative employment or because the relationship with the employer is sufficiently poor after bringing the claim that future employment would seem to be untenable. If the employee is reinstated, he/she returns to the job previously held and the employer must treat the employee as if he/she had not been dismissed. This means that all monies that would have been paid to the employee (salary and any benefits) during the time between the dismissal and the order to reinstate must be paid. All rights and privileges that the employee previously enjoyed must be reinstated.

If the employee is re-engaged, he/she returns to the employer but in a different role. The Employment Tribunal must state the nature of the employment and the benefits that accompany the role. Again, the employee must be treated as if he/she had not been dismissed and any monies he/she would have earned during the period between dismissal and the order to re-engage must be paid.

If the Employment Tribunal makes an order for reinstatement or re-engagement and it is not carried out by the employer, the tribunal will then award compensation to the employee in the way we outline later in this section. In addition, there will be an additional award of not less than 26 weeks', and not more than 52 weeks', pay.

8.9.2 Compensation

If compensation is awarded it will consist of two parts (according to section 118 of the Employment Rights Act 1996). These two parts are the basic award and the compensatory award.

The basic award is calculated by determining the employee's period of continuous service with the employer (up to a maximum of 20 years). The following amounts are awarded:

- one and a half weeks' pay for each year when the employee was between the ages of 41 and 64 years;
- one week's pay for each year when the employee was between the ages of 22 and 40;
- half a week's pay for each year of employment when the employee was aged under 21 years.

The statutory definition of the maximum limit on a week's pay is reviewed each year by the government. It is currently £508 (as of April 2018). If an employee is paid more than this, the figure of £508 will be used for all calculations.

If the employee has been unfairly dismissed for a reason relating to health and safety, being a trustee of an occupational pension scheme or an elected employee representative, there is a minimum basic award of £6,203 (as of April 2018). (Note that the figures quoted are reviewed every April.)

The compensatory award is that which the Employment Tribunal sees as fair given all of the circumstances and the loss that the employee has suffered. The aim is to compensate the employee for the loss he/she has suffered, not to punish the employer. The items that are taken into consideration when determining the compensatory award are:

- Loss of earnings from the date of dismissal to the date of the Employment Tribunal hearing.
- Potential future loss of earnings (the tribunal will give consideration to the degree of difficulty the employee might encounter in getting alternative employment and the likelihood of obtaining employment at a similar level of remuneration to the role from which he/she was dismissed).
- Loss of statutory industrial rights (the employee has lost the continuous service he/she had accrued with the previous employer and will have to start the process of accrual anew with a new employer – this item aims to compensate the employee for that loss).
- Loss of pension rights.
- Loss of benefits (eg health insurance, company car).
- Expenses incurred in seeking alternative employment.

The maximum compensatory award is £83,682 (as of April 2018) or the employee's annual salary – whichever is lower (up-to-date figures for all awards can be found at www.gov.uk).

8.9.3 Injury to feelings

The issue of damages for injury to feelings has been contentious. In section 123 of the Employment Rights Act 1996, the compensatory award in unfair dismissal cases is defined as that which is 'such amount as the tribunal considers just and equitable in all the circumstances having regard to the loss sustained by the complainant in consequence of the dismissal'.

In determining the amount of compensation in the case of *Norton Tool Co Ltd v Tewson* (1972) ICR 501, a clear statement was made that the compensatory award for unfair dismissal could only reflect economic loss.

This interpretation of section 123 of the ERA 1996 remained unchallenged until a ruling in the following case:

- *Johnson v Unisys Ltd* (2001) ICR 480
  In this case Johnson claimed he had suffered psychological problems due to the nature of his dismissal. He won a claim for unfair dismissal, but the compensatory award did not include any damages for injury to feelings. He tried to pursue a claim for breach of contract in the County Court, on the basis that the nature of the dismissal had breached the term of mutual trust and confidence. However, it was ruled that such a claim could not be made because the term of mutual trust and confidence applied to preserving the relationship and not terminating it.

In making the House of Lords judgment, specific reference was made by one of the judges to the *Norton Tool Co Ltd v Tewson* case. It was commented that the interpretation of the compensatory award was too narrow and the definition of compensatory award should include damages for distress, humiliation, damage to reputation or family life and psychiatric injury, when appropriate. (Note that in the *Johnson v Unisys Ltd* case the House of Lords did not go on to review the unfair dismissal compensatory award because they were hearing an appeal relating to a breach of contract claim.) This judgment was then tested in the case of:

- *Dunnachie v Kingston upon Hull City Council* (2004) EWCA Civ 84
  Dunnachie worked for the council and had been subjected to a long campaign of bullying and undermining by his colleague and former line manager. The council failed to resolve the situation and eventually Dunnachie resigned and successfully claimed constructive dismissal.

  Although there was no evidence of Dunnachie's suffering from a recognised psychiatric disorder, he had been reduced to a 'state of overt despair'. In light of the ruling in the *Johnson v Unisys Ltd* case, the Employment Tribunal included a £10,000 award within the compensatory award for injury to feelings flowing from the dismissal.

  Although the EAT overturned the tribunal's decision, the Court of Appeal supported the £10,000 award and thus supported the tribunal's calculation of the compensatory award. The Court of Appeal decision was later overturned by the House of Lords, which determined that damages for non-economic loss (which would include injury to feelings) are not recoverable in the situation of unfair dismissal.

8.9.4 Reductions

The amount of compensation can be reduced due to the employee's contribution to the dismissal. For example, in *Parker Foundry Ltd v Slack* (1991) IRLR 11, Slack was dismissed following a fight with a fellow employee. The Employment Tribunal found that Slack had been unfairly dismissed because of procedural irregularities relating to the way that the claim had been handled. However, they reduced his compensation by 50 per cent because they believed that his conduct had made him 50 per cent to blame for the dismissal.

There is also the possibility to make a reduction to the compensatory award when the procedure for dismissal has not been followed fairly but the Employment Tribunal judges that (even if the procedure had been followed) the employee would still have been dismissed. This approach refers back to the case of *Polkey v A E Dayton* (1988).

- *Polkey v A E Dayton* (1987) AC 344
  In this case Polkey was one of four van drivers working for A E Dayton. There was a need to cut costs for commercial reasons and it was decided that the four van drivers would be replaced by three van salespeople. A E Dayton decided that Polkey was unsuitable for the role of van salesperson and accordingly decided to make him redundant. The first Polkey knew about it was when he was given a letter setting out his redundancy payments and he was dismissed.

  On hearing his claim of unfair dismissal it was determined that the employers had not acted correctly because they had not consulted with Polkey or warned him of the possible redundancy (we explore this procedure more in Chapter 9). However, they also concluded that even if the procedure had been followed, Polkey would still have been made redundant. On that basis his dismissal was found to be fair. The case was eventually referred to the House of Lords, which found that the Employment Tribunal had taken the wrong approach. It found that the dismissal was unfair. However, a compensatory award can be reduced to reflect the likelihood that an employee would have been dismissed anyway, if the correct procedure had been followed.

Clearly, this leads to a rather subjective decision of the tribunal. However, in assessing compensation the tribunal can assess what chance the employee would have had of keeping his/her job if a correct procedure had been followed and that percentage chance can be applied to reduce the compensation awarded.

8.9.5 *Mitigation*

The employee also has a duty to take reasonable steps to mitigate his/her loss (by making serious efforts to find alternative employment). The basic rule of mitigation is that the employee must take all reasonable steps to mitigate the loss to him/her resulting from the employer's actions and he/she cannot recover compensation for any such loss that he/she could have avoided but failed to avoid through unreasonable action or inaction. The duty is to act reasonably, although the level of requirement on the employee is not high – given that the employer is the wrongdoer.

- *Kelly v University of Southampton* (2010) UKEAT/0295/07
  Kelly was an academic of US citizenship. There had been some confusion over the length of time that she was entitled to work in the UK and she had been dismissed because it was thought by the university that continuing to employ her would have been illegal. In the meantime Kelly had been granted indefinite leave to remain working in the UK.

  It was found that she had been dismissed unfairly. When considering compensation the EAT concluded that she had failed to mitigate her loss by not applying for two posts for which she was qualified within the university where she worked. As a result the compensation was limited to the date when it was presumed that she would have been appointed to one of the two posts had she applied.

KEY LEARNING POINTS

1 A contract of employment can be terminated without a dismissal taking place.
2 There are five potentially fair reasons for dismissal – capability, conduct, redundancy, statutory ban and some other substantial reason.
3 There are some employees who are unable to take a claim of unfair dismissal – these include employees with less than two years' continuous service of employment.
4 For a dismissal to be fair, a correct procedure must be followed. The Acas Code of Practice: Disciplinary and Grievance Procedures should be followed.
5 Employees have the right to be accompanied at a disciplinary hearing.
6 Constructive dismissal occurs where the conduct of the employer breaches the contract of employment, making it intolerable for the employee to continue working according to that contract.
7 There are a number of situations in which it is automatically unfair to dismiss an employee.
8 The remedy for unfair dismissal is reinstatement, re-engagement or compensation.
9 Compensation consists of a basic award and a compensatory award.
10 Compensation can be reduced on the basis of the employee's contribution to the dismissal, or the failure of the employee to mitigate his/her loss.

 Case summaries

- *Hare v Murphy Brothers Ltd* (1974) ICR 603 – Hare was imprisoned for 12 months following his involvement in a fight (unconnected with work). When he was released from prison, he was told his job was no longer available and he claimed unfair dismissal or, alternatively, redundancy. The Court of Appeal ruled that his contract had been frustrated, due to the length of the prison term.
- *Horkulak v Cantor Fitzgerald International* (2003) EWHC 1918 (QB) – Horkulak was subjected to a series of bullying behaviour from his line manager. He eventually resigned in response to this. It was held that the behaviour had breached mutual trust and confidence, and Horkulak was therefore successful in his claim of constructive dismissal.
- *Stanley Cole (Wainfleet) Ltd v Sheridan* (2003) IRLR 52 – Sheridan had been an employee for more than five years and had no record of disciplinary action. She had a heated discussion with a colleague that upset her and she then left the office for one and a half hours (which included her half-hour lunch break). She was given a final written warning and this amounted to a breach of the contract of employment because it breached the implied term of trust and confidence and/or the implied term that the disciplinary procedure would be used fairly. Her claim for constructive dismissal was upheld.

(Continued)

(Continued)

- *Phoenix House Ltd v Stockman* (2016) UKEAT/0264/15
  The employee was dismissed when the relationship between the employer and the employee broke down. It was ruled that there was no requirement to follow the Acas Code of Practice: Disciplinary and Grievance Procedures because this only applies when there is something for which the employee is culpable.
- *Holmes v Qinetiq Ltd* (2016) UKEAT/0206/15
  The employee was unwell and was dismissed because he could not continue in his role. The Acas Code of Practice: Disciplinary and Grievance Procedures did not have to be applied because the reason for the dismissal was not something for which the employee was culpable.
- *Ramphal v Department for Transport* (2015) UKEAT/0352/14
  The investigating officer concluded that an employee should be given a final written warning. HR intervened, and after discussions lasting some time, it was decided to go ahead and dismiss the employee. The EAT referred this back to the Employment Tribunal – HR should advise but not interfere with a disciplinary decision.

? Examples to work through

1 Jenny, a long-serving employee, has recently been making a lot of errors. Some of these errors have resulted in a financial loss to the organisation. The problems seem to have started when a new computer system was installed. Jenny was given full training and says she has no problems with using the system. Today she has made an error that has resulted in a customer complaint and her line manager is demanding that action should be taken. What is your advice?

2 Bill and Fred were fighting in the office. Bill says that Fred started it by taunting him about a recent disciplinary warning that he had received for poor performance. Fred says that Bill is just too sensitive, and everyone laughs and jokes in the office. What action should you take?

3 Today you have received a letter of resignation from Judy. She has a new job to go to. She has also informed you that she is taking a claim of constructive dismissal to the Employment Tribunal due to the ongoing bullying that she has received from a number of colleagues. This is the first time she has raised any allegations of bullying. What action should you take?

4 It is alleged that Julia has been stealing from the organisation. She was issued with a letter inviting her to a disciplinary meeting, setting out the detail of what she was alleged to have stolen and when. When she attended the disciplinary meeting she gave evidence that showed it was unlikely to be her that was responsible for the thefts. However, her evidence demonstrated that she had been breaching a number of health and safety rules – and she has now been dismissed for that reason. Is the dismissal potentially fair?

09
Redundancy and transfers of undertaking

CHAPTER OBJECTIVES

The objectives of this chapter are:

- to explain the concept of wrongful dismissal and the associated remedies;
- to outline the differences between wrongful and unfair dismissal;
- to analyse the concept of termination by summary dismissal;
- to outline the procedures required to ensure that a redundancy is a fair dismissal;
- to explain transfers of undertakings.

9.1 Wrongful dismissal

Wrongful dismissal occurs when the employer terminates the contract of employment and in doing so breaches the contract of employment. For example, the breach of contract can be:

- giving no notice of termination, or insufficient notice (assuming that a summary dismissal was not justified – see section 9.2);
- where the dismissal is in breach of a contractual disciplinary procedure;

- where the dismissal is in breach of a contractual redundancy procedure;
- the termination of a fixed-term contract before the date it is due to expire.

If the employee is claiming that a wrongful dismissal has taken place, he/she must be able to show that the employer has terminated the contract of employment and that such termination has been a breach of the contract. To defend the action of termination the employer must demonstrate that the employee had conducted himself/herself in such a way as to show no intention to be bound by the contract of employment.

If an employee successfully shows that wrongful dismissal has taken place, he/she is entitled to compensation for the breach of the contract. This will usually be equal to the loss of salary between the date of the termination and the date of the hearing when wrongful dismissal is determined.

Alternatively, the employee can ask for an injunction against the dismissal being carried out or a declaration by the court that the dismissal is invalid. In most cases the remedy given is that of damages.

Although injunctions are not common, the granting of one was allowed in the case of:

- *Irani v Southampton and SW Hampshire Health Authority* (1984) IRLR 203
  Irani was a part-time ophthalmologist working in a clinic within the health authority. Irreconcilable differences developed between Irani and the consultant in charge of the clinic. The health authority decided that the only solution was for one of the employees to leave the clinic. Because Irani was the junior employee and worked part-time, he was dismissed. The health authority did not determine that there was any particular fault with Irani. Irani successfully obtained an injunction against the dismissal because the correct procedures had not been followed. The injunction meant that the dismissal was suspended until the issues had been correctly considered. Irani did not work during this period.

The salary lost during the period between the termination and the hearing determining wrongful dismissal will include any pay awards agreed during that period or agreed at a later date and backdated. Compensation for share options, discretionary bonuses and enhanced pension rights has also been awarded by the courts.

- *Clark v Nomura plc* (2000) IRLR 766
  Clark was dismissed and was not paid his discretionary bonus (which he would have expected to amount to around £1.5 million), although he had been in employment at the time that annual bonuses were paid. He had earned significant profits for his employer and argued that he should have received the bonus.

  The employer argued that the 'performance' that the bonus depended on was much more widely defined than achieving financial success. They cited a number of aspects about Clark's performance (eg his dress and appearance, erratic timekeeping and attendance and not attending management meetings) that gave cause for concern and claimed that these had resulted in his bonus being assessed as 'nil'.

  The High Court held that these issues had not been the subject of any warnings and it was not convinced that the employer would have assessed the bonus as 'nil' if Clark had not been dismissed. It therefore upheld that the bonus should be paid.

If an employee is wrongfully dismissed because the employer did not follow the correct disciplinary procedure, the employee is entitled to damages reflecting the time that it would have taken for the procedure to operate. This is illustrated in the case of:

- *Gunton v London Borough of Richmond-upon-Thames* (1980) IRLR 321
  Gunton was dismissed and given one month's notice. The dismissal did not follow the correct procedure and so Gunton claimed wrongful dismissal. He was successful in his claim and, on outlining his damages, claimed loss of earnings up to retirement age, stating that he would have remained with the employer until that time unless he were made redundant or dismissed in accordance with the disciplinary procedure. The employers appealed against this assessment of the damages.

  The Court of Appeal supported the finding that he had been wrongfully dismissed, but stated that the damages should be limited to the period from when the dismissal took place until the contract could have been properly brought to an end. In this case it would have been when the disciplinary procedure had been properly carried out plus the one-month notice period.

If an employee has lost the right to claim unfair dismissal because of the wrongful dismissal, there is the possibility that extra damages can be received. This could occur, for example, when an employee with 10 months' service with a three-month contractual notice period is wrongfully dismissed by reason that the contract was terminated without notice. If the correct notice period had been given, the employee would have had 13 months' service at the time of termination and thus would have been eligible to bring a claim of unfair dismissal if he/she had started work before 6 April 2012.

This was shown in:

- *Raspin v United News Shops Ltd* (1998) IRLR 9
  Raspin was dismissed because her employers suspected that she had stolen money from them. Raspin successfully claimed wrongful dismissal because she was dismissed without notice and the Employment Tribunal found no evidence that she had been stealing the money. In awarding compensation for the wrongful dismissal, an additional three weeks' pay was considered that would reflect the time it would have taken to reach the decision to dismiss if the correct procedure had been followed. This additional three weeks would have increased Raspin's service to an extent that she would have been eligible to make a claim for unfair dismissal.

  The Employment Tribunal rejected this claim, relying on case law that suggested that a tribunal must restrict its deliberations to what has happened and not consider what might have happened. However, this decision was overturned by the EAT and the claim for damages relating to the lost opportunity of claiming unfair dismissal was allowed. It should be noted that if there is a clause in the contract of employment allowing the employer to pay in lieu of notice (see Chapter 5), such a claim would not be allowed. This would be because the ending of the contract without the employee working through the period of notice is expressly allowed by the contract.

9.2 The differences between unfair and wrongful dismissal

In studying both unfair and wrongful dismissal, many of the differences will have already become apparent. A summary of the main differences can be found in Table 9.1.

Table 9.1 The difference between unfair and wrongful dismissal

	Wrongful Dismissal	Unfair Dismissal
Basis	Based on breach of contract	Based on statute and the concept of fairness
Right to claim	No qualifying period required to make a claim	Unless the reason for dismissal is automatically unfair, one year's continuous service is required to make a claim, or two years if the employee started work on or after 6 April 2012
Time limit	Claim must be made within six years of the dismissal	Claim must be made within three months of the dismissal
Damages	No limit to damages that can be awarded	Maximum compensatory award currently (as of April 2018) £83,682 or the employee's annual salary, whichever is lower
Court	Only dismissal claims for damages less than £25,000 are heard in the Employment Tribunal; other claims are heard in the County Court or the High Court – although an employee claiming for damages less than £25,000 can be heard at these courts if he/she so elects	All claims heard in the Employment Tribunal
Future loss	Future loss is not considered	Future loss may be considered when compensation is being calculated
Remedy	The remedy is damages	The remedy can be reinstatement, re-engagement or compensation

9.3 Termination by summary dismissal

A termination by summary dismissal occurs where the employer terminates the contract of employment without giving the employee a period of notice. The contract is terminated because the employee has breached the contract of employment. If the employer can show that the employee has breached the contract of employment, the act of summary dismissal can be lawful.

The nature of the behaviour that causes the breach of contract can be varied. As a general principle, the behaviour must be shown to have disregard for the essential conditions of the contract. For example, if the employee has stolen from the employer, there is a potential breach of mutual trust and confidence (the employer can no longer trust the employee because of his/her actions) and summary dismissal results because of this breach of contract.

In determining whether the employee has breached the contract of employment, the Employment Tribunal will consider whether the act is one serious isolated incident or indicative of a pattern of behaviour.

This is illustrated in:

- *Pepper v Webb* (1969) WLR 514
  Pepper was employed as head gardener by the Webbs. After a period of time both his standard of work and his attitude deteriorated. One day he refused to carry out their instructions and used foul language to them. He was summarily dismissed. In considering his claim for unfair dismissal the Court of Appeal found that his manner and his standard of work showed that he had no intention to be bound by the fundamental aspect of service within a contract of employment. By taking such a stance he had breached the contract of employment and so summary dismissal was justified.

In another case of a gardener, the courts found that an isolated incident of foul language and not obeying an instruction did not amount to a breach of contract, and summary dismissal was therefore unfair:

- *Wilson v Racher* (1974) ICR 428
  Wilson was the head gardener employed by Racher. One afternoon he was cutting the hedges using an electric hedgecutter when it started to rain. He stopped the hedgecutting and busied himself with other jobs. Two days later Racher accused him of stopping work early when he stopped cutting the hedge. There followed a heated exchange during which Wilson used a range of foul language. He was summarily dismissed.

An interesting question is whether an employee who is under notice and is then discovered to have breached the contract can be summarily dismissed:

- *Williams v Leeds United Football Club* (2015) EWHC 376
  Williams was working his notice, having been made redundant. During his notice period his employer found that he had sent obscene and pornographic e-mails to two male friends and a junior female colleague. They found that this amounted to gross misconduct, and hence dismissed him without him concluding his notice period. He was unsuccessful in arguing that this was wrongful dismissal, because his acts had breached his contract and summary dismissal was appropriate.

Task

If your organisation, or an organisation with which you are familiar, has a dismissal procedure, look to see if it has a part of the procedure dealing with summary dismissal. If it does, read it, and then read section 9.3 to gain a better understanding of the legal requirements of such a procedure.

 Explore further

Students who wish to explore this area in more detail should consider the relationship of wrongful and summary dismissal. In one the employer breaches the contract of employment; in the other the breach is by the employee. Compare and contrast the cases cited in sections 9.1, 9.2 and 9.3 and referenced in the 'Case summaries' section. In each case identify which part of the contract of employment has been breached. Are there any cases where the breach of the contract seems to be carried out by both the employer and the employee?

9.4 Redundancy

9.4.1 Definition of redundancy

As we saw in Chapter 8, redundancy is one of the five potentially fair reasons for dismissal – as listed in the Employment Rights Act 1996. According to section 139(1) of this Act, employees are regarded as redundant if their dismissals are attributed, primarily or partly, to any one of three reasons:

1 The fact that the employer has ceased, or intends to cease, to carry on the business for the purposes for which the employee was employed.
    This is illustrated in the case of:

    – *Hindle v Percival Boats* (1969) WLR 174
    Hindle was employed as a boatbuilder. Percival Boats moved from their traditional methods of making boats from wood to making them from fibreglass. Hindle was unable to adapt to the new methods of working and was made redundant on the grounds that the employer had ceased to carry on the business for which Percival had been employed.

    However, it was ruled that Hindle was not in fact redundant. He was employed to make boats and Percival Boats were continuing as boatbuilders. Therefore, there was no redundancy.

Task

If Hindle was unable to make boats out of fibreglass and could not be lawfully made redundant, what action could Percival Boats take? Would a dismissal on the grounds of capability be potentially fair?

2 The fact that the employer has ceased, or intends to cease, to carry on that business in the place where the employees were employed.

   If the employee has a clause in their contract of employment requiring them to be 'mobile', it is possible that a redundancy will not occur if the location where the employee works is closed but other locations remain open. The mobility clause may allow the employer to move the employee to a different location. The employer would have to show that such a request was reasonable.

   This is demonstrated in:

– *Bass Leisure Ltd v Thomas* (1994) IRLR 104
   Thomas worked at the employer's Coventry depot, which it closed. She was asked to move to another depot that was 20 miles away and refused because of family commitments. There was a mobility clause in her contract, which the employer relied on in requesting her to make the move. After a trial period she left employment and claimed a redundancy payment. The EAT ruled that she should be paid a redundancy payment because, given her family commitments, travelling 20 miles was an unreasonable request.

3 The fact that the requirement of that business for employees to carry out work of a particular kind, or for employees to carry out work of a particular kind in the place where they were employed, has ceased or diminished or is expected to cease or diminish.

In the case of *Safeway Stores plc v Burrell* (1997) IRLR 200, the EAT gave a clear approach to follow in determining whether there has been a reduction in the need for employees. In this case Burrell was employed as a petrol station manager. Following a reorganisation the role of manager disappeared and was replaced with the role of filling station controller, at a lower salary and lower level of status. Burrell decided that he did not want this role and he was dismissed with a redundancy payment. He claimed the dismissal was unfair because there was no diminution in the duties that he had been carrying out – they were being carried out by someone else. The Employment Tribunal supported his claim.

In considering the appeal made by Safeway against the decision, the EAT laid out the following approach to determining whether someone has been dismissed for redundancy:

• Has the employee been dismissed?
• Have the requirements of the employer's business ceased or diminished, or are they expected to do so?

- If so, is the dismissal the whole or primary result of the cessation or diminution?

In applying this test the EAT found that the dismissal of Burrell was due to redundancy and was fair. His duties as a manager had diminished because not all the duties would be carried out by someone of a lower status – so applying this test showed there was a redundancy situation.

9.4.2 Consultation

The length of time that must be spent in collective consultation is laid down in the Trade Union and Labour Relations (Consolidation) Act 1992:

- If the proposed redundancies involve more than 100 employees, the consultation must take place over at least 45 days.
- If the proposed redundancies involve more than 20 but fewer than 100 employees, the consultation must take place over at least 30 days.
- If fewer than 20 employees are to be made redundant, the redundancy is not covered by the above legislation relating to collective redundancies. However, case law has demonstrated a clear requirement on the employer to consult with the individual who is potentially affected by the proposed redundancy. This consultation must take place over a 'reasonable' period of time.

The consultation over collective redundancies must be with trade union representatives or with elected employee representatives if the organisation is not unionised. It should be noted that any employer intending to make more than 20 employees redundant at one establishment is required to inform the Secretary of State for Trade and Industry in writing at the time that the intention is announced. This is done by using the form HR1.

Some key requirements of the consultation period were laid down in the Court of Session's ruling in:

- *King and others v Eaton Ltd* (1995) IRLR 199
  Eaton Ltd announced a redundancy and consultation took place with the trade union representatives. During this consultation period the issues relating to selection were not addressed. The Employment Tribunal found that the redundancies were unfair because there had been insufficient consultation. The EAT disagreed with this view, but it was supported by the Court of Session. In making the decision they laid down the following guidelines:
  - The consultation must take place when the proposals are still at a formative stage (ie starting the consultation when all decisions have already been made does not lead to a meaningful consultation).
  - The employer must give adequate information and give adequate time for a response to be given.
  - The employer must give 'conscientious consideration' to the points made during the consultation process.

This was further supported in the case of *Junk v Kuhnel* (2005) IRLR 310, where the ECJ ruled on when, in the consultation period, notices of dismissal can be issued. Consultation must be concluded before any dismissal notices are given. (Clearly, if dismissal notices had actually been issued, any further consultation is probably meaningless anyway.) If consultation has concluded, actual dismissal notices can be issued within the 30/45-day periods described in the beginning of section 9.4.2. However, no dismissals should actually take place within the consultation period.

Consultation must, however, be taken before the decision to dismiss has been made.

- *Leicestershire County Council v Unison* (2005) IRLR 920
  In this case an officer of the council made a recommendation to the Employment Committee on 18 November that, following a job evaluation exercise, redundancies should occur. The formal decision to proceed with the dismissals took place at a meeting of the committee on 12 December. The trade union, Unison, was informed of the decision on 18 December and there was then total failure to consult.

  The EAT ruled that the actual decision to proceed with dismissals was taken on 18 November and that consultation should have commenced at this point. Consultation should have commenced before decisions on dismissals had been reached.

Section 188(4) of the Trade Union and Labour Relations (Consolidation) Act 1992 also determines that certain information must be given in writing by the employer at the start of the consultation:

- the reason for the proposed redundancies;
- the number and description (ie the types of jobs involved) of the employees who it proposes to make redundant;
- the total number of employees at the establishment who are to be affected;
- the proposed method of selection;
- the procedure to be followed in dealing with the redundancies;
- the method of calculating the redundancy payment, if it differs from the statutory payment.

As a result of the Agency Worker Regulations 2010 the following information must also be given to the representatives:

- the number of agency workers working under the supervision and direction of the employer;
- which parts of the organisation the agency workers are engaged in;
- the type of work that the agency workers do.

A meaningful period of consultation cannot start until the employees (or employee representatives) have been supplied with all the required information regarding the redundancy. In *Green and Son (Castings) Ltd and others v ASTMS and AUEW* (1983) IRLR 135, a redundancy was announced but details of the proposed selection methods were given to the trade unions only eight days before the dismissals took effect. In this case it was ruled that there was insufficient time for meaningful consultation to take place regarding the selection criteria.

If the employer fails to consult, the dismissal will not be automatically unfair, although that is a possible conclusion. However, a protective award will be made when the appropriate length of consultation has not been observed. The protective award is the wages that the employee would have earned during the consultation period, if that period of consultation had taken place.

- *Shanahan Engineering v Unite the Union* (2010) UKEAT/0411/09
  Shanahan Engineering was working as a sub-contractor in the construction industry. The main contractor ordered Shanahan Engineering to change the work schedules with immediate effect and the result was a downturn in work for Shanahan, leading to inevitable redundancies. Due to the immediacy, Shanahan Engineering did not enter into the required 30-day period of consultation, but made the workers redundant with immediate effect. It argued that the specific situation made it impractical to consult for the full period.

  The EAT found that Shanahan Engineering could have consulted for a few days and it was not correct to ignore all consultation requirements. However, it found that it was not appropriate to award a full protective award.

Another question to be determined is how the total number of employees should be calculated when deciding on the length of consultation:

- *USDAW & Wilson v Woolworths & Ors* (2015) Case C-182/13
  In 2008 Woolworths went into administration. Some of the stores had fewer than 100 employees, and hence the consultation at those stores was for the shorter length of time (at the time of these redundancies the consultation period for 100+ redundancies was 90 days, so quite a significant period of time). USDAW, the trade union, argued that Woolworths should be seen as one establishment, rather than each store being seen as a separate establishment, and therefore all employees should have benefitted from the longer consultation. This issue was referred to the Court of Justice of the European Union.

  The Court of Justice has said that there is no requirement under the EU Directive to add all the redundancies together if they are being made across more than one location, but neither does the directive say that each location should be treated separately. Hence, the ruling is that individual countries within the EU have to determine the approach for themselves. However, it has recommended that redundancies should be determined with reference to the 'local employment unit'. This suggests that each location could be treated separately, or only added together if the locations are geographically close to each other.

9.4.3 Voluntary redundancy

Many organisations will ask for volunteers for redundancy in order to reduce the number of compulsory redundancies. Sometimes this call will be accompanied by an offer of enhanced redundancy terms, to encourage volunteers.

There is no reason not to do this, but legally there is no obligation to ask for volunteers. It is important to note that volunteers are still counted in the number of redundancies, so when determining the length of consultation they must be included. For example, if there are 15 compulsory redundancies and six volunteers there would be a total of 21 redundancies, and hence the requirement for collective consultation is triggered.

9.4.4 *Selection for redundancy*

Although an employer might have a situation that classifies as a redundancy under the definition we have just considered, it is still possible for the dismissal to be unfair if the selection of the redundant employee(s) is unfair. It is important to emphasise that it is the job that is made redundant. Therefore, if there is more than one person carrying out similar jobs and only some of those jobs are to be made redundant, there must be a fair way of determining who is to be selected for redundancy. The first step is to determine the selection 'pool'. These are the employees who all carry out a similar job and so are all potentially at risk from the redundancy. In some cases this is quite straightforward. For example, assume that a company operating a call centre needs, for economic reasons, to make 10 call-centre operators redundant. The call centre has 50 call-centre operators who all do broadly similar work. The call centre has no other operations.

In this case the selection of 10 redundant employees must be made from the 50 call-centre operators. However, consider the example of another call centre that handles three separate contracts. One is for a car-breakdown company, one is for a home-shopping company and one is for a tourism-information company. The home-shopping company's business has reduced and there is therefore a need to make five employees redundant. Should the selection be made from only those call-centre operators working on the home-shopping company? Would your decision change if you were told that the employees working on each contract do move around when necessary to cover absence? The general rule gleaned from case law is that the employer should err on the side of including employees in a pool:

- *Bristow and Roberts v Pinewood Studios Ltd* (1982) EAT 600/81–601/81
  Bristow and Roberts were two of 14 drivers employed by Pinewood. The drivers were employed in four different sections of the business. Bristow and Roberts were employed in the commercial section, along with two other drivers. Pinewood announced the need to make two drivers redundant and, following consultation with the trade union, it was agreed that the selection would be made solely from the commercial section. As a result Bristow and Roberts were selected for redundancy. The EAT ruled that the redundancy had been an unfair dismissal because no good reason had been given for the restriction of the selection pool.

Having determined the correct selection pool, the method of selection must then be agreed. The process of selection must be fair and must be as objective as possible. In the past the most common method of selection has been last in, first out (LIFO). It is often preferred because it is a clearly objective method of making selection. However, the courts have increasingly been unhappy with LIFO as the only method of selection. In addition, it is likely to be indirect age discrimination because young people cannot have longer periods of service.

The approach of LIFO was challenged in the case of:

- *Rolls-Royce v Unite the Union* (2009) IRLR 576
  Rolls-Royce had a collective agreement with Unite, relating to redundancy. This set out a matrix of selection criteria that would be used to select employees for redundancy; one of the several criteria in this matrix was length of service. Unite

the Union wanted length of service to remain as one of the criteria, but Rolls-Royce argued that it should be removed as it was indirect age discrimination.

Unite argued that the use of length of service was potentially discriminatory, but that it was justified as a 'proportionate means of achieving a legitimate business aim'. The High Court, supported on appeal by the Court of Appeal, accepted that the criterion was justified. It agreed that there was a legitimate business aim – namely the advancement of an employment policy that achieved a peaceful process of redundancy selection. They also noted that the criterion rewarded loyalty and experience, and avoided putting older people into the labour market at a difficult time (during a recession) when they would be particularly vulnerable. However, it is important to note that length of service was just one of many criteria – and not the only means of selection.

However, in looking more widely than length of service as a selection tool, the employer must choose appropriate criteria. Guidelines for this were laid down in:

- *Williams v Compair Maxam* (1982) IRLR 83
  In this case employees were selected for redundancy by the three departmental managers listing those employees they felt should be retained for the best long-term viability of their departments and the company. The employer justified this approach because the reasons for the redundancy were that the business was struggling and long-term viability was a real issue.

  However, the EAT found that the selection criteria were completely subjective. There had been no attempt to agree objective criteria with the trade union representatives and the selection was therefore unfair. In making the ruling on this case a number of points were made that should be followed to ensure a fair redundancy:
  - As much warning as possible should be given of any impending redundancies.
  - Consultation must take place over the selection criteria, with a view to agreeing those criteria.
  - The criteria chosen must be able to be checked objectively (eg against attendance records or records of performance).
  - The criteria must be applied fairly in carrying out the selection.
  - If possible, alternative employment must be offered in preference to making an employee redundant.
  - Any selection that is carried out must be completed by assessors who know all the employees in the selection pool and are able to assess each of the criteria correctly.

This last point is important: there must be some consistency in the selection process and it is preferable that there are at least two assessors who know all the employees. In reality, this might not always be possible. However, an organisation must do everything that it can to make the selection as fair and objective as possible:

- *Dabson v David Cover and Sons Ltd* (2011) UKEAT/0374/10
  Dabson worked as a transport manager, with Taylor operating as the depot manager. Taylor and Dabson did not get on well. A redundancy situation arose. It was decided that the roles of depot manager, transport manager and transport assistant would be reduced to two roles of transport manager and transport administrator.

After the initial selection Taylor was appointed as transport manager. He then scored the other two employees for the post of transport administrator. Dabson scored the lower mark and hence he was made redundant. He complained that his marks were low due to past disputes between him and Taylor, and hence a director of the firm carried out a moderation process. This did result in Dabson's marks being increased, but they were still the lowest and hence he made redundant. He took a claim of unfair dismissal. The dismissal was found to be fair because there was no evidence of improper assessment and the organisation had put in place a moderation process.

It is also important to ensure that the selection is applied fairly with the avoidance of discrimination. However, in the case of *De Belin v Eversheds* (2011) the efforts to avoid discrimination against a woman on maternity leave went too far, resulting in discrimination against the man in the selection pool:

- *De Belin v Eversheds* (2011) UKEAT/0352/10
  There were two employees in the selection pool – De Belin, a 45-year-old male, and a 40-year-old female who was on maternity leave. One was to be selected for redundancy using a matrix that assessed a range of abilities including financial performance, discipline history and absence records. One of the factors was the ability to swiftly secure 'lock up' payments from clients. The female employee was absent on maternity leave during the period that was assessed for this criteria and hence she was given a maximum notional score against this criteria.
  De Belin was selected for redundancy, having scored half a point less than the female lawyer. He later discovered that she had been given a maximum score

---

 Explore further

Consider the impact of discrimination legislation on redundancy selection criteria. Think broadly about the type of criteria that an employer might want to use. Consider whether there are any circumstances in which indirect discrimination might possibly occur. How can the need to make a fair selection be balanced with the requirements of this legislation?

---

for the 'lock up' payments element, as a notional score because she was on maternity leave. He took a claim of sex discrimination. De Belin won his case. The selection process had favoured the woman rather than ensuring fairness.

There have been various challenges relating to the right to see a selection assessment that has been made. The ruling in *British Aerospace v Green and others* (1995) is of relevance here:

- *British Aerospace v Green and others* (1995) IRLR 433
  British Aerospace announced the need to make 530 of its 7,000 employees redundant. They used agreed selection criteria in identifying the employees to be made redundant; 235 of the employees made redundant claimed unfair dismissal. In preparing for their claims at the Employment Tribunal the employees asked for sight of their own assessments (which were provided)

and the assessments of those employees who had not been made redundant – so the reason for selecting the redundant employees could be examined. This disclosure was refused.

There are occasions, however, when a ruling has been made that such assessments should be revealed for specific reasons:

- *Eaton Ltd v King and others* (1996) EAT 1353/96 – because the employer was unable to explain how the selection criteria had been applied.
- *British Sugar plc v Kirker* (1998) IRLR 624 – because the employee alleged that a disability had been taken into account when making the assessment and it was important to see how the criteria had been applied to employees who were not disabled.
- *Pinewood Repro Ltd t/a County Print v Page* (2010) UKEAT/0028/10 – because the employee was not able to enter into appropriate consultation due to a lack of information about the scores that he had been given.
- *E-Zec Medical Services Limited v Gregory* (2009) EAT/0192/08 – because the selection criteria were not explained sufficiently, they were too subjective and Gregory was only given her total score.

It should be noted that any employee wanting to see their own assessment criteria would have the right to do so under the Data Protection Act 1998. Similarly, the employer might fall foul of the Act if they allow employees to see assessments made of other employees (see Chapter 11).

In devising selection criteria, it is important to note that no criteria must be directly or indirectly discriminatory (see Chapters 6 and 7).

9.4.5 Dismissal

Once the collective consultation is over and the selection has been completed, there will be individual employees whose jobs have been identified as potentially being redundant. At this stage the employer must consult with the individual employees before making a final decision to dismiss.

The employer must write to the employee informing him/her that she/he is at risk of redundancy and detailing the reasons for this. The employee must then be invited to a meeting to discuss it.

It is very likely that one meeting with the employee will not be sufficient for proper consultation to take place. It will largely depend on the response from the employee and any evidence that the employee might bring. If the employee does raise information that requires exploration, the meeting will have to be adjourned and then reconvened when the necessary investigations have taken place.

When the decision to dismiss has been communicated, the employee has the right to appeal against the decision.

9.4.6 Redundancy compensation

An employee is entitled to a statutory redundancy payment if he/she has been employed for more than two continuous years at the time of the dismissal. The statutory redundancy payment is calculated in the same way as the basic award (see Chapter 8).

If an employee is offered suitable alternative employment and refuses it unjustifiably, he/she loses the entitlement to a redundancy payment.

9.4.7 *Suitable alternative employment*

Section 141 of the Employment Rights Act 1996 provides that: if the employer makes an offer to renew the contract of employment, or to re-engage the redundant employee under a new contract that is to take place when the old contract expires, or within four weeks of the contract expiring:

- if the capacity and place of employment, and the other terms and conditions of employment do not differ from the previous contract, or
- the terms and conditions of the proposed contract differ, but the proposal constitutes an offer of suitable employment, and
- in either case the employee unreasonably refuses that offer, the employee will not be entitled to a redundancy payment.

The employer has the burden of showing that the offer of employment was a suitable alternative and that the refusal of it was unreasonable. In assessing these points, consideration has to be given to the extent that any terms and conditions might vary and the impact that this might have upon the individual employees concerned:

- *Readman v Devon Primary Care Trust* (2013) EWCA Civ 1110
  Readman was identified as being at risk of redundancy. She had worked as a community nurse since 1985, and a hospital-based job was identified as being available. She refused this, as she had not worked in a hospital since 1985 and did not want to return to that job. The Court of Appeal ruled that the Employment Tribunal must consider whether it is reasonable to refuse a job that has significant differences to the work that the employee is currently doing. The case was remitted to consider that point.

- *Bird v Stoke-on-Trent Primary Care Trust* (2011) UKEAT/0074/11
  A physiotherapist refused an offer of alternative employment because it was primarily clinical, and her job was primarily a management position. The EAT did not agree that her refusal was unreasonable, and set out that a tribunal must question whether the job as a whole, including the skills, aptitude and experience required, is suitable for a person. If a job is different it is not necessarily unsuitable, but the more different it is the more difficult it will be to show that refusal is unreasonable.

If the employee accepts an offer of alternative employment, he/she is entitled to a statutory minimum trial period of four weeks. That four-week period can only be extended if retraining is required. If, during that period, the employee finds the job

 Explore further

Acas has written a guide to managing redundancies. Access this at their website at

http://www.acas.org.uk/index.aspx?articleid=747 to explore the process further.

to be unsuitable, he/she can resign and claim a redundancy payment. However, if the employer does not agree that the job is unsuitable, it could refuse to make the payment. If the employer determines that the job is not suitable during, or at the end of, the trial period, the employee is still entitled to a redundancy payment.

9.5 Transfer of undertakings

The Transfer of Undertakings (Protection of Employment) Regulations 1981 (known as TUPE) were introduced as a result of the Acquired Rights Directive 77/187/EEC. These regulations were replaced by the Transfer of Undertakings (Protection of Employment) Regulations 2006, and it is the 2006 regulations that we now refer to.

Further, relatively minor amendments were made by the Collective Redundancies and Transfer of Undertakings (Protection of Employment) (Amendment) Regulations 2014.

The rights protect employees who work in an organisation that is transferred to a new owner. When a transfer of an undertaking takes place, all the contractual rights of an employee are transferred from the old owner to the new owner. This includes continuity of service, contracts of employment, trade union recognition, collective agreements and all rights and obligations contained within the contract of employment.

- *Taylor v Connex South Eastern Ltd* (2000) EAT 1243/99
  In this case the employer sought to change the employee's terms and conditions of employment two years after the transfer had taken place. The proposed change was minor, but the employee refused to agree to it. As a result the employee was dismissed. The EAT ruled that this was an unfair dismissal because it related to the transfer, even though two years had passed since the transfer had taken place.

The case of Taylor illustrates an important point – there can be no dismissal or variation of contractual terms as the result of a transfer unless there is an economic, technical or organisational (ETO) reason for that change. There is no time limit on this, so there is not a time in the future at which changes can be made.

The 2014 regulations tightened up the definition of an ETO reason, stating that:

A variation to the contract of employment can be permissible if the reason for the variation is an economic, technical or organisational (ETO) reason entailing changes in the workforce.

'Changes in the workforce' includes a change to the place where employees are employed by the employer to carry on the business of the employer or to carry out work of a particular kind for the employer.

The law does not specifically define an ETO reason, which means that it is tricky to apply. However, the courts have determined that this must be concerned with the daily running of the business. For example:

- Reasons relating to profitability or performance (economic reason).
- Reasons relating to a change of equipment or production process (technical reason).

- Reasons relating to management or organisation structure (organisational reason).

9.5.1 *Collective agreements*

A collective agreement is an agreement that has been reached following a collective bargaining process between management and a recognised trade union. The 2014 regulations allow for a collective agreement to be altered after one year as long as the overall affect is not less advantageous to the employees concerned.

Note also that the 2014 regulations state that a collective agreement will not transfer if the provisions in the agreement come into effect after the date of the transfer, and the new employer is not party to the negotiations relating to that provision:

- *Alemo-Herron and others v Parkwood Leisure* (2013) UKSC26
  The employees originally worked for Lewisham Council, and were covered by terms of employment that were negotiated by the National Joint Council (NJC) for Local Government Services. There were a number of transfers, and they were eventually moved into the private sector. They argued they should still benefit from annual pay increases that were negotiated with the NJC, but their employer argued that it would not adhere to these increases as it was not involved in the bargaining process. The Court of Justice of the European Union found in favour of the employer, which led to the 2014 changes as explained in section 9.5.

9.5.2 *Pensions*

An occupational pension scheme does not transfer. However, if the transferor has a contractual obligation to pay an amount into a pension scheme of the employee's choice (a non-occupational scheme), that obligation will transfer.

In studying this area we will be referring to the 'transferor' – the old employer who is selling the business – and the 'transferee' – the new employer who is buying the business.

9.5.3 *Definition of a transfer*

The Acquired Rights Directive and the TUPE Regulations 1991 gave unclear definitions of a transfer. It therefore took a great deal of case law to build up a picture of what actually defines a transfer of undertaking.

The 2006 TUPE Regulations aimed to address that confusion by giving clearer definitions. A transfer can be of two kinds (although they are not mutually exclusive). These are:

1 The transfer of an economic entity that retains its identity. For example, a national transport company decides to sell 'South West Buses' to another transport company. The routes run by 'South West Buses' remain the same, the buses transfer to the new company and the customers and suppliers remain the same. This would be the transfer of an economic entity that retained its identity.

2 A change of service provision in which:

 – Activities are currently carried out by one person on his/her own behalf and transfer to another person on the client's behalf. For example, if an organisation carried out its own catering and then decided to offer the catering contract to a catering organisation.

– Activities are currently carried out by one contractor and are then transferred to another contractor. For example, if 123 Catering currently ran the catering within an organisation and the contract was transferred to 456 Catering.

– An organisation decides to carry out activities itself that are currently carried out by a contractor.

For example, 123 Catering currently runs the catering within an organisation, but that organisation decides to employ its own catering staff and run the operation itself. In all the three situations listed here there must, immediately before the transfer, be an organised group of employees whose principal purpose is carrying out the activity – and it is intended that the activities will be carried out by the transferee after the transfer. Note that a service provision change does not apply to one specific event. For example, if our organisation currently ran its own catering but for one major conference decided to use a catering contractor, this would not amount to a transfer.

Cases that relate to the definition of a transfer include:

- *Spijkers v Gebroeders Benedik Abattoir CV and another* (1986) CMLR 296
  In this case a slaughterhouse was sold to a new owner, who kept all the existing employees apart from Spijkers and one other. At the time of the sale the existing owner had ceased trading. The buildings and equipment were transferred to the new owner, but the question posed to the ECJ was whether the transfer of assets was sufficient to determine that a transfer had taken place and whether the fact that the business had ceased trading before the change of ownership precluded a transfer's taking place.

Because a clearly defined economic entity had not been transferred, there was not a transfer of undertaking. In making this judgment the ECJ determined that all the factors of the situation had to be considered in deciding whether a transfer had taken place. These included such things as the transfer of tangible assets (eg buildings and equipment), the similarity of activities before and after the transfer, the period of time for which the business is interrupted (if it is) before and after the transfer, and the value of any intangible assets. An important case that caused considerable confusion in the interpretation of the 1981 regulations was:

- *Süzen v Zehnacker Gebäudereinigung GMBH Krankenhaus Service and Lefarth GMBH* (1997) IRLR 255
  Süzen was a cleaner employed by a contract cleaning company to work in a school. The contract ended and one month later was taken over by a new contractor – Süzen was not offered work with the new contractor. Süzen claimed her employment should have been protected by the Transfer of Undertakings Regulations. The ECJ ruled that in this case a transfer of an entity did not take place. There was no transfer of assets or taking over of the majority of the workforce: all that happened was a transfer of an activity.

This case caused confusion because it seemed to be contrary to judgments in other similar cases. It is noted here because it is a good example of how the 2006 regula-

tions have aided the courts by being specific about the definition of a transfer. The
Süzen case would now be seen as a transfer of an undertaking because there was a
change of service provision in which an activity performed by one contractor was
transferred to another contractor.

Note that a transfer situation can relate to just one employee:

- *Hunt v Storm Communications and others* (2007) ET2702546/06
  Hunt worked as a PR account manager, with around 70 per cent of her time
  being spent on work for a client called Brown Brothers. Brown Brothers moved
  its account from Storm Communications to Wild Card. The Employment
  Tribunal confirmed that this was a transfer situation, and that Hunt should
  transfer to Wild Card.

9.5.4 *Protection by the TUPE regulations*

The regulations give protection to employees of the company being transferred at the
time of the transfer. If employees are unfairly dismissed for a reason relating to the
transfer immediately prior to the transfer, they will still be covered by TUPE.

In some situations it can be unclear who, if anyone, should transfer. It is only
those employees who are specifically assigned to the work that is transferring who
are included:

- *Eddie Stobart v Moreman* (2012) UKEAT 0223/11
  Eddie Stobart provided warehousing and logistics to five clients from the
  Nottinghamshire site. This reduced to two clients, and it was decided to close
  the site. One of the clients decided to move their work to another logistics
  company. At the Nottinghamshire site the employees were organised according
  to their shifts. They were not organised in teams relating to different clients.
  Hence, it could not be argued that there was an 'organised group of employees'
  who worked specifically on the work that was transferring, so the EAT
  concluded that there was no one to transfer.

An employee can refuse to transfer to the new employer. This right does not prejudice the employee's right to resign and claim constructive dismissal. If the employee
objects, the transfer goes ahead and the employee resigns:

- *Capita Health Solutions Ltd v McLean* (2008) IRLR 595
  McLean was a nurse working for the BBC. It was decided that her role would
  be transferred to a contractor and she was not happy with this. She did agree
  to work for the contractor for six weeks after the transfer date. The EAT found
  that, based on the facts, she had been unhappy with the transfer rather than
  objecting to it and, by working for six weeks, she had agreed to it and hence
  her employment had transferred to the employer.

Any dismissal because of a transfer of undertaking will be automatically unfair.
However, unlike other categories of automatically unfair dismissal there is still a
requirement to have qualifying service of one year (two years if the employee started
work on or after 6 April 2012) to take up a claim of unfair dismissal. As already stated, the new employer is not entitled to make any changes to the employee's contract
of employment. The only exception to these rules is where the employer can show

an 'economic, technical or organisational' (ETO) reason for its actions. An example of the use of the ETO defence is found in:

- *Whitehouse v Chas A Blatchford & Sons Ltd* (1999) IRLR 492
  In this case the contract provision of certain hospital supplies was transferred to the new employer. A condition of the contract was that the costs of running the contract would be reduced, in line with the reduction of the hospital's budget. In order to make the required cost savings the new employer had to make an employee redundant. The employee claimed that this redundancy was an unfair dismissal because it resulted from a transfer of the undertaking. The employer successfully argued the ETO defence, showing that the dismissal was essential in order to fulfil the economic requirements of the contract.

9.5.5 Consultation

The regulations specify that consultation must take place with the relevant employee representatives. These representatives may be trade union representatives or elected employee representatives. The following information must be supplied to the representatives:

- that a transfer is to take place;
- the reason for the transfer and when it is expected to take place;
- the implications for the employees (legal, social and economic);
- the measures that the employer expects to take in relation to the employees;
- the measures that the transferee expects to take in relation to the employees.

If the consultation does not take place, or is ruled to be inadequate, the liability for this is jointly the responsibility of the transferee and the transferor. Up to 13 weeks' pay may be awarded as compensation to each of the employees affected by the transfer.

- *Ilab Facilities v Metcalfe and others* (2013) UKEAT/0224/12
  One part of the company was sold, with employees transferring, and the other went into liquidation. The employees working for the part that went into liquidation argued that they should have been part of the consultation because the transfer meant that the rest of the business was not viable. Their argument was unsuccessful – the only requirement is to consult with those who are transferring. Any consultation with the employees who did not transfer would have related to their redundancy, and not the transfer.

Note that the 2014 regulations added in the right for employers of micro-businesses (those with fewer than 10 employees) to consult directly with the employees if there are no representatives.

9.5.6 Employee liability information

The transferor is legally required to provide the transferee with certain information about the employees who are transferring. This must be provided at least 28 days prior to the date of the transfer. The information that must be given includes:

- the names of the employees who will transfer and their ages;
- the details of the employees' statement of employment particulars;
- details of any applicable collective agreements;
- details of any disciplinary action taken against any of the employees in the past two years;
- details of any grievances raised by any of the employees in the past two years;
- details of any legal action against the transferor taken by any of the employees in the past two years.

 Task

Try to find an example of a transfer of an undertaking in an organisation with which you are familiar. Take time to understand why the events that took place were defined as a transfer.

 KEY LEARNING POINTS

1 Wrongful dismissal is when the employer terminates the contract of employment and, in doing so, breaches that contract.

2 A wrongful dismissal can relate to a dismissal that does not follow the correct procedure, a dismissal without appropriate notice being given or the termination of a fixed-term contract before the agreed date.

3 Summary dismissal is where the employee breaches the contract of employment and as a result the contract is terminated without notice.

4 Redundancy is one of the five potentially fair reasons for dismissal.

5 If an employer is proposing to make more than 20 employees redundant, it must engage in collective consultation.

6 The consultation period must be meaningful and employees must be supplied with certain minimum information in writing.

7 Statutory redundancy payments are calculated in the same way as the basic award.

8 An employee who refuses an offer of suitable alternative employment forgoes the right to a redundancy payment.

9 A transfer of undertaking takes place when there is a transfer of an economic entity, or a change of service provision.

10 An employee transfers to a new organisation with no change to his/her contract of employment.

11 Any changes to the contract, or dismissals associated with the transfer, can only be allowed if they can be supported by the 'economic, technical or organisational' (ETO) defence.

Case summaries

- *Levett v Biotrace International Ltd* (1999) IRLR 375 – Levett was dismissed after disciplinary proceedings. The rules of the share option scheme were that the ability to exercise the options was removed if the employee was dismissed on disciplinary grounds. However, Levett argued that the dismissal was in breach of contract and, if he had received the correct notice period, he could have exercised his right during this period. This was upheld.

- *Murray and another v Foyle Meats Ltd* (1999) IRLR 562 – Murray worked in a slaughterhouse where there was a downturn in business. He was made redundant as a result of this downturn and this was held to be a fair dismissal. The Supreme Court ruled that there are two questions that need to be answered to show that there was a redundancy: have the requirements of the employer's business, or the requirements for certain work, diminished? Was the dismissal of the employee due to this?

- *Mugford v Midland Bank plc* (1997) IRLR 208 – The employer was proposing 3,000 redundancies and collective consultation took place. Mugford was selected for redundancy and a number of individual meetings took place with him regarding redeployment – but these discussions came to nothing. Although the individual consultation was not thorough, it was seen as adequate in the circumstances.

- *High Table Ltd v Horst and others* (1998) ICR 409 – The employees worked as waitresses for a contract catering company. They primarily worked at one location, although there was a clause in their contract requiring them to work at other locations if the needs of the business changed. Due to a reduction in the contract at their usual place of work, they were made redundant. They argued that this was unfair dismissal because there should have been regard to the clause requiring mobility. The Court of Appeal ruled that it was of primary importance to look at what happened in the job. Because they usually worked in one location, a downturn in business at that location could result in a fair redundancy dismissal.

- *Inex Home Improvements Ltd v Hodgkins* [2015] UKEAT/0329/14
A group of employees had temporarily been laid off and then their work transferred. They were successful in arguing that they should transfer to the new employer, despite being laid off at the time of the transfer.

- *BT Managed Services Ltd v Edwards & Anor* [2016] EWCA Civ 679
The employee had been absent due to sickness for five years. The section that he had worked in when his absence started had transferred. The EAT ruled that he did not transfer, because it could not be said that he was assigned to the section that was transferring as he had not worked for them for so long. This was appealed to the Court of Appeal, but settled out of court.

- *Middlesborough Borough Council v TGWU and another* [2002] IRLR 332
Consultation about redundancies began on 25 June and on 3 July notices of redundancy were sent to 325 employees. The union successfully argued that there had been a breach of the requirement to consult, because the decision to have redundancies had been made before consultation began.

Examples to work through

1 Peter was dismissed on the grounds of capability, without notice, on 31 August 2017. He joined the company on 1 October 2016 and his contract allowed for a three-month notice period. Following a High Court hearing it has been ruled that he was wrongfully dismissed. What impact does this have on Peter and potential future hearings?

2 There is a redundancy taking place in your organisation and your managing director has drawn up potential criteria for selection. He has asked for your views on whether these are acceptable criteria. If you judge any to be unsatisfactory, give your reasons and suggest alternatives:
   - length of service;
   - willingness to work from other locations within the region;
   - performance;
   - physical strength (because the work requires a lot of manual lifting);
   - absence.

3 Following collective consultation regarding redundancies you have now identified the individuals who are at risk of redundancy. You have written to all of these employees asking them to come to individual meetings to discuss the situation. One employee has written back immediately stating that he does not want to 'waste his time at such a meeting – management won't change their mind'. How should you react?

4 Upon hearing the news of a possible transfer of undertaking, three employees started a petition against it. The transferor was furious about this lack of co-operation and summarily dismissed all of them. They have now taken up claims of unfair dismissal. What will be the liabilities of both the transferee and the transferor in this situation?

 Case study 9.1

You are the HR manager in a manufacturing organisation and you have just returned to work after a two-week holiday. You find four e-mails in your inbox that seem to need immediate attention. These are the e-mails:

E-mail 1

Hi Gemma, hope that you had a lovely time. Can't wait to see the photos! Whilst you were away Pete and Tom got involved in a fight. Apparently Pete was teasing Tom because he has started going out with Tom's ex-girlfriend. They only split up two weeks ago, so Tom was still a bit upset about the whole thing. It seems that Pete was actually seeing the girlfriend before the split as well. Anyway, to cut a long story short, it ended in a fight in the factory and I suspended them both. They are coming in to a disciplinary hearing later today. I am going to dismiss Tom because he started the fight, but just give Pete a final written warning because he reacted in self-defence. Is that okay?

(continued)

(Continued)

E-mail 2

Hi Gemma, we missed you whilst you were away! Steve, one of our drivers, has been banned from driving for 12 months. It was a drink-driving offence, which occurred in his own vehicle out of working hours. I have dismissed him. I know that all the drivers also work in the warehouse, etc etc, but I do think we have to make a stand against drink driving. Just thought I would let you know.

E-mail 3

Gemma – you must never go on holiday again! I missed you so much. We had yet more complaints about Ann, the receptionist, so I decided to make her redundant. I have given her a redundancy letter and she is now on garden leave. In the meantime, I have advertised for a receptionist/secretary in the local paper. I thought that would be okay as it is a different job from receptionist. Hope you are okay with that.

E-mail 4

Hi Gemma, I bet you have got a fantastic tan! Whilst you were away Katerina made more errors (she is the one we gave a written warning to, the day before you went away). So, I have dismissed her on the grounds of capability. Just thought I would let you know so that you can update the records.

Explain any concerns that you have about each situation and how you would respond to each e-mail.

10
Trade union legislation

CHAPTER OBJECTIVES

The objectives of this chapter are:

- to define and describe a trade union;
- to explain the role of the Certification Officer and the Central Arbitration Committee;
- to outline the legislation relating to the recognition and derecognition of a trade union;
- to analyse the legislation relating to collective bargaining;
- to explain the legislation relating to industrial action;
- to analyse the legislation relating to consultation.

10.1 Trade unions

 Task

Before studying this chapter about trade union legislation, find out if your organisation, or an organisation with which you are familiar, recognises a trade union. Try to understand the reasons behind the recognition or lack of it and the impact it has on the relationships between the employer and employees.

Section 1 of the Trade Union and Labour Relations (Consolidation) Act 1992 (TULRCA) defines a trade union as:

> An organisation consisting wholly or mainly of workers of one or more descriptions and whose principal purposes include the regulation of relations between workers of that description or those descriptions and employers or employee associations.

This definition shows us that the group of people wishing to be defined as a trade union must be workers who are concerned with relations with employers. This was demonstrated in the case of:

- *Midland Cold Storage v Turner* (1972) ICR 230
  In this case the employees took industrial action against the employer, instructed by the Joint Shop Stewards Committee (JSSC – the employee representative body within the organisation). The company tried to sue the JSSC because of its actions in threatening drivers who attempted to cross picket lines set up to deter anyone from working during the industrial action. Section 10 of TULRCA allows for a trade union to be sued. The courts held that the JSSC was not a trade union – rather it was a pressure group, because it was not primarily concerned with the relationships between workers and employers – and so it could not be sued.

A list of trade unions is kept by the Certification Officer. The post of Certification Officer was established under Section 7 of the Employment Protection Act 1975. The Certification Officer (https://www.gov.uk/government/organisations/certificationofficer) is an independent statutory authority appointed by the President of the Board of Trade.

A trade union can be included on this list by paying the appropriate fee and submitting a copy of its rules, officers, address and the name under which it is known. The list of trade unions is available for public inspection. If a trade union wants to apply for a certificate of independence, it must be on this list held by the Certification Officer.

There are clear advantages to a trade union in receiving a certificate of independence. If it is successful, its members can:

- appoint safety representatives (see Chapter 12);
- receive information for bargaining purposes (see section 10.2);
- be consulted in the situation of redundancies and transfers of undertakings (see Chapter 9);
- take time off for trade union activities (see section 10.3).

In addition, its members cannot have action taken against them because of their membership or trade union activities.

The Certification Officer determines whether the trade union is independent or not. In making that decision the Certification Officer must consider the definition of independence given in Section 5 of TULRCA:

- The trade union is not controlled or dominated by an employer or a group of employers.
- The trade union cannot be interfered with by an employer or group as a result of the giving of financial or material support or by any other means that could tend towards control.

The process of determining whether a trade union is truly independent was laid down by the EAT in the case of *Blue Circle Staff Association v Certification Officer* (1977) ICR 224.

The Blue Circle group of companies formed a staff consultative organisation. Initially it was under the control of the management and received financial support from the company. The organisation wanted to move away from this control and instituted a new set of rules and agreed a negotiating procedure with the management in a bid to achieve this independence. Five months after agreeing the rules it applied to the Certification Officer for a certificate of independence. This was refused on the grounds that there had been no clear move away from the former dependence on the employer.

In giving its judgment the EAT gave some clear guidelines in what issues should be considered when assessing independence. These were:

- Finance – if the organisation is getting any financial help from an employer, it is clearly not independent.

- Other assistance – being given assistance such as free premises from which to operate is likely to rule out independence, although the extent of the support has to be considered.

- Employer interference – if the organisation gets considerable help from the employer, it is unlikely to be independent.

- History – it is quite possible for an organisation to start as dependent and then to grow into independence. However, the recency of this will be relevant. In the case of Blue Circle the dependence was still very recent.

- Rules – is there anything in the rule book of the organisation that allows the employer to interfere or control it? If so, this is likely to contradict independence.

- Single company unions – although it is possible to have an independent trade union within a single company, it is more likely to be interfered with than a trade union that represents workers across a range of organisations.

- Organisation – who is in charge of the group that wants it to be recognised as an independent trade union? If it is the senior management of the employer, it is likely to have more interference.

- Attitude – is there a record of a robust attitude to negotiation, giving a sign of genuine independence?

10.2 Recognition and derecognition

Recognition of a trade union means that the employer is required to negotiate with the trade union on matters covered by collective bargaining such as redundancies or pay negotiations. It is possible for an employer to agree to negotiate on a limited range of issues (maybe just disciplinary and grievance matters). There are four routes to recognition:

- voluntary – when the agreement is made voluntarily between the employer and the trade union;

- semi-voluntary – when the trade union makes a formal approach to the employer in writing, which the employer then agrees to;
- automatic recognition;
- recognition by ballot.

The last two routes can be a result of the statutory recognition procedure. This applies only when the employer has at least 21 employees (although the employees potentially represented by the trade union can be of a smaller number). For the statutory recognition procedure to be invoked, the trade union making the request must have a certificate of independence.

The statutory recognition process is as follows:

The trade union seeking recognition makes a written request to the employer for recognition. This must identify the trade union and the bargaining unit. The bargaining unit is the group of workers that the trade union is seeking to represent. This might be all employees or it could be a specific group within the organisation. If the employer and the trade union cannot agree on the definition of the bargaining group, the Central Arbitration Committee (CAC) will decide. The CAC can only become involved in the discussions if there are at least 10 per cent of trade union members in the proposed unit and the majority of workers in the unit are likely to favour recognition. The CAC is an independent body that has statutory powers, the main one being the adjudication on decisions relating to recognition or derecognition of trade unions.

 Explore further

In considering the important issue of independence, students should examine the status of a range of trade unions. Start by looking at some of the larger and well-known trade unions and understand why they are clearly independent (eg Unite, USDAW, Unison). Then look at some smaller trade unions – maybe those that are specifically focused on an industry. Do these have a certificate of independence? Why/why not? Information about this can be found on the Certification Officer website.

The Employment Relations Act 2004 determined the process that must be followed if the employer and trade union have been unable to agree on an appropriate bargaining unit. At this stage the CAC becomes involved and must start by considering the bargaining unit that has been proposed by the trade union. If the CAC does not consider that this bargaining unit is appropriate, it must make an alternative proposal taking account of the need for the unit to work within the current management and bargaining arrangements. The CAC must try to avoid small, fragmented bargaining units within an organisation.

Once the bargaining unit has been decided, the next question is whether the trade union should be recognised as representing the workers. If the CAC is satisfied that at least 50 per cent of the workers in the unit are union members, the CAC will issue a declaration that the trade union is recognised for the purpose of collective bargaining. This is the route of automatic recognition.

However, the CAC can decide to proceed with the route of a ballot if one of three qualifying conditions is fulfilled. These are:

- The CAC determines that a ballot is the best way of proceeding for the purpose of good employee relations.
- A significant number of the members of the trade union within the bargaining unit tell the CAC that they do not want the trade union to carry out collective bargaining on their behalf.
- The CAC has evidence that leads to doubts that a significant number of trade union members do want the union to represent them.

In addition, if fewer than 50 per cent of the workers are union members, a ballot of the workers in the bargaining unit will be held.

If the CAC decides to proceed with a ballot, it will appoint an independent person to carry it out. The ballot must take place within 20 days of the appointment, unless there are good reasons for an extension. If the result of the ballot is such that: 1) a majority of those who voted supported recognition; and 2) at least 40 per cent of the workers within the bargaining unit supported recognition, the CAC will issue a declaration that the union is recognised.

- *Amicus and Solent & Pratt* (2002) TUR 1/168
  Union membership amounted to 68 per cent, but the employers wanted a ballot due to concerns about union recognition that had been expressed by one worker (who stated that many of his colleagues felt similarly). There was also concern about some level of misrepresentation of the company's position on a range of issues. The CAC ruled that a ballot was not in the best interests of employee relations because of the high level of union membership.

- *R v Central Arbitration Committee* (2006) IRLR53
  The National Union of Journalists (NUJ) approached the employer seeking recognition. A significant number of employees were NUJ members. At the same time the British Association of Journalists (BAJ) sought recognition, even though they only had one member working in the bargaining unit – their request was accepted. The NUJ was then told that they could not proceed with their request for recognition, because another agreement was already in place.

Once the declaration of recognition has been given, the two parties have 30 days to agree a process for conducting collective bargaining. They can agree an extension to this period of time if required. If the two parties are unable to reach an agreement, the CAC may be asked to assist. The CAC has 20 days in which to help the parties reach agreement, although this period of time may be extended by agreement. If the parties are unable to reach agreement, the CAC will specify the method of collective bargaining that is to be used. Once an agreement is reached, it is a legally enforceable contract.

If there are significant changes to the original bargaining unit, either party may apply to the CAC asking for a decision on the appropriate bargaining unit. If the CAC accepts that the bargaining unit has changed, it can issue a declaration ending the current bargaining arrangements or making a declaration on a more appropriate bargaining unit. An application for derecognition of the trade union can only be made after a minimum of three years after the declaration of recognition. The application can only be made if:

- the size of the workforce is now less than 21;
- there is no longer majority support for the collective bargaining arrangements;
- the original declaration was made on the basis of 50 per cent union membership and the rate of membership has now fallen below this level.

 Explore further

Students who want to know more about the work of the CAC and recent judgments it has made should look at its website: https://www.gov.uk/ government/organisations/central-arbitration-committee

10.3 Time off for trade union duties

Employers must allow a reasonable amount of paid time off during working hours for official representatives of independent trade unions that they recognise. The allowed time should be for the purpose of:

- carrying out duties relating to negotiations with the employer;
- carrying out duties connected with their role (specifically listed in section 178(2) of TULRCA) and duties that the employer has agreed they may carry out – the most likely examples are representing their members at disciplinary and grievance hearings;
- receiving information from the employer;
- undergoing training relevant to their trade union duties, which is approved by their trade union or the TUC (Trades Union Congress).

A trade union representative is not required to have a minimum length of service before these entitlements apply.

- *Edwards and another v Encirc Ltd* (2015) UKEAT/0367/14
Edwards worked on the night shift, and was also a trade union representative. He was required to attend meetings with his employer, as a trade union representative, during the day. He argued that he was not getting the rest periods as set out in the Working Time Regulations 1998 when he was at meetings during the day and then working during the night. The EAT agreed that attendance at the union meetings counted as working time. Although Edwards was not carrying out his contractual duties at these meetings he was required to be present by his employer.

10.4 Collective bargaining: disclosure of information

As we saw in section 10.2, a recognised trade union negotiates with the employer on issues covered by collective bargaining. Examples of such issues are terms and conditions of employment, disciplinary matters and grievances. Sections 181–85 of TULRCA give the regulations relating to information that the employer is required to disclose in order for the bargaining process to proceed effectively.

Information should be disclosed that:

- is information without which the union would be impeded to a material degree in carrying out collective bargaining with the employer;
- it would be good industrial relations practice to disclose.

Clearly, there could be a range of interpretations of these two definitions. The Code of Practice produced by Acas (Disclosure of Information by Trade Unions for Collective Bargaining Purposes) gives useful additional guidance. Some important guidelines to consider are:

- Any information that is requested must be relevant to the issue being addressed through the collective bargaining.
- The information must be of importance to the negotiations.
- The level at which the negotiations are taking place must be considered.
- The relevance of the type and size of the organisation must be taken into account.

 Task

Students are recommended to read the Acas Code of Practice to gain a fuller outline of the disclosure process. This can be accessed from the Acas website: www.acas.org.uk

---

The need for the requested information to relate to the matters being discussed in the collective bargaining is illustrated in the case of:

- *R v Central Arbitration Committee ex parte BTP Tioxide Ltd* (1981) IRLR 60
  In this case BTP Tioxide entered into a limited bargaining agreement with the trade union ASTMS. ASTMS thereafter asked the employer to disclose information regarding a job evaluation process that was not part of the area covered by the bargaining agreement. BTP Tioxide refused to disclose the information and ASTMS took a complaint to the CAC. The CAC ordered BTP Tioxide to disclose the information and they appealed to the High Court. The appeal was upheld – the High Court stated that the CAC had been misdirected because the information did not relate to the representational function of the trade union.

There are certain classifications of information that the employer is not required to disclose. These include:

- information that might affect national security;
- information that can only be disclosed by contravening other legislation (maybe relating to data protection – see Chapter 11);
- information that has been given to the employer in confidence;
- information relating specifically to an individual, unless he/she gives consent;
- information that could significantly damage the employer's undertaking;
- information obtained by the employer for the purpose of defending or bringing legal proceedings.

Any information that is disclosed by the employer can be used only for the purposes of collective bargaining. If the trade union considers that the employer is failing to comply with the requirement to disclose information, it can make a complaint to the CAC. If the CAC considers the complaint can be resolved by conciliation, it must refer the case to Acas. If the case is not referred to Acas, or if any conciliation is unsuccessful, the CAC must hear the complaint.

If the complaint is upheld, the CAC can require the employer to release the information, specifying a period in which the disclosure must be made.

10.5 Industrial conflict

Within the law there is a right to organise strikes and other industrial action. This right is supported by giving statutory immunity from liability at common law for civil wrongs or torts, provided that certain conditions are met. Whenever workers strike or take some other form of industrial action, they are acting in breach of their contract of employment. So when a trade union calls for organised industrial action, it is inducing its members to take action in breach of their contracts.

Under common law it is unlawful to induce people to act in breach of a contract and so trade union officials would face legal action each time they called for strike action if there were not special immunities granted. The immunity from legal action only applies to actions that are in preparation for, or in the activities of, a trade dispute. The immunities relate to:

- inducing a breach of contract;
- intimidation;
- conspiracy;
- interference with a business by unlawful means;
- inducing a breach of a statutory duty.

A trade union's immunity from any legal action only applies to actions that are in contemplation or furtherance of a trade dispute. This immunity is known as the 'golden formula'. To understand the immunity in more detail we will look at the first three of those listed because they are most commonly encountered.

10.5.1 *Inducing a breach of contract*

Direct inducement is when pressure is put on a person to break a contract. A tort (wrong) is committed if the person putting the pressure on knows that the result of the pressure will be a breach of the contract.

Indirect inducement is where pressure is put on a person to do an unlawful act to another body, which then results in that other body breaching a contract. Section 219 of TULRCA gives immunity from any legal action in relation to the tort of inducing a breach of contract, presuming that the inducement relates to the contemplation of furtherance of a trade dispute.

The issue of inducement is illustrated in:

- *Timeplan Education Group Ltd v National Union of Teachers* (1997) IRLR 457
  In this case Timeplan (a recruitment agency for teachers) had agreed to place a series of advertisements in a magazine run by a teachers' union in New Zealand (NZEI). However, the National Union of Teachers (NUT) was in dispute with Timeplan at this time, regarding terms and conditions of the teachers that it supplied. Because the NZEI was a sister organisation of the NUT, the NUT contacted it to inform it of the ongoing dispute with Timeplan and to request that the advertisements cease. After some correspondence, NZEI agreed to withdraw the advertisements. Timeplan then took action against the NUT, claiming that it had unlawfully interfered with the contract between Timeplan and NZEI.

The Court of Appeal held that the NUT had not been aware of any contract that existed between NZEI and Timeplan and so could not be found guilty of persuading, procuring or inducing the NZEI to breach a contract. The NUT had therefore not committed the tort of inducement to breach a contract.

10.5.2 *Intimidation*

This tort is committed when a person is threatened. For example, Fred is convicted of stealing the funds of the local football club. He is also an employee at Bloggs Ltd. A number of the employees at Bloggs Ltd are also members of the football club. They are no longer prepared to work with Fred, and their trade union representative tells the management of Bloggs Ltd that the employees will take industrial action unless Fred is dismissed. If such a threat is made in contemplation or furtherance of a trade dispute, section 219 of TULRCA gives immunity from any legal action.

10.5.3 *Conspiracy*

This occurs when two or more people combine to damage the employer by unlawful means (for example, gathering together to take industrial action to protect jobs). Clearly, any industrial action is likely to damage the employer.

Section 219 of TULRCA gives immunity if the action is taken in contemplation or furtherance of a trade dispute, unless the act would be subject to legal action if it had been carried out by one person (eg criminal action).

If a trade union is involved in action without the support of a ballot, unlawful picketing, secondary action or action to enforce union membership, it forfeits statutory immunity. Although there is immunity from these torts, the golden formula does not allow immunity from all torts:

- *Gate Gourmet Ltd v TGWU* (2005) IRLR 881
  The organisation provided catering services at Heathrow Airport and most of the employees were represented by the TGWU. Discussions were taking place over changes to working practices and staff reductions, and mediation talks were due to take place. However, before mediation started, employees staged a sit-in without a ballot; 622 workers were dismissed and it was alleged that picketing at the sites included harassment and intimidation of remaining employees. An interim injunction was granted due to the unlawful activity. The TGWU had not repudiated the unlawful activities and hence the injunction could be directed at the union.

 Task

In understanding the legislation relating to industrial conflict it would be useful to consider occurrences within recent employment disputes.

Find articles relating to disputes in newspapers, magazines or relevant websites to broaden your understanding of the processes of such disputes.

10.5.4 Lawful industrial action

Sections 226 to 235 of TULRCA 1992, further altered by the Employment Relations Acts of 1991 and 2004 and the Trade Union Act 2016, explain the process that must take place for any industrial action to be lawful.

At least seven days before any ballot is held, the trade unions must inform the employers (in writing) of all employees involved in the ballot. They must tell the employers that a ballot is to be held, when the ballot will take place and give the employer information that the trade union holds that will help the employer to make plans and bring information to the attention of those employees who are to be balloted. This requirement does not mean that the trade union must supply the names of all those who are to be involved in the ballot, but the numbers, categories of employees and workplaces are to be disclosed. If the trade union intends to organise industrial action at more than one place of work, it must carry out separate ballots at each of those places of work. An independent scrutineer must be appointed to oversee the ballot process and the counting of the votes. It has been shown that a trade union is not deprived of its immunity from the tort of inducing a breach of contract if additional members join the trade union after the ballot has taken place.

- *London Underground v National Union of Rail, Maritime and Transport Workers* (1995) IRLR 636
  The National Union of Rail, Maritime and Transport Workers (RMT) held a ballot of members, receiving a clear majority in favour of strike action (over a number of one- and two-day periods). After the ballot a further 20 members joined the trade union, which London Underground was prepared to accept.

However, around one month later, notice was given of further industrial action and this time a further 672 new members had joined the RMT. London Underground claimed that the action could no longer be supported by the original ballot and a further ballot was required. However, the RMT argued that the original ballot still held because a clear majority had voted for industrial action.

The Court of Appeal ruled that the industrial action is supported by the view of the majority of those who are eligible to vote in a ballot and that this ballot was not rendered invalid if new members joined the trade union, because the ballot is still relevant to the dispute in question. The industrial action was therefore still lawful and the RMT still had immunity from the tort of inducing breach of contract.

All those who are entitled to vote must be given a reasonable opportunity to vote. This includes giving the opportunity for a postal vote when it is appropriate. The voting paper must clearly state the name of the independent scrutineer, the address to which the ballot paper is to be returned (assuming there is the option of a postal vote) and the date by which it must be returned. It must be marked with a number that is one of a series of consecutive numbering, must allow the voter to clearly indicate a 'yes' or 'no' response to the willingness to participate in strike action and identify the person authorised to call industrial action.

- *Connex South Eastern Ltd v National Union of Rail, Maritime and Transport Workers* (1998) IRLR 249

  The issue of the definition of a strike was addressed. The members of the RMT were balloted for industrial action that was to include an overtime ban and refusal to work on rest days. On the ballot paper they were asked to vote 'yes' or 'no' for strike action, with no mention of action short of a strike. Following a majority vote the RMT informed Connex of a subsequent overtime ban and refusal to work on rest days. Connex immediately applied for an injunction, claiming that such action had not been addressed by the ballot paper.

  The Court of Appeal refused the injunction. It agreed that the definition of a strike used by the RMT in this situation was not the usual definition. However, 'strike' is defined in TULRCA 1992 as any concerted stoppage of work. Clearly, the proposed action of the RMT fell into this definition and thus lawful industrial action was being proposed.

The ballot paper must also contain a clear statement as follows:

> If you take part in a strike or other industrial action, you may be in breach of your contract of employment. However, if you are dismissed for taking part in a strike or other industrial action that is called officially and is otherwise lawful, the dismissal will be unfair if it takes place fewer than twelve weeks after you started taking part in the action, and depending on the circumstances may be unfair if it takes place later.

The ballot paper must also include:

- a summary of the issue that has led to the proposed industrial action;
- if the proposed action is short of a strike, the proposed action;
- when it is planned that any action will take place.

For a ballot to be valid at least 50 per cent of those who are entitled to vote must vote, and the majority of those who vote must be in favour of taking action.

In essential public services (defined as health services, education of those aged under 17 years, fire service, transport services, border security, and decommissioning of nuclear installations and management of radioactive waste and spent fuel) at least 50 per cent of those entitled to vote must do so, and at least 40 per cent must be in favour of taking action. These requirements relating to turnout at a ballot were introduced by the Trade Union Act 2016.

The voting must be secret and the ballot papers must be fairly and accurately counted, and the counting must be overseen by an independent scrutineer. As soon as reasonably possible the trade union must inform all those concerned of the result of the ballot. Those who voted must be told:

- the number of individuals who were entitled to vote;
- the number of votes cast;
- the number who said 'yes';
- the number who said 'no';
- the number of spoiled/invalid papers;
- if the 50 per cent threshold was met;
- if the 40 per cent threshold (in essential public services) is relevant, whether it was met.

If the result is in favour of industrial action, the trade union must give the employer 14 days' notice of the industrial action (if the employer and trade union agree this can be reduced to 7 days). Any industrial action must commence within an agreed period. This is usually four weeks, but could be longer if agreed between the employer and the trade union. If the industrial action does not commence within the agreed period, a new ballot must take place.

A ballot for industrial action has a six-month life. This can be extended to nine months if the trade union and employer agree. Once the ballot has expired there is a requirement to have a further ballot if industrial action is going to continue.

The notice to take industrial action must give the employer sufficient information to make plans and to bring information to the attention of those who are likely to be involved in the action. The trade union must explain whether the industrial action is intended to be continuous or on specific days or at specific times (and explain what days and times those are to be). If the action is to be continuous, the date it will start must be given. If this procedure is not followed in any significant way, the ballot can be declared void.

- *British Airways v Unite the Union* (2010) IRLR 809
  A challenge was made relating to a ballot. The union had balloted its members on industrial action and there was a majority in favour of taking industrial action. Following the ballot the union sent out e-mails, tweets and texts to members informing them that the result was in favour of action. It gave the detail of the number of votes, the number of 'yes' and the number of 'no' votes and the number of spoiled papers on the notice boards, its website and in a newsletter. British Airways argued that this was a breach of procedure, as the detailed information had not been provided to all who had voted, and the

company hence sought an injunction to stop the industrial action from going ahead. The High Court allowed the injunction, but this was overturned by the Court of Appeal. The Court of Appeal ruled that communication via websites and noticeboards was sufficient.

This case followed a challenge against an earlier ballot in 2009. On this occasion the union had included members who had accepted voluntary redundancy from British Airways in its ballot. Although they were in employment at the time of the ballot, it was known that they would have left the organisation by the time that the industrial action would take place. On this occasion the injunction was awarded.

 Explore further

To understand how much industrial action occurs in the UK, and the trends over recent years, access statistics at www.ons.gov.uk

---

10.5.5 *Unlawful industrial action*

If unlawful industrial action is taken (which could be action following a void ballot or action taken without a ballot – known as a 'wildcat strike'), the employer can apply for an injunction to stop any further action being taken.

Given the immediacy of the situation (ie the desire to stop unlawful action that is already occurring), it is usual for an employer to start by trying to obtain an interim injunction. This gives an order for the unlawful action to cease until a particular date. It is hoped that by the given date the matter will have been considered at a full hearing and either the application will have been refused or a permanent injunction will have been granted.

In deciding whether to grant an interim injunction the courts will consider first whether there is a serious issue to address. The courts will then have to consider the balance of convenience – in other words, is the granting of an interim injunction in the interests of both parties (and is there any relevant public interest)? The court also has to consider the likelihood of the trade unions being able to give a defence under the immunities that we examined earlier in this chapter. If it can be shown that a person has suffered loss as a result of unlawful industrial action, he/she can bring an action for damages. Claims are usually brought against trade unions, although they can be brought against individual participants.

In August 2007 the Prison Officers Association (POA) called an unofficial strike over their pay dispute. Without warning, all prison officers took industrial action from 7 am on 29 August. The government went to the High Court to seek an injunction, which would demand that the prison officers returned to work. The injunction was granted, but the prison officers did not return to work immediately. However, after a few hours passed they started to return to work. If they had ignored the court order, they could have faced prison or unlimited fines. In addition, the government (as the employer) could have sued the POA, as outlined below.

The level of damages against a trade union that can be awarded by the court is subject to limits imposed by section 22 of TULRCA. The limits vary according to the size of the union:

- £10,000 if the union has fewer than 5,000 members;
- £50,000 for 5,000–25,000 members;
- £125,000 for 25,000–100,000 members;
- £250,000 for 100,000+ members.

 Task

The somewhat lengthy procedure for ensuring lawful industrial action, introduced by TULRCA 1992, was criticised for weakening the employees' strength in an industrial dispute. Some believe that by the time the balloting process is completed, some of the initial 'passion' has gone out of the situation and employees are less likely to vote in favour of industrial action. Others would argue that this is the very point of the legislation – making sure that any action taken has been thought about, rather than being an emotional reaction to a set of circumstances. Consider these two arguments and evaluate the impact this might have on the employment relationship.

10.6 Picketing

Section 220 of TULRCA 1992 allows for a person who is contemplating or acting to further a trade dispute to attend at or near his/her place of work or (if he/she is a trade union official) at or near the place of work of a member of the trade union he/she is representing for the purpose of peacefully communicating information or peacefully persuading a person to abstain from working.

The Trade Union Act 2016 made a number of changes to the rules relating to picketing. The trade union must appoint a person to supervise the picketing. That supervisor must be an official or other member of the trade union who is familiar with the Code of Practice relating to picketing. The trade union must tell the police the name of the supervisor, how to contact the supervisor and where the picketing will take place. The trade union must give the supervisor a letter that says the picketing is approved by the trade union, and the supervisor must show this letter to the employer or an individual operating on behalf of the supervisor, if asked to do so. The supervisor must be present at the picketing, and must wear something that identifies him/her as the supervisor, and must be readily contactable by both the trade union and the police.

Picketing is therefore not unlawful in itself, although there are situations in which actions taken in relation to picketing may be deemed to be unlawful. It should be noted that mass picketing is likely to be unlawful because it may no longer be picketing for the purposes of 'peaceful persuasion'. This is illustrated in the case of:

- *Thomas v National Union of Mineworkers (South Wales) (1985) IRLR 136*
  This case took place during the miners' strike of 1984–85. When a number of miners started to return to work, although the dispute continued, large groups of pickets assembled at the entrances to the mines. Although there were only six official picket groups, 60 to 70 miners would gather, shouting abuse at those who crossed the picket lines. It was found that this was no longer 'peaceful persuasion' and was also restricting the miners from using the highway to get to work. An injunction was placed on the National Union of Mineworkers (NUM) restricting it to the placing of just six pickets at the mine gates.

There are other civil and criminal offences that could potentially be committed in the process of picketing:

- Civil:
  - Inducing a breach of contract. This could occur if a driver from another organisation is persuaded not to cross a picket line. In this situation the driver is being induced to breach his/her contract of employment.
  - Trespass to the highway. This could occur if the regular passage along the highway is disrupted.
  - Private nuisance. This could be interference with a person's use of nearby land or premises. It could also be action that makes it unpleasant for a person to access premises, such as using foul language or beating on cars as they drive through.

- Criminal:
  - obstruction of the highway;
  - causing a breach of the peace;
  - obstruction of a police officer in the execution of his/her duty;
  - riot, affray, violent disorder;
  - public nuisance;
  - criminal damage to property;
  - harassment.

 Explore further

Students who wish to consider the issue of industrial action in more detail would be well advised to look at any current employment disputes and note what is occurring. Although there are not always high-profile disputes happening, a careful read of any newspaper over a number of days usually uncovers some dispute. Alternatively, read about recent disputes that have been reported in the news.

Read the summaries of the actions taken and the reasons for them. Then apply the relevant legislation. In applying legislation try to understand any limitations that were placed on either the employers or the trade unions in their activities.

It might also be useful to read about threatened industrial action, which is resolved before any action takes place. It is interesting to track the process that takes place in resolving the situations.

10.6.1 Dismissal of employees

The Employment Relations Act 1999 provided that it is unfair to dismiss those involved in strike action for the first eight weeks of any strike. This period was extended to 12 weeks by the Employment Relations Act 2004. After that time the dismissal is fair if the CAC judges that all reasonable action has been taken by the employer to end the strike.

This 12-week period does not include any period of 'lock-out'. Lock-out occurs when an employer closes the place of employment or suspends all work, or refuses to continue to employ the employees because of a dispute. The action is taken with a view to compelling the employees to accept the terms and conditions that are the focus of the dispute. If an employer unreasonably refuses to use conciliation or mediation services, the 12-week period of protection against dismissal can be extended. This was inserted by the Employment Relations Act 2004 with the aim of encouraging employers to resolve disputes.

If an employer dismisses all employees involved in industrial action and then re-engages a selection of those employees within a three-month period, the dismissal of those who are not re-engaged is likely to be unfair.

It is automatically unfair to dismiss an employee because he/she is a member (or proposes to become a member) of an independent trade union, or has taken part (or proposes to take part) in activities of an independent trade union or refuses to join, or proposes to resign from, a trade union.

10.7 Consultation

10.7.1 The Transnational Information and Consultation of Employees Regulations 1999

The European Works Council Directive was implemented in the UK by the Transnational Information and Consultation of Employees Regulations 1999, which came into force on 15 January 2000. The regulations require that a European Works Council (EWC), or an alternative process for consulting and informing employees, is set up for 'community-style undertakings' if a valid request to do so is received. A valid request must include at least 100 employees from at least two member states. A 'community-style undertaking' is defined as an undertaking with at least 1,000 employees within the member states, with at least 150 members in each of at least two of the states.

The purpose of the EWC is for the employees to receive information on, and to be consulted about, matters that concern the company as a whole. These include issues such as business structure, economic and financial situation, mergers, cutbacks, redundancies, production and sales.

There should be a minimum of three members of an EWC and a maximum of 30. The EWC is required to meet at least once every year. The organisation is required to pay the costs of the EWC, which can include costs relating to travel, accommodation, interpretation and any resources required for members to carry out their duties. Members of the EWC are entitled to paid time off for the carrying out of their duties. Any dismissal or detriment relating to membership of an EWC is automatically unfair. There has been general concern that EWCs have little impact on organisations, with the difficulty of representing such a diverse range of employees and issues being seen as one of the major difficulties. The Transnational Information and Consultation of Employees (Amendment) Regulations 2010 were introduced in June 2011 to try to address some of these concerns. These regulations apply to any EWC or information and consultation process set up on or after 5 June 2011. The regulations place new obligations on central management relating to the way that information and consultation take place; tighten the definition of a transnational issue that can be considered by an EWC (hence extending the remit); require EWCs to be adapted after a significant structural change to an organisation to ensure that all employees are represented; and create a new right for members of EWCs to receive appropriate training.

10.7.2 *The Information and Consultation of Employees Regulations 2004*

Clearly, the EWC regulations apply only to multinational companies. The Information and Consultation of Employees Regulations 2004 addresses the need to establish a general framework for the rights to information and consultation of employees in undertakings within the European Community. As with works councils, there is only the requirement to take action if a valid request is made. In this case, to be valid, the request must come from at least 10 per cent of the employees (or at least 15 employees if the workforce comprises fewer than 150 staff, or at least 2,500 employees if it comprises more than 25,000 staff). The regulations apply to all businesses with 50 or more employees. The rights given to employees are to receive information relating to such issues as activities within the organisation, economic position, the development of employment (particularly when this might involve a threat to employment) and any proposed substantial changes in work organisation or contractual relations. The information must be given in sufficient time to allow the employees to prepare for consultation.

Consultation must then be carried out with appropriate timing and content at the relevant level of management. The consultation must involve the employees' representatives having ample opportunity to express their opinions and take place with a view to reaching agreement.

If there are already existing agreements about information-giving and consultation, the employer may hold a ballot to seek the endorsement of the employees for these agreements.

A pre-existing agreement must:

- be in writing;
- cover all employees;
- have been approved by the employees;
- set out how the employer is to give information to employees, and how the employer will seek their views on this information.

- *Stewart v Moray Council* (2006) IRLR 592
  This case centred on the definition of a pre-existing arrangement. Stewart, on behalf of 500 colleagues, submitted a request to Moray Council asking for negotiations to be held on an information and consultation agreement. The

council took the view that it already had a number of existing agreements with employees and so it would hold a ballot for those agreements to be endorsed.

Stewart argued that the agreements had been made with trade union representatives and therefore just covered employees who were trade union members and had not been approved by non-union members. The CAC, later supported by the EAT, held that the agreements did cover all employees and were not restricted to trade union members only. However, it was upheld that the existing agreements did not clearly set out how the council as employer was to give information and to seek views of employees on the information. The agreements in place thus did not meet all the requirements of pre-existing agreements and the council was ordered to negotiate on that point.

- *Lee and others v Cofely Workplace Ltd* (2015) UKEAT/0058/15
This case looked at the definition of a 'valid request'. Twenty-eight employees had asked for their employer to set up an information and consultation body. They worked in a team of 210 employees providing facilities services to the University of London.

However, Cofely (their employer) employed a total of 9,200 employees across 600 sites. They argued that the request was not valid because it should come from a minimum of 10 per cent of the 9,200 employees, not the 210 employees in the local team.

Their argument was successful. The regulations state that at least 10 per cent of the employees in the undertaking must make the request in order for it to be valid. The undertaking is the legal entity employing the individuals – and hence it was the 9,200 employees.

10.7.3 Collective redundancies, health and safety, and transfers of undertaking

It should also be noted that employers have specific requirements to consult with employees (elected employee representatives if there are no trade union representatives in place) in the situations of collective redundancies and transfers of undertaking (see Chapter 9), and health and safety (see Chapter 12).

 KEY LEARNING POINTS

1 A trade union is a group of workers that is concerned with the relationship between the workers and employers.
2 A certificate of independence is issued to a trade union by the Certification Officer.
3 Recognition of a trade union means that the employer and trade union negotiate on issues covered by collective bargaining.
4 There are four routes to recognition – voluntary, semi-voluntary, automatic and by ballot.
5 If the employer and trade union cannot agree on the definition of a bargaining unit, they can ask the Central Arbitration Committee (CAC) for assistance.

6 The CAC is an independent body with statutory powers.

7 An application for derecognition of a trade union can only be made three years or more after the declaration of recognition.

8 A trade union representative is allowed a reasonable period of paid time off work to carry out his/her duties.

9 An employer is required to disclose to the trade union any information without which the trade union would be impeded in the process of collective bargaining or information that should be disclosed in accordance with good employee relations.

10 If a trade union takes lawful industrial action, it has immunity from certain torts, as long as the relevant actions are taken in contemplation or furtherance of a trade dispute.

11 For lawful action to take place a process must be followed that involves notifying the employer of a ballot, holding a ballot and giving notice of any industrial action.

12 If unlawful action takes place, the employer may seek an injunction to halt the action.

13 Picketing is lawful as long as it is done with the aim of 'peaceful persuasion'.

14 Although picketing is lawful, certain actions that might take place during picketing could breach civil or criminal legislation.

15 An organisation that has at least 1,000 employees within the member states of the European Community, and at least 150 employees in each of at least two of the states, is required to establish a European Works Council.

 Case summaries

- *TGWU and Economic Skips Ltd* (2002) TUR 1/121 – The CAC ordered that a ballot be carried out, although 55 per cent of the bargaining unit were union members. The union and the company had carried out their own surveys, which gave greatly differing figures of support for recognition (73 per cent and 10 per cent).

- *UNIFI and Bank Tejarat* (2002) TUR 1/144 – 54 per cent of the bargaining unit were union members. The employer argued that it was inappropriate to proceed with the recognition process because of an impending merger. The CAC ruled that the process could continue and, indeed, no ballot was necessary. If the bargaining unit changed significantly as a result of the merger, there could be an application for a review.

- *R v Central Arbitration Committee* (2005) IRLR641 – A ballot was arranged for trade union recognition, but the numbers in favour fell short by four votes. It was found that four employees had not been given voting papers, so the CAC ordered that the ballot should be rerun. The Court of Appeal ruled that the CAC was right to do this.

(continued)

(Continued)

- *Bone v North Essex Partnership NHS Foundation Trust (No 2)* (2016) IRLR 295 – The employee was a member of Unison, and also of the Workers of England Union (WEU). He was bullied by colleagues who were in Unison, and the employer took informal action. He successfully argued that not taking more serious action amounted to a detriment because the employer was trying to deter him from being involved in the WEU.
- *Post Office v Union of Communication Workers* (1990) IRLR 143 – The Union of Communication Workers balloted its members, asking if they supported 'industrial action up to and including strike action'. They received a majority vote and

strike action followed. After a lull for a publicity campaign, further industrial action took place. However, the Post Office successfully argued that the trade union had not sought a vote on 'action short of strike action' and therefore could not rely on the existing ballot for taking such action. Separate questions must be asked for each type of action.
- *Monk Staff Association v Certification Officer and ASTMS* (1980) IRLR 431 – A staff association applied for a certificate of independence, which was refused. All the officers of the association, and members, were employed by the company and hence it was not seen to be independent.

 ### Examples to work through

1 Your organisation has received an application from a trade union asking for recognition. It claims that 65 per cent of the workforce are asking for trade union recognition. Your managing director does not want to have a unionised workforce and suggests that an agreement be set up under the Information and Consultation of Employees Regulations 2004. What is your response?

2 For several weeks you have been carrying out pay negotiations in your organisation and the negotiations have not been going very well. At the end of a meeting with the trade union representatives this morning, they reported back to their members that they did not think they would succeed in reaching a good settlement. After lunch around 75 per cent of

your employees refused to return to work. They have said they will not return until management agree to their pay claim. What should you do?

3 Over recent years trade union recognition in your organisation has decreased from 76 per cent to 34 per cent. A number of employees have now claimed that the trade union is not relevant in the organisation and so they want to agree a process for information-giving and consultation that is not part of the current union agreement. How should you proceed?

4 You are the HR manager. The employees at your organisation are currently taking strike action. When you drove into work this morning, passing the picket line, your wing mirror was damaged by one of the pickets. What action can you take?

11
Privacy and confidential information

CHAPTER OBJECTIVES

The objectives of this chapter are:

- to outline the provisions of the Human Rights Act that are relevant to employment law;
- to analyse the legislation relating to data protection;
- to understand issues relating to the use of social media and the workplace;
- to outline the main issues relating to inventions, patents and copyright;
- to explain the importance of restraints of trade;
- to explain the relevance of public interest disclosures;
- to outline the requirements imposed by the Access to Medical Reports Act.

11.1 The Human Rights Act 1998

Of the 14 articles within the Human Rights Act (HRA), there are six that have potential relevance to employment law. It is those six articles that we examine in the following sections. The Act, which came into effect in England and Wales on 2 October 2000, incorporates the provisions of the European Convention on Human Rights into UK law. It is important to note that the Human Rights Act applies only to those employed by public bodies – and to private organisations carrying out public functions.

11.1.1 Article 6(1): the right to a fair trial

This article states that everyone is entitled to a fair and public hearing in the determination of civil rights and obligations within a reasonable time by an independent and impartial tribunal established by law. This article is of particular relevance to the Employment Tribunal system. As we noted in Chapter 2, Employment Judges do have the power to 'strike out' cases that have very little chance of success. When this happens, the applicant is not allowed to bring the case before the tribunal and there is the possibility that the claimant could argue that his/her rights under Article 6 have been ignored.

It is also important to note the requirement that the article places to hear any case within a 'reasonable period of time'. This was challenged in the case of:

- *Somjee v United Kingdom* (2002) IRLR 886
  Somjee was a doctor who worked for a hospital in Merseyside. She brought cases against the hospital relating to race discrimination and unfair dismissal. The applications went through a series of hearings and appeals and there were a number of delays in the proceedings. The cases were reasonably complex and the reasons for the delays were varied. Somjee took a complaint to the ECHR relating to the length of time taken to hear the cases. There were three claims she had brought: the first took eight years and nine months to reach a conclusion, the second took seven years and eleven months, and the third took eight years and eight months. The ECHR ruled that there had been unreasonable delays, although they did note that some of the reasons for the delays were the fault of Somjee.

 Explore further

The reasons for the many delays in the *Somjee v United Kingdom* case were complex. Students who wish to understand the requirements of Article 6(1) in more detail are advised to read a full synopsis of the case to obtain further insight.

There is the concern that employers can apply the concept of legitimate business purposes to almost anything – but they still must have regard to data protection, which we examine later in section 11.2.

11.1.2 Article 8: the right to respect for private and family life

The first part of this article determines that everyone has the right to respect for his/her family life, home and correspondence. However, this first part of the article is subject to the provisos included in the second part, which allow for there to be 'interference' with this right when it is necessary for reasons of public safety, national security, the economic well-being of the country, the prevention of crime or disorder, the protection of health or morals, or the protection of the rights and freedom of others.

- *Barbulescu v Romania* (2017) ECHR 61496/08
  An employee was asked to set up a Yahoo Messenger account to be used by customers. There was a strict company rule that no computer, photocopier, fax or other machine should be used for personal purposes. The employee used the Yahoo Messenger account to send a large number of messages to his girlfriend and brother. He was dismissed. He successfully argued that he had suffered a breach of his rights under Article 8, because his personal messages had been accessed by the employer. Although it was a company account he had never been told that any personal messages might be accessed.

The issue of surveillance and monitoring of employees has been debated in some detail in recent years, partly because of the increased ability to carry out sophisticated surveillance.

The use of CCTV (closed-circuit television) is becoming increasingly common. In addition, the use of e-mails and the internet has become widespread and some employers do have concerns about the use that employees might be making of such tools. There has been specific legislation to address these issues. The Regulation of Investigatory Powers Act 2000 made it a civil wrong to intercept communications on private and public systems. Section 3 of this Act does allow for interception if the parties to the communication have consented to it. This emphasises the need for organisations to have clear policies on e-mail and internet use and to make it very clear that the employer reserves the right to monitor such use.

The Telecommunications (Lawful Business Practice) (Interception of Communications) Regulations 2000 nonetheless allowed exceptions for 'legitimate business purposes'. There is considerable breadth to the legitimate business purposes allowed, which include monitoring quality, investigating unauthorised use and ensuring compliance with internal procedures.

An area where this has become of particular importance is the use of social media. If an employee posts something on their personal social media page that criticises the organisation in some way, or potentially brings the organisation into disrepute, what action can the employer take? Some recent cases help us to answer this:

- *Preece v JD Wetherspoons plc* (2011) ET/2104806/10
  In this case a pub manager was dismissed for placing insulting comments about two customers on her Facebook page. This was found to bring the company into disrepute, and was in breach of the company policy on internet usage, which she was aware of. This was found to be a fair dismissal.

- *Smith v Trafford Housing Trust* (2012) EWHC 3221
  Smith posted some comments that were opposed to gay marriage on his Facebook page. His page identified that he worked for the housing trust, and

some of his friends were work colleagues. He was demoted because of his comments, but this was found to be a breach of contract. There was nothing to suggest that he was saying that his views were those of the housing trust, and he was entitled to his personal opinions.

- *Game Retail Ltd v Laws* (2014) UKEAT/0188/14
Laws was a risk investigator with responsibility for 100 stores. He set up a Twitter account, and 65 of the stores followed him. He made a number of rude and abusive posts, and was dismissed for gross misconduct. This was found to be a fair dismissal, because he knew the stores were following him and his posts brought the company into disrepute.

Two cases in this general area are well worth noting as well:

- *Copland v United Kingdom* (2007) ECHR 62617/00
The events in this case took place before the Regulation of Investigatory Powers Act 2000 was enacted – the outcome of the case therefore does not address the application of this Act.
   In this case the European Court of Human Rights ruled that the college at which Copland worked had breached her right to privacy. Over a prolonged period the college monitored her phone calls, e-mails and internet use. The college argued that it merely kept a log of the use and did not actually intercept any communications.
   However, the ECHR ruled that it was a breach of Copland's privacy because she was not informed that any monitoring was taking place. She thus had a reasonable expectation that all her communications were private.

- *Long and others v SP Dataserve Ltd* (2005) ET 103200/05
In this case Long and others were dismissed by the company for sending and receiving an excessive number of personal e-mails. Over three days one employee had received or sent 537 personal e-mails, and another employee had sent or received 745 personal e-mails over six days. There was a company e-mail policy in place, which allowed 'limited and reasonable' internet/e-mail use for personal reasons. However, the organisation argued that the use by these employees fell outside the definition of 'limited and reasonable'.
   The employees successfully argued that the definition of 'limited and reasonable' was not clear and so the dismissal was unfair.

The important message from all these cases is that employers must have a clear internet and e-mail usage policy that is clearly communicated to all employees.

 Task

Find out if your organisation, or an organisation with which you are familiar, has a policy relating to privacy in the workplace. If there is a policy, do you think it adequately addresses all the issues? If there is no policy, what problems might the organisation face in addressing any issues relating to privacy?

Explore further

In the light of the current relevance of the topic, students might find it interesting to explore the issue of privacy relating to e-mails, internet use, etc, in more detail. Explore the cases listed here, as well as others that have been reported.

11.1.3 Article 9: freedom of thought, conscience and religion

This article gives the freedom of thought, conscience and religion, and the freedom to manifest the religion or belief. This freedom is subject to limitations prescribed by law and those limitations necessary for public safety, public order, health or morals, and the protection of the rights and freedom of others.

There is some overlap between the provisions of this article and the legislation relating to discrimination on the grounds of religion or belief that is included within the Equality Act 2010.

- *Eweida and others v UK* (2013) 48420/10
  Four individuals, who were all Christians and had all had their claims of discrimination rejected, joined together to bring a claim under Article 9 of the Human Rights Act 1998. Eweida, a British Airways check-in operative, had been refused permission to wear a cross as an item of jewellery because the company had a no-jewellery rule. Chaplin was a nurse and she had also been refused permission to wear a cross for health and safety reasons – a patient might reach up and grab the chain, hurting him/herself and Chaplin. Ladele was a registrar and had been told she would have to carry out civil partnership ceremonies. MacFarlane was a therapist with Relate and was told he would have to counsel same-sex couples. Eweida was successful in her claim that this breached Article 9 because there was no good reason to refuse her request. The others were unsuccessful – there was a health and safety reason for Chaplin, and the other two were required to provide a public service and could not choose who should receive this service.

11.1.4 Article 10: freedom of expression

This article allows everyone freedom of expression, including the right to hold opinions and to give and receive information relating to these opinions without interference. Again, there are restrictions given in the second part of the article relating to the interests of such things as national security, public safety, the prevention of disorder or crime, and the protection of health, morals and the reputations of others.

The ECHR has determined that freedom of expression can relate to the way the employee dresses – because dress can be a form of expression. However, there may be circumstances in which an employer can show that a dress code at work is reasonable because of the nature of the work. This could include the need to tie back long hair for hygiene reasons. Less clear could be a dress code that the employer justifies on the grounds that the employer's reputation is related to the appearance of the employees.

Freedom of expression can also relate to the employee's interests outside of work. This is shown in the case of:

- *Pay v Lancashire Probation Service* (2003) ICR 1138
  Pay was employed as a probation officer specialising in the treatment of sex offenders.

  His employers became aware that he was involved in an organisation that promoted the sale of items relating to sadomasochism and also that he performed acts in hedonist and fetish clubs. The employers decided to dismiss Pay because they considered that these outside activities were inconsistent with his role as a probation officer, particularly in the light of his work with sex offenders. Pay applied to the Employment Tribunals claiming unfair dismissal and contravention of Articles 8 and 10 of the Human Rights Act.

  It was ruled that the dismissal was fair. In specific relation to Article 10 it was agreed that the continuing employment of Pay, given his outside interests, was not justified in the light of the need to protect the reputation of others – in this case the reputation of the Probation Service.

In considering the case it is important to note the relevance of the nature of Pay's job. If his employment had not involved work with sex offenders, it might well be that any dismissal would have been found to be unfair.

11.1.5 *Article 11: freedom of assembly and association*

This article gives everyone the right to peaceful assembly and association with others and includes the right to form and join trade unions for the protection of one's interests. Again, there are provisos that include potential restrictions on the grounds of national security or public safety interests, the protection of health or morals and the rights and freedoms of others, and the prevention of disorder or crime.

The restrictions that can be imposed on this article are clearly illustrated by the decision in the case of *Government Communications Staff Federation v Certification Officer and the Council of Civil Service Unions* (1992) ICR 163, which was later referred to the ECHR for its judgment.

- In 1984 the rights of employees of the Government Communications Headquarters (GCHQ) to join a trade union were withdrawn. The employees were allowed to join a staff association, which was set up at GCHQ, known as the Government Communications Staff Federation. In 1989 the federation applied for a certificate of independence (as explained in Chapter 10) but was refused because it was not truly independent – the GCHQ director could 'interfere' with its operation, and indeed its existence was subject to the approval of the GCHQ director.

  The UK Government argued that the refusal to allow GCHQ employees to join an independent trade union was justified because the employees were involved with matters of national security. Their rights to freedom of association under Article 11 were therefore restricted by the interests of national security. This case was referred to the ECHR, which ruled in favour of the UK Government.

An interesting question occurs when the rights of different groups, under the Human Rights Act, seem to clash:

- In the case of *ASLEF v United Kingdom* (2007) ECHR 110022/05, the trade union ASLEF expelled a member who was also a member of the British National Party (BNP). It argued that it did not support the values of the BNP and under Article 11 had the freedom of association, which included the freedom to choose who it associated with.

    The ECHR found that the right of ASLEF to choose its members outweighed the right to freedom of expression of the BNP members, and so ASLEF did not have to accept them into membership.

 Explore further

The impact of Article 11 on trade union recognition and activities is potentially wide-ranging. Exploring this matter further the student should consider the impact on:

- the right to picket;
- the unlawfulness of the closed shop;
- the right to strike;
- the refusal to recognise a trade union.

(See Chapter 10 for some relevant case law to start the exploration.)

11.1.6 *Article 14: prohibition of discrimination*

Article 14 specifically relates to discrimination relating to one of the articles within the HRA. It does not, therefore, give protection against discrimination in all circumstance. The areas of discrimination covered in the article are sex, race, colour, language, religion, political or other opinion, national or social origin, association with a national minority, property, birth or other status.

To illustrate the essential relationship between the discrimination and an article within the Human Rights Act, consider this example: if an organisation introduced random drug testing for all employees aged over 50 years, this would be discrimination in contravention of Article 14. This is because the random drug testing relates to Article 8 – the right to privacy – and discrimination on the grounds of age is specifically listed within Article 14.

However, if the organisation introduced the requirement that all employees aged over 50 years who applied for promotion had to give a presentation to the senior management, this would not be in contravention of Article 14 because the issue of giving a presentation does not fall under any article of the Human Rights Act.

 Explore further

Students who wish to explore the issues of the Human Rights Act and the work of the European Court of Human Rights in more detail are advised to start by looking at the ECHR website (www. echr.coe.int). This website gives summaries of recent judgments and advice on further reading.

11.2 The Data Protection Act 2018

Data Protection has been addressed by legislation since 1994. The protection was further enhanced by the Data Protection Act 1998. On 25 May 2018 the General Data Protection Regulation (GDPR) was implemented. This is a European Union Regulation addressing data protection and privacy for all EU citizens. The Data Protection Act 2018 implements the GDPR and also covers other aspects of data protection that are not covered by EU law.

The legislation applies to a wider remit than employment, although we concentrate on employment in this chapter. The legislation applies to any personal data, which is defined as any data that can be used to identify an individual. This includes:

- any information that is processed by equipment operating automatically in response to instructions given for that purpose;

- any information that is recorded with the intention that it should be processed by means of such equipment;

- any information that forms part of an accessible record, but is not covered in the earlier definitions.

It is clear from this definition, therefore, that the Act covers information that is held manually as well as electronically. It could also include information such as an IP address, if a person can be identified this way.

One area where the GDPR has added in much more stringent requirements is consent. For an employer to store or process personal information there must be unambiguous and specific consent. This means that it is not permissible to have a general statement in a contract of employment that the employer would hold data relating to employment, and it is not allowable to have a 'pre-ticked' consent box that an employee has to 'untick' to indicate a lack of consent. Rather, the employee must give specific consent. However, the employer is allowed to store and process data that is needed for the fulfillment of the employment contract or for legitimate interests.

The employer needs to think broadly about the personal data that might be held. For example, an individual might apply to the organisation for a job and might be unsuccessful. It could be standard practice to inform the applicant that the application will be held on file in case a suitable vacancy occurs. The individual would need to give their consent for that to happen, and would have to have the right to ask for their application and any documentation relating to it to be destroyed.

In the same way, an employer will need to have permission to keep documents about an employee once that individual has left the organisation, if the documentation is not needed to fulfil the employment contract or for a legitimate interest. Again, the individual can ask for the documentation relating to them to be destroyed.

Within the DPA 2018 is a list of six data protection principles. The Act requires each data controller (in the case of employment this corresponds to the employer) to abide by these principles in all keeping and processing of personal data. The six principles are:

- All personal data must be processed lawfully and fairly. To achieve this, the processing of the data must be necessary for the reasons already listed or the data subject (the employee) must give permission for the data to be processed. The employee should be made aware of the processing of the data that is to take place. Without this knowledge the employee cannot give informed consent and so the processing is unlikely to be fair.

- The processing of the data must be specified, explicit and legitimate. The Act does allow an employer to list such purposes in a note to employees.

- The personal data must be adequate, relevant and not excessive in relation to the purpose for which it is required.

- The personal data should be accurate and be kept up to date. The employer must keep an accurate record of the information provided by the employee. There should be opportunity for the employee to advise the employer of any changes, but the employer is not necessarily at fault if the information is inaccurate due to the employee's not notifying the employer of changes.

- Personal data should not be kept for longer than is necessary. This is particularly relevant to employees who have left employment. Some information must be kept in case an employee makes a claim against an employer and in case there is a need to supply references. The employer must consider what information to keep – it might not be necessary to keep all information for an extended period of time (and the employer will need consent to keep information, as already noted).

- The personal data must be processed in a secure manner.

The main rights of the data subjects are:

- To have access to personal data. The employee is allowed to ask the employer to inspect all records held about him/her. Prior to the GDPR it was possible to ask the employee to pay a fee for this, but this is now removed. The employer should respond in one month to a request to access personal data. If the request is particularly complicated to address, more time can be requested. A very complex request that would take a long time to address can be refused.

- To correct any data that is inaccurate.

It should be noted that there are additional restrictions relating to the holding and processing of 'sensitive personal data'. This is data relating to such things as racial or ethnic origin, political opinions, religious belief, trade union membership, health, sexuality and committing a criminal offence. Before any such data can be processed, specific consent must be obtained from the employee.

In determining the restrictions placed by the Data Protection Act, the reasons for processing the data must be considered. This is shown in the case of:

- *Blackpool and the Fylde College v National Association of Teachers in Further and Higher Education* (1994) IRLR 227
  In this case the trade union, the National Association of Teachers in Further and Higher Education (NATFHE), had informed the college of the intention of its members to take industrial action. However, the college argued that it did not know the full list of the teachers who were members of NATFHE and the trade union had thus not met its obligations under TULRCA 1992 – see Chapter 10. The college successfully applied for an injunction against the industrial action. NATFHE challenged the injunction, claiming that to disclose the names of its members would contravene the Data Protection Act. NATFHE was unsuccessful in its challenge because although it was trying to

adhere to the Data Protection Act, in doing so its actions had breached the legislation relating to industrial action and ballots. It was noted that the union could ask members to give their permission for their names to be given to the college because this detail was required by law when giving notice of proposed industrial action.

Another example of the correct use of information is illustrated in:

- *Dalgleish v Lothian and Borders Police Board* (1991) IRLR 422
  In this case the local authority asked the employer to provide details of employees' names and addresses to help them trace those who were in arrears with their community charge payments. The employees applied for an injunction stopping the employer from complying with this request. It was ruled that the information held by the employer was for the sole purpose of employment-related issues and was not information that was generally available to the public. The employer therefore had no right to disclose the information to the local authority.

 Task

Find out if your organisation, or an organisation with which you are familiar, has a data protection policy. If there is such a policy, read it and consider whether it meets the requirements of the revised data protection legislation and the GDPR.

 Explore further

Any student who wishes to examine the legislation relating to data protection in more detail, or wants to understand further the impact of the GDPR, is advised to refer to the Information Commissioner's website – www.ico.org.uk

11.3 The Access to Medical Reports Act 1988

This Act covers any medical report that is supplied before employment commences or during employment by a medical practitioner who is or has been responsible for the clinical care of the individual.

The Act thus covers any information sought from an employee's GP because that medical practitioner is responsible for the clinical care of the individual. However, if the employer asks an independent doctor for a report on an employee (for example, if the employee has had long periods of absence due to illness), the report is not covered by this Act unless the doctor is going to be involved in treating the employee in some way. If an employer wants to apply for a medical report that is covered by the Act, the employer must seek the consent of the employee and specifically inform the employee that:

- he/she has the right to refuse consent for the application for the medical report;
- he/she can request access to the medical report before the employer sees the report;
- he/she can request that the report is amended or is allowed to record, in writing, a difference of opinion over any details within the report;
- he/she can refuse consent for the report to be disclosed to the employer.

An employee can be denied access to a medical report if the medical practitioner considers that the disclosure would be likely to:

- cause serious physical or mental harm to the employee;
- reveal information about another individual;
- reveal the intentions of the practitioner in relation to the individual;
- reveal the identity of another person (non-medical) who has supplied information to the medical practitioner.

If the medical practitioner decides to withhold part or all of a report, he/she must inform the employee. The employee then has the right to refuse consent to the report's being disclosed if he/she wishes.

11.4 Patents, inventions and copyright

Section 39 of the Patents Act 1977 provides that an invention made by an employee shall belong to the employer if one of the following conditions is met:

- The invention was made in the course of the employee's normal duties and an invention might reasonably be expected to result.
- The employee had a special obligation to further the interests of the employer's undertaking because of his/her duties and the particular responsibilities arising from those duties.
- Although the invention was not made in the normal course of duties, it was made in the course of duties specifically assigned to the employee so that an invention would be expected to result.

In every other situation the patent will lie with the employee.

The issue of 'normal duties' was examined in the case of *Reiss Engineering v Harris* (1985), which we looked at briefly in Chapter 1:

- *Reiss Engineering v Harris* (1985) IRLR 23
  Harris was manager of a department within a company that sold and assembled valves. It provided an after-sales and advice service for its customers, but it had never designed a valve or a modification to a valve.

Harris was given six months' notice of his impending redundancy. During this time he invented a new valve that overcame some of the problems that existed with valves currently sold by Reiss Engineering. There then was a dispute over who owned the patent to the valve. Reiss Engineering argued that Harris had developed the valve in the course of his 'normal duties' and in addition that he had a special obligation to further the interests of his employer. The patent should therefore belong to them. Harris challenged this.

The High Court ruled that the patent should belong to Harris. Because Reiss Engineering was not involved in any way with the design or modification of valves, it was not correct to claim that Harris had developed the valve in the course of his normal duties.

In addressing the issue of his responsibility the court held that this requirement had to relate to some extent to the employee's status and responsibilities within the organisation. Harris was not employed in a senior role and it was also noted that he was actually under notice of redundancy when he made his invention. On this basis, Harris had no special obligation placed upon him.

Clearly, it can be difficult to determine exactly what might result from an employee's normal duties. However, it is unlikely to be found that an invention belongs to an employer for this reason if the employer does not design and develop similar products to the invention. If it is found that a patent does belong to an employer, the employee can still apply to the Controller of Patents for compensation on the grounds that the invention is of 'outstanding benefit' to the employer. The controller can then consider whether the employee is entitled to a share of the benefits, giving regard to the nature of the employee's duties, the effort and skill involved in making the invention, the effort and skill of any third party, and the significance of any contribution made by the employer towards the invention.

If an employee produces any literary, musical, dramatic or artistic work in the course of employment, the copyright is owned by the employer unless there is any agreement to the contrary (section 11 of the Copyright, Designs and Patents Act 1988).

An employee must not act in such a way that might damage the protection of a patent owned by an employer:

- *Hedgehog Golf Company Ltd v Hauser* (2011) EWHC 689
  Hedgehog was a business involved in the development of a patented device that would allow a golf cart to be used in wet weather. Hedgehog had previously had two directors – Hauser and one other. There had been previous court proceedings between the two directors, which had resulted in certain orders being made against Hauser. As a result he had resigned, leaving the other director as the sole director of the company. Another company brought a claim in the courts that the device developed by Hedgehog infringed a patent that it owned. Allegedly Hauser made threats that if proposals that he had made to Hedgehog were not accepted, he would stop assisting Hedgehog in defending the patent infringement claim and he would also offer his services to the other company's patent attorneys.

  Hedgehog applied to the High Court for a perpetual injunction (an injunction awarded at the end of a trial as part of the final judgment) that would stop Hauser disclosing any confidential information about Hedgehog.

The perpetual injunction was granted, stopping Hauser from disclosing confidential information without the consent of Hedgehog. The High Court found that Hauser's conduct suggested that he intended to damage Hedgehog by revealing information that might damage the business and that he would also be in breach of orders that had been made in previous court proceedings.

11.5 Restrictive covenants

There are situations in which an employer might wish to restrict the activities of an employee. This is normally after the employee has left the employer's employment, but it might refer to the desire to restrict an employee from engaging in certain other work. If the employer wishes to restrain the employee in some way, a restrictive covenant may be put in place within the contract of employment.

However, a restrictive covenant must be reasonable, otherwise it will be deemed to be void. To be reasonable the covenant must be in the interests of both parties and the public. There must be a clearly enforceable interest to protect. This could include the knowledge of trade secrets, particular influence over customers, or situations in which the employee might entice other employees away from the employer after his/her employment has terminated. If a restrictive covenant simply seeks to restrict competition, it will not be deemed to be reasonable.

There are four types of restraint:

- *Non-competition*
  This stops the employee from working in a role that directly competes with the old employer.

- *Non-solicitation*
  This stops the employee from contacting customers to ask them to take their custom to the new employer that the employee is working for.

- *Non-dealing*
  This is stronger than a non-solicitation restraint, because it stops the employee from having any dealings with a former customer. A non-solicitation clause does not cover the situation where the former customer makes contact with the employee, but a non-dealing clause does.

- *Non-poaching*
  This stops the employee from enticing former colleagues to leave their employer to join the employee at the new organisation.

All of these restraints can only be in place for a limited period of time, and it might be appropriate for them to be limited to a specific geographical area. If the restraints are excessive they will be unreasonable and unenforceable.

An example of a restraint that was not reasonable is shown in the case of:

- *Greer v Sketchley Ltd* (1978) IRLR 445
  Greer was a director of Sketchley's dry-cleaning business. At the time of this case Sketchley operated only in the Midlands and the south of England. After Sketchley was taken under new management, Greer proposed to leave and

join a competitor. Sketchley tried to stop him because there was a restrictive covenant in his contract of employment. This covenant restricted Greer from working in any organisation where his knowledge of trade secrets/special processes was of relevance. The restriction was in place for 12 months and geographically the restriction applied to the whole of the UK.

Greer successfully applied for a declaration that the restriction was invalid. The Court of Appeal ruled that the geographical restriction was unreasonably valid (primarily because Sketchley did not operate throughout the UK) and thus the restraint was void. It is important to note that the whole restrictive covenant was ruled invalid because of the unreasonableness of one aspect of the restraint.

Although this restraint was declared void because of its unreasonable scope, there are many occasions where restraints are successfully used:

- *Bullivant Ltd and others v Ellis* (1987) IRLR 491
  Ellis was the managing director of an organisation and left to set up a competing business. He used information relating to the customers of his old organisation to assist him in setting up his own business. Within his contract of employment there was a restraint of trade clause that prohibited him from carrying out any business with any organisation or person with whom he had carried out business activities during his time working for Bullivant. This restraint was for a period of 12 months following the end of his employment. Bullivant successfully sought an injunction enforcing the restraint.

  It was found to be a reasonable restraint, protecting the business of Bullivant for a reasonable period of time.

Some useful guidelines for restraints of trade were set out in the following case:

- *TFS Derivatives Ltd v Morgan* (2004) EWHC 3181
  In this case the High Court set out that for a restraint including a non-competition clause to be valid:

  - there must be a legitimate business interest that needs protecting;
  - the clause must be no wider than that required to protect that interest;
  - the reasonableness of issues such as geographical location, time and other issues will depend on the extent and nature of the threat to the employer's business.

Other rulings have suggested that the seniority of the employee within the organisation might be relevant:

- *Thomas v Farr plc and Hanover Park Commercial Ltd* (2007) EWCA Civ 118
  Thomas, who was a former managing director, appealed against a non-competition clause that lasted for 12 months. However, the court upheld the restraint due to the seniority of Thomas's position and with it the likelihood that he would know confidential information that would be of interest to a competitor.

Task

Find out if your organisation, or an organisation with which you are familiar, uses restrictive covenants. If possible, read one. Do you think that the provisions within the covenant would be judged to be reasonable by a court? If not, what problems do you foresee?

11.6 Confidential information

A restraint of trade often refers to confidential information and all employees (whether they have a restraint clause or not) have a duty of fidelity to their employer, which includes an obligation not to disclose or misuse confidential information. However, it is not always clear what information is to be classed as 'confidential'. The guidelines to addressing this were set out in the following case:

- *Faccenda Chicken Ltd v Fowler* (1986) IRLR 69
  Faccenda Chicken Ltd prepared and sold chickens to a range of customers. Fowler was the sales manager. He left Faccenda and set up an organisation in competition – selling chickens to customers in the same area. His eight recruits included five salespeople from Faccenda. In setting up his business he used information that he had gained from Faccenda, including names and addresses of customers, their usual requirements and the prices they were charged. Faccenda brought an action for damages against Fowler. Faccenda Chicken was unsuccessful in its application. In making its judgment the Court of Appeal gave some clear guidelines about the use and misuse of confidential information:

  - When assessing what is confidential information it is first important to consider the express terms of the contract of employment.
  - When the employment ends, the requirement to keep information confidential only applies to information that can be clearly defined as a trade secret.
  - In determining what is a trade secret, regard must be given to the nature of the employment, the nature of the information and whether the employee was clearly told that the information was confidential.

The case demonstrates, therefore, that the employer must address the issue of confidentiality by an express term within the contract of employment. This can relate back to the introduction of a restrictive covenant, as described in section 11.5. Again, it is important to be specific and reasonable – and this can be difficult for employers because it is difficult to consider the varied range of information to which the employee might be exposed during employment.

As we have already noted, the issue of computers and their use in the workplace causes new issues for employers. A case linking computers and confidentiality of information is:

- *Brandeaux Advisers Ltd and others v Chadwick* (2010) EWHC 3241
  Chadwick was given notice that her job was likely to be made redundant and was placed on garden leave. Before she went on leave she e-mailed a number of confidential documents to her personal e-mail account. When this was discovered she was dismissed for breach of contract. The High Court found that the dismissal was fair and issued an order that the documents be returned. However, they refused a claim for damages from the employer as it could not be shown that the employer had suffered any loss due to Chadwick's actions.

11.7 Public interest disclosures

The Public Interest Disclosure Act (PDA) 1998 makes additions to the protection already offered to employees in sections 43 and 47 of the Employment Rights Act 1996. The Act specifically addresses situations when the employee knows of (or suspects) some wrongdoing within the organisation. The Act was further amended by the Enterprise and Regulatory Reform Act 2013.

In order to gain the protection offered by the Act the disclosure must be in the public interest. There is no longer a requirement for the disclosure to be made in good faith, but if it is not and the employee subsequently is awarded compensation for a detriment suffered due to making a disclosure, the compensation can be reduced by up to 25 per cent.

The employee must act reasonably in making the disclosure. In determining this reasonableness regard will be given to issues such as the identity of the person to whom the disclosure has been made (if the employee has gone straight to the media it is quite likely that the disclosure will not be protected), the seriousness of the matter, the likelihood of the issue recurring (and the number of times it has already occurred), and whether the disclosure results in a breach of a duty of confidence.

If the disclosure deals with a failure of an exceptionally serious nature, the employee is not obliged to work through any existing internal procedures. In this case the employee can go straight to an appropriate body. The type of disclosures that are protected include those where the employee has a reasonable belief that a criminal offence has been committed, where there has been a failure to comply with a legal obligation, where health and safety is endangered, and where a miscarriage of justice has occurred.

The Small Business Enterprise and Employment Act 2015 includes the requirement for 'prescribed persons' (those to whom a disclosure is made) to produce an annual report summarising the disclosures that have been made.

11.7.1 Reasonable belief

The need for an employee to have a reasonable belief in the truth of his/her allegations was illustrated in the case of:

- *Babula v Waltham Forest College* (2007) EWCA Civ 174
  Babula was a college lecturer and he was concerned that remarks made by one of his colleagues amounted to racial hatred. The college did not seem to react

to his concerns and so he reported the concerns to the police. It was eventually determined that no criminal offence had taken place, but Babula felt that the college had reacted sufficiently badly to his making the disclosure that it gave him no option other than to resign.

He resigned and made a claim for unfair constructive dismissal on the basis that he had been treated unfairly under the Public Disclosure Act. The employer argued that he did not merit protection under the Act because the disclosure he had made was not shown to be true (ie there was no criminal act of racial hatred). However, the Court of Appeal ruled that the test was whether he reasonably believed, at the time that he made the disclosure, that a criminal activity was being committed.

Because the events did allow for him to reach this conclusion, they ruled that he was protected under the Act. An employee should not be subjected to any detriment as the result of making a protected disclosure. Any dismissal as a result of making a disclosure is automatically unfair. However, for the detriment to be unfair it must relate specifically to the disclosure.

11.7.2 Public interest

The need for the disclosure to be in the 'public interest' was introduced by the Enterprise and Regulatory Reform Act 2013. This was introduced to stop individuals using a public interest disclosure to address an individual contractual complaint.

- *Chesterton Global Ltd v Nurmohamed* (2017) EWCA Civ 979
  Nurmohamed made a disclosure that the employer was overstating its costs, which meant that bonuses for him and 100 other managers were reduced. The employer argued that this was not in the public interest, because it amounted to a contractual dispute. The Court of Appeal disagreed. A significant number of people were affected, and hence it was in the public interest to make the disclosure.

11.7.3 Detriment

- *BP plc v Elstone (1) and Petrotechnics (2)* (2010) EAT/0141/09
  Elstone worked for BP for a considerable length of time, but then moved to work for Petrotechnics in 2006. While at Petrotechnics he was required to evaluate safety procedures for a number of clients, including BP. While he was working for Petrotechnics he made a protected disclosure about safety procedures to BP. When Petrotechnics found out about this he was dismissed.

  He then entered into a consultancy agreement with BP. However, they found out that he had been dismissed from Petrotechnics due to disclosing confidential information and hence they did not give him any further contracts. Elstone took a claim that he had been subjected to a detriment by BP because of a disclosure that he had made while employed by Petrotechnics. He argued that it was not relevant who employed him when he made the disclosure; rather, the law protected him against detriment for making a disclosure.

  This argument was supported by the EAT.

11.8 Bribery Act 2010

A further piece of information that impacts on employers is the Bribery Act 2010, which was introduced in July 2011. Within the Bribery Act 2010 there are four possible offences:

- bribery;
- being bribed;
- bribing a foreign public official;
- the corporate offence – where an organisation fails to stop someone acting on its behalf from being bribed or accepting bribes.

It is the corporate offence that has caused employers most concern, as it applies more widely than employees, including anyone operating on behalf of the organisation (eg an agent or representative). An organisation can put forward a defence to the corporate offence.

To do this it would have to show that it had adequate procedures in place to stop bribery occurring. The government has published guidelines about adequate procedures, which are based around six guiding principles:

- proportionate procedures;
- top-level commitment;
- risk assessments;
- due diligence;
- communication;
- monitoring and review.

🔑 KEY LEARNING POINTS

1 Article 6(1) of the Human Rights Act determines the right to a fair trial.

2 Article 8 of the HRA determines the right to respect for private and family life.

3 Article 9 of the HRA determines the right to freedom of thought, conscience and religion.

4 Article 10 of the HRA determines the right to freedom of expression.

5 Article 11 of the HRA determines the right to freedom of assembly and association.

6 Article 14 of the HRA prohibits discrimination.

7 The Data Protection Act 2018 addresses the introduction of the General Data Protection Regulation.

8 The Access to Medical Reports Act 1988 covers medical reports made by a medical practitioner who is responsible for the clinical care of the employee.

(Continued)

(Continued)

9 The Patents Act 1977 specifies when an invention will belong to an employer.

10 A restrictive covenant can protect an employer against certain activities of an employee once that employee has left employment – but all aspects of the restriction must be reasonable.

11 An employer must determine what information is confidential as an express term within the contract of employment.

12 An employee must suffer no detriment from making a public interest disclosure, as long as the disclosure is protected and is made in good faith.

 ## Case summaries

- *Halford v United Kingdom* (1997) IRLR 471 – The assistant chief constable of the Merseyside police force claimed that there was an invasion of her privacy during investigations into allegations that had been made against her, which included alleged bugging of her phones – contrary to Article 8 of the HRA. The ECHR upheld her claim.

- *Aspinall v MSI Mech Forge Ltd* (2002) EAT 891/01 – Aspinall asked a colleague to take a video of production processes to demonstrate how he had been injured at work. The employer was concerned about this because of the secrecy of the production processes. Aspinall was asked to name the person who made the video, but refused. He resigned – but was asked to reconsider. He claimed he had suffered detriment because he had made a public disclosure. However, the EAT ruled that he had resigned of his own accord.

- *Crisp v Apple Retail Ltd* (2011) ET/ 1500258/11 – Crisp posted a number of derogatory comments about Apple products on his Facebook page. He worked in sales for Apple, and was dismissed. This was a fair dismissal because his comments could have damaged Apple's brand, and he had been made aware of the importance of not publicly criticising any products.

- *Trasler v B&Q plc* (2013) ET/1200504/12 – Trasler made a number of negative comments about his workplace on Facebook. He did not name his employer, but it could be deduced from other information on the page. He was dismissed, but this was found to be unfair because he had not damaged the company in any way. The compensation was reduced by 50 per cent because he knew the comments were unfavourable, and hence had contributed to his dismissal.

- *Romero Insurance Brokers Ltd v Templeton and another* (2013) EWHC1198 – The restrictive covenant restricted the senior insurance broker from working for a competitor for 12 months. This was upheld, because insurance contracts are typically renewed every 12 months and he had been specifically recruited to build up the employer's business.

- *Patsystems Holdings Ltd v Neilly* (2012) EWHC2609 – When the employee joined in a junior role there was a 12-month restrictive

(Continued)

(Continued)

covenant. When he was promoted this was not specifically referenced. The covenant was excessive when he was junior, and it was not specifically addressed on promotion – it was not 'brought to life' and therefore was not enforceable.

 Examples to work through

1 There have recently been a number of thefts from the warehouse where you work. The managing director has decided to install CCTV, partly as a security measure – and he says it is also to protect employees. A number of employees have signed a petition stating that the CCTV is a violation of their human rights. Advise the managing director of how to proceed.

2 One of the sales team in an organisation that designs, manufactures and sells cosmetics has invented a new face cream, which he claims will be better than anything else on the market. He is trying to register the patent as his own. The organisation states that the patent should belong to the company – because he works for it selling cosmetics. Advise the two parties.

3 You have concerns that the accounts in the small organisation where you work are incorrect. In particular, you think you have evidence that shows that some customers are paying cash and the transactions are not being recorded – in an attempt to avoid VAT payments. What should you do to ensure that any action you take is covered by the Public Interest Disclosure Act 1998?

12
Health and safety

12.1 Health and safety legislation

In this chapter we examine a range of issues relating to health and safety. The legislation underpinning all that we look at may be summarised as follows:

- **Health and Safety at Work Act (HASAWA) 1974**
  This is the main statute relating to health and safety. It sets out the main duties of the employer and the employee. It also provides for a variety of means of enforcement of the legislation, which are wide-ranging and can include criminal action.

- **Workplace (Health, Safety and Welfare) Regulations 1992**
  The regulations impose a duty on employers to maintain places of work, equipment and systems in an efficient state of good order and repair.

- **Personal Protective Equipment Regulations 1992**
  An employer must identify the protective equipment that is needed by the employee, provide that equipment and ensure that it is kept in a good state of repair. The employee must be trained in the correct and appropriate use of the equipment.

- **Health and Safety (Display Screen Equipment) Regulations 1992**
  These regulations focus on the specific risks associated with the use of display screens. They specify the need for regular breaks when using display screens, the optimal layout of workstations and provision of regular eye examinations where appropriate.

- **Reporting of Injuries, Diseases and Dangerous Occurrences Regulations (RIDDOR) 1995**
  These regulations set out the need to report events arising at work, ranging from injury requiring hospital treatment to the death of the person involved in the incident. There is a requirement to report any incidents that lead to an individual being absent for a continuous period of more than seven days. There is also the requirement to report the occurrence of certain diseases at work.

- **Manual Handling Operations Regulations 1998**
  The regulations require an employer to examine all work involving lifting and manual handling, looking at ways to eliminate the amount of lifting and handling involved, and ensuring that all employees are trained in the correct ways to lift and move heavy objects.

- **Provision and Use of Work Equipment Regulations 1998**
  These regulations specify the need to supply appropriate equipment for use at work, with special emphasis on particular dangers such as fires and explosions. There is a duty to give employees information and training with regard to the equipment.

- **Management of Health and Safety at Work Regulations 1999**
  The main object of these regulations is to use risk assessments to improve health and safety at work. Employers are required to look at each activity within the organisation, consider the potential risks and look at ways to reduce or to eliminate those risks.

- **Control of Substances Hazardous to Health (COSHH) Regulations (amended 2002)**
  These regulations set out the requirements for the storage, use and risk assessments of materials that can be hazardous if incorrectly used.

From this list of legislation you will note that whereas the HASAWA addresses a full range of general issues associated with health and safety, the other legislation focuses on specific areas of health and safety activity. It should also be noted that the Working Time Regulations 1998 might also have been included in this list. As we noted when we examined these regulations in Chapter 5, their basis is in health-and-safety concerns.

Task

Talk to the person responsible for health and safety in your organisation, or an organisation with which you are familiar. Find out what processes the organisation has in place to ensure that it meets the requirements of health-and-safety legislation.

12.2 Duties of the employer

The HASAWA, section 2(1), clearly states that the employer has a duty to ensure, as far as is reasonably practicable, the health, safety and welfare at work of all employees. This requirement includes the following aspects of work:

Safe and adequate plant and equipment

In *BAC Ltd v Austin* (1978) IRLR 332, Austin's job required the wearing of eye goggles. She had to wear these over her own spectacles, which resulted in the goggles becoming misted up and light reflecting. She complained, but her employers did nothing. She was left with the option of dropping her complaint, not wearing the goggles and risking an eye injury, or leaving her job. She chose to leave her job and took up a claim of constructive dismissal. Her claim was successful because her employers had breached the implied contractual requirement to provide safe equipment for her use at work.

Safe premises and/or place of work

The case of *Latimer v AEC Ltd* (1953) AC 643 illustrates this point, with emphasis on the requirement to act as far as is 'reasonably practicable'. Here, Latimer slipped on an area of floor where oil had become mixed with water. The employer was aware that this had happened and had put sawdust across the floor to make the place of work safe. However, it had not had enough sawdust to cover the whole floor. Latimer argued that AEC had breached the requirement to provide a safe place of work. However, it was ruled that the employer had acted as far as was practicable because the only alternative would have been closing the factory.

Competent and safe fellow employees

In *Hudson v Ridge Manufacturing Co Ltd* (1957) QB 348, an employee had carried out practical jokes for many years, which included tripping up fellow employees. He had been warned against such behaviour by his supervisor, but no further action had been taken. He tripped up Hudson, who was disabled, and Hudson sustained an injury. It was found that the employers had breached the requirement to provide safe fellow employees because they were aware of the employee's behaviour and had not stopped it.

A safe system of work

In *Crouch v British Rail Engineering* (1988) IRLR 404, the Court of Appeal ruled that, where the employee is regularly performing tasks that involve potential risk to the eyes, the employer has the duty to actually put the goggles into the hands of the employee.

It is an implied term of the contract of employment that the employer will provide a workplace that, as far as is reasonably practicable, is suitable for the employee to perform his/her contractual duties. If the employee is subjected to poor quality of air because of the smoking habits of colleagues, the employer could be in breach of this implied term.

The Health Act 2006 made it unlawful to smoke in an enclosed public space, and hence some of the issues that employers have had to address in the past in relation to smoking are no longer relevant. However, the effects of being in such an environment can have an impact on health that is not evident until some years later, and so it cannot be presumed that the Health Act 2006 will see the immediate end of any claims similar to the following:

- *Waltons & Morse v Dorrington* (1997) IRLR 488

  Dorrington worked as a secretary in a firm of solicitors. She worked in an open-plan area with other secretaries, some of whom smoked. She also worked near the offices of solicitors who smoked and their smoke drifted to her place of work. After her complaint the solicitors decided to ban smoking in open-plan areas, but solicitors were still allowed to smoke in their offices and a smoking area was set up for other smokers. Unfortunately, Dorrington had to work near one of these smoking areas. She asked to be moved, but her request was refused – and when she moved her own desk she was instructed to move back. Eventually, she resigned and claimed constructive dismissal.

  The Employment Tribunal, supported by the EAT, upheld Dorrington's claim. They decided that there was a requirement to provide a suitable place of work in comparison with other similar places (ie other offices based in London). They decided it was not enough to consider how the needs of non-smokers could be balanced with smokers, because the choice of an employee not to smoke had no adverse impact on smokers, whereas the choice to smoke did have an adverse impact on non-smokers. They found, therefore, that the employer had breached the contract of employment and thus that there had been a constructive dismissal.

It is interesting to note the way the courts defined a suitable workplace in this case. They compared the situation Dorrington was working in with what could generally be expected of offices in London. Clearly, different workplaces have different levels of noise, smells and other potentially irritating factors. This case suggests we have to consider what might be reasonable, given the type of workplace in which the employee is operating.

12.3 Duties of the employee

Section 7 of the HASAWA states that employees have a duty to:

- take reasonable care for the health and safety of themselves and others who may be adversely affected by their acts or omissions at work;

- co-operate with their employer as is necessary to enable health and safety requirements to be met.

More specific duties on employees are laid down in other health and safety legislation that was cited in section 12.1. Examples include:

- the requirement to use any personal protective equipment that is provided, to ensure it is stored correctly and to report any loss or obvious defect of the equipment (from the Personal Protective Equipment at Work Regulations 1992);
- the requirement to follow appropriate systems of work laid down by the employer to ensure safety during manual handling operations (from the Manual Handling Operation Regulations 1992);
- the requirement to inform the employer of any serious and imminent dangers to health and safety, and to inform the employer of any shortcomings in the employer's protection arrangements for health and safety (from the Management of Health and Safety at Work Regulations 1999).

An employer is expected to bring the attention of employees to the requirements that are placed upon them. The Health and Safety Information for Employees (Modifications and Repeals) Regulations 1995 require employers to inform employees of what is expected of them through the distribution of leaflets or the displaying of posters giving the appropriate information.

Although any prosecutions relating to health and safety are more typically brought against the employer, employees can be prosecuted for not complying with certain safety laws. In a Magistrates' Court there can be a fine of up to £50,000, and claims in the Crown Court can bring the penalty of an unlimited fine.

12.4 The employer's liability relating to claims of work-related stress

Work-related stress is an area of health and safety that has attracted a number of high-profile claims in recent years. Claims for stress have been based on the tort (wrong) of negligence – that the employer's duty of care to the employee has been breached. Most of the claims have related to the duty to provide a safe system of work. One of the first, and often quoted, claims relating to stress (which we looked at briefly in Chapter 1) was *Walker v Northumberland County Council* (1995).

- *Walker v Northumberland County Council* (1995) IRLR 35
  Walker was a social worker. There was a heavy workload in the area that he worked, largely because of the increased reporting of child abuse cases. On a number of occasions Walker discussed the workload with his employer, expressing his concern at the pressure he was under. No solution was found. In November 1986 Walker suffered a nervous breakdown and he was absent due to this breakdown until March 1987. During his period of absence he discussed the workload with his employers again and certain support mechanisms (including the temporary assignment of extra staff to help with the work) were

agreed. When Walker returned to work most of this support mechanism did not materialise and any that did was withdrawn within a month. Walker suffered a second breakdown and in February 1988 was dismissed on the grounds of permanent ill-health.

He claimed that the employers had been negligent in not providing him with a safe system of work. The High Court ruled that the employers were not liable for Walker's first breakdown because it was not reasonably foreseeable that it would occur. However, they were liable for the second breakdown because he had already suffered the first breakdown and the agreed support mechanisms had been withdrawn. An out-of-court settlement of £175,000 was eventually agreed.

The fact that the damages were awarded for the second breakdown only is very significant. For an employer to be liable for damages resulting from the stress of an employee, the illness resulting from the stress must have been reasonably foreseeable.

This point was emphasised further in a judgment given by the Court of Appeal when considering appeals on four cases that were grouped together: *Sutherland v Hatton, and other cases* (2002). In this appeal, damages had been awarded in four unrelated cases and in each one the employer was appealing against the decision.

- *Sutherland v Hatton, and other cases* (2002) IRLR 263
  Hatton had been awarded £90,766. She was a teacher who had suffered stress and depression and had eventually retired early on the grounds of ill health. Her workload had not been exceptionally heavy and she had not told the school she was struggling. The history of events included her being attacked in the street in January 1994 and suffering the anxiety of her son being hospitalised in April 1994 for a considerable period. Neither of these events related to her work. In August 1994 she first saw a stress counsellor, but did not tell the school. In October 1995 she went absent due to sickness and never returned to work. She eventually took ill-health early retirement in August 1996. The appeal of the employer succeeded and the award of damages was withdrawn. There could be no liability because the illness relating to stress was not foreseeable because the school had not been made aware that she was struggling.

- Barber was also a teacher. He worked at a difficult school, but did not have a particularly heavy workload in comparison with other teachers. He became depressed in August 1995 and did not tell his employers at that time. In October 1995 he talked to the deputy headteacher and told him he was struggling, and he helped Barber to prioritise and delegate some work. He continued to experience symptoms of stress and in May 1996 was absent for three weeks due to stress and depression. On his return he discussed his problems with the headteacher and two deputy headteachers, but no real help was forthcoming. He eventually collapsed in November 1996. In March 1997 he took early retirement on the grounds of ill health. He took up a claim for damages relating to stress-induced injury and was awarded £101,042. In the Court of Appeal the employers won the appeal. However, this was later overturned by the House of Lords (2004). They concluded that Barber had given the employer sufficient indication that he was struggling and that the employer had been negligent by not offering any assistance to Barber.

- Jones worked as an administration assistant. Hers was a unique job in the organisation that involved working very long hours. The employer commented that it was a gamble to expect one person to do the job, which was really two or three people's work. Jones complained of the workload and was offered extra help – but that never happened. She then wrote a five-page document explaining the problems in detail and invoked the formal grievance procedure. She was threatened with the loss of her job if she continued to complain. In January 1995 she became ill with anxiety and depression and never returned to work. Towards the end of 1996 the centre where she worked closed and she was therefore made redundant. She was awarded £157,541 upon her claim for damages relating to stress-induced illness on the grounds of the employer's negligence. The employers lost this appeal. The outcome was clearly foreseeable – Jones had complained in detail about the problems and the employer had accepted that the workload was too great.

- Bishop was a factory worker. His organisation was bought by another and there was a reorganisation. He had to move to a new job and found it hard to adjust. He complained and asked for his old job back, but it no longer existed. The pressures in the new job were not seen to be excessive, but Bishop could not cope with the changes. He saw his GP due to symptoms of depression, but did not tell his employer. His employer knew he was unhappy, but was not aware of any medical impact it was having on him. In February 1997 he had a breakdown and attempted suicide. In 1998 his employment was terminated. He brought a claim for damages relating to a stress-induced illness and was awarded £7,000 plus loss of earnings.

  The employer won the appeal. At no time had the employer been made aware that the difficulties at work were having any impact on Bishop's health and so the outcome was not foreseeable.

These rulings are important because they result in some clear guidelines for dealing with claims of negligence relating to stress. The key points to note are:

- The ordinary principles of employer's liability apply to any psychiatric injury in the same way as they apply to any physical injury.

- An essential question is whether the harm was reasonably foreseeable – in particular, was an injury to health attributable to stress at work (as opposed to stress from personal difficulties)?

- Foreseeability has to depend on what the employer knows (or ought to know – the employer cannot decide to ignore obvious signs and then claim ignorance). If the employer is not aware of any problems, it is entitled to assume that there aren't any.

- In deciding whether an event was reasonably foreseeable, consideration must be given to the type of work being carried out and the demands placed upon an employee in comparison with other employees in similar work.

Cases include:

- *Intel v Daw* (2007) IRLR 346
  Daw complained of excessive work in e-mails and had been found in tears by one of her managers, but no urgent action had been put in place to address the issue. She suffered a breakdown and took up a claim of negligence against

her employer. The employer argued that there were confidential counselling services in place that she had not opted to use. However, the Court of Appeal held that this could not have addressed the underlying problem, which was the excessive workload. It also held that having a counselling service in place did not absolve the employer of its duty of care to the employee.

- *Dickens v O2 (2009) IRLR 58*
A similar situation to Daw arose in this case. Dickens was struggling with the amount of work and made her managers aware. She was advised to make use of the organisation's counselling service. She subsequently went off sick and her employment was terminated.

   She successfully brought a claim of personal injury due to stress. In this case, the courts ruled that her illness was foreseeable and just having a counselling service in place did not let the employer 'off the hook' in terms of responsibilities to the employee.

Task

Find out what safeguards your organisation, or an organisation with which you are familiar, has put in place to guard against claims of work-related stress. Do you think that sufficient has been done?

Explore further

Read about other cases concerning stress-induced illness and damages sought for the employer's negligence. Apply the guidelines given by the Court of Appeal in the four appeals grouped together in *Sutherland v Hatton, and other cases* (2002). Try to understand what the courts see as 'reasonably foreseeable' when dealing with these cases. Cases that might be of interest can be found in the 'Case summaries' section at the end of this chapter.

12.5 Penalties for breaches of health and safety

12.5.1 *The tort of negligence*

We have seen from the cases that we have examined so far that the focus in determining the outcome of a claim has been on the breach of the employer's duty of care. As explained in section 12.2, the employer's duty of care extends to a range of different aspects of health and safety (eg a safe system of work, a safe place of work).

   These claims are based on the tort (wrong) of negligence. In order to demonstrate that the tort of negligence has occurred, and so succeed in a claim for damages, the employee must be able to show that:

- the employer owed the employee a duty of care;
- the employer breached that duty through negligence;
- the employee suffered damage as a result of that negligence.

Having established that the employer has been negligent in some way, the courts will consider any contribution that the employee has made to the situation before determining what damages should be awarded. This is known as contributory negligence.

The Law Reform (Contributory Negligence) Act 1945 provides that where an employee has contributed to his/her injuries by his/her own negligence, his/her damages may be reduced by the percentage by which he/she is to blame. An example of this is not wearing the protective equipment that has been provided by the employer.

In addition, the courts will give consideration to any consent the employee has given to the act concerned. This is known as 'volenti non fit injuria' – the employee was aware of the risk associated with a particular act and voluntarily consented to continue. In reality, there are difficulties with this defence because it can be argued that an employee never gives completely 'voluntary' consent to anything. However, if this defence is successfully argued, any compensation will be reduced to nil.

A claim for damages for negligence is brought in the County Court if the amount claimed is less than £50,000 and in the County or the High Court if the amount claimed is greater than £50,000.

12.5.2 Contractual claims

As we have also seen in the cases we have looked at in section 12.2, there is the possibility of bringing a claim of constructive dismissal if the employee has resigned as a result of the employer's breach of the duty of care. As we determined in Chapter 8, the employer's breach must go to the root of the contract and the employee's resignation must be as a result of that breach.

12.5.3 Criminal action

If the employer is successfully prosecuted under the HASAWA, the penalty is either a fine or imprisonment. The severity of the penalty will depend on the actual breach of the legislation that has been proved.

In deciding on the level of fine to be imposed the courts will consider the penalty that the offence merits. However, the fine is not usually so large as to create a risk that the organisation might itself collapse – unless the breach is so serious that the organisation should not be trading. The courts will also consider such things as whether any warnings had been given (and if so, whether any action was taken), any profit the employer made from the failure to take adequate health and safety measures, prompt admission of guilt, the action that has since been taken to remedy the problem and the previous safety record.

In April 2008 the Corporate Manslaughter and Corporate Homicide Act 2007 came into force. This Act introduced the offence of 'corporate manslaughter' in England, Wales and Northern Ireland and 'corporate homicide' in Scotland. An organisation will be guilty of the offence if the way in which senior management has organised or managed the activities amounts to a gross breach of the duty of care that the employer has to employees, the public or others, and if that gross breach resulted in a fatality. Companies and public bodies face prosecution if a death results from health and safety failings. The possible penalties include an unlimited fine, a remedial order and a publicity order (making it public that the organisation has been convicted and giving details of any remedial order and fine that has been imposed).

- *R v Cotswold Geotechnical Holdings Ltd* (2011) Crown Court 020110037
  The first conviction of an organisation under the Corporate Manslaughter and Corporate Homicide Act 2007 was in this case. The case relates to events in 2008 when Mr Wright, a junior geologist, was crushed to death. Wright had been left alone working in a 3.5-metre-deep trench collecting soil samples. The company director left for the day, but the two people who owned the development plot stayed at the site because they knew that Wright was working alone. After around 15 minutes they heard a noise and went to investigate. They found that the sides of the trench had fallen in and buried Wright. Wright died of traumatic asphyxiation.

  Cotswold Geotechnical Holdings were prosecuted because it was argued that Wright was working in a dangerous trench and the organisation had not taken reasonable steps to protect him. The organisation had ignored well-recognised industry guidance that prohibited entry into excavations more than 1.2 metres deep and did not allow junior employees to work in unsupported trial pits. As a result of this, the organisation was fined £385,000.

12.6 Enforcing good standards of health and safety

Much of the health and safety legislation is focused on putting systems in place to ensure that employers are providing a healthy and safe place of work. Within that legislation there are specific requirements placed on the employer:

12.6.1 Written statements

Section 2(3) of the HASAWA requires every employer who employs more than five people to prepare (and revise as often as required) a written statement of the general policy with respect to the health and safety at work of the employees and the process in force for carrying out that policy. The statement, and any revisions of it, must be brought to the attention of all employees.

No guidance is given in the HASAWA as to what the statement should include or how it should be brought to the attention of employees. However, advice is available from the Health and Safety Executive (HSE – see section 12.6.5). Generally, the statement should include the responsibilities of all employees in relation to health and safety and general safety precautions.

12.6.2 Safety representatives

Section 2(4) of the HASAWA refers to the appointment by recognised trade unions (see Chapter 10) of safety representatives. The safety representatives must be employees and may be elected or appointed. The employer has a duty to consult with these representatives about all measures to ensure the health and safety of employees at work.

The main duties of the safety representatives are to investigate potential hazards and dangerous occurrences, investigate complaints by their colleagues about health-and-safety-related issues, make general representations regarding health and safety to their employer, carry out inspections and attend safety committees.

A trade union safety representative is allowed paid time off to carry out his/her duties during normal working hours. The safety representative is also allowed paid time off for relevant training.

12.6.3 Safety committees

If at least two trade union safety representatives submit a written request, employers must establish a safety committee. This must be formed after consulting with those who made the request and any other representatives of recognised trade unions, and within three months of the request being made. The function of the committee is to review measures being taken to ensure the health and safety at work of employees.

 Task

Find out if your organisation has a safety committee. If it has, ask if you can attend a meeting to see what issues are discussed and the decisions that are made.

12.6.4 Consultation with employees

The Health and Safety (Consultation with Employees) Regulations 1996 require that employees or their representatives are given sufficient information to enable them to participate effectively in consultation about health and safety matters. Employers are required to consult with employees and/or their representatives about all questions relating to health and safety at work.

12.6.5 The Health and Safety Executive (HSE)

The HSE (www.hse.gov.uk) was set up by the HASAWA to help enforce the requirements of the Act. (Initially there were two bodies – the HSE and the Health and Safety Commission – but they have now merged.) One role of the HSE is to carry out research into health-and-safety-related issues, to provide information and training, to advise employers and employees with regard to health and safety issues and to develop and submit proposed regulations.

Another key role of the HSE is to enforce the HASAWA. The HSE appoints inspectors who have the right to enter an employer's premises at any reasonable time and to carry out any necessary investigations. Since April 2013 inspectors have only carried out such inspections in high-risk sectors (eg construction) or if an organisation has a poor record of compliance with health and safety legislation. In addition, they will carry out an inspection if there has been a fatality or serious injury in the workplace.

If there has been an incident that requires investigation, they have the authority to demand that premises are left undisturbed for as long as it takes them to carry out any investigation and to take any necessary evidence. They also have the right to see any documents or books that contain information relating to the issue under investigation.

If an inspector is concerned that a practice is contravening a statutory requirement, such that the contravention is likely to continue, the inspector can serve an Improvement Notice. The notice must specify the area of concern and the reasons that the inspector has the concerns, and must give a time period within which action must be taken to address the issue. The period must not be less than 21 days. (If the employer wishes to appeal against the Improvement Notice, it must also do so within 21 days.)

If the inspector believes that the contravention of the statutory requirement is such that there is a risk of serious personal injury, he/she may serve a Prohibition Notice. Again, the notice must specify the issue and the reasons for the concerns. This notice usually takes immediate effect – and the activity cannot continue until the problems have been remedied. An employer who has received an Improvement Notice or a Prohibition Notice can appeal to the Employment Tribunal – who can cancel the notice, affirm the notice or modify it. If an appeal is made against an Improvement Order, it is suspended until the appeal is heard. If an appeal is made against a Prohibition Order, it is only suspended if the Employment Tribunal specifically directs that this be so. Failure to comply with either order is an offence under the HASAWA and could lead to a fine or imprisonment.

 Explore further

Read the annual report of the Health and Safety Executive (www.hse.gov.uk). Study some of the incidents that they cite. What legislation has been breached, or could be breached, in these incidents?

 KEY LEARNING POINTS

1 The main duties of the employer and employee, with relation to health and safety at work, are set out in the Health and Safety at Work Act (HASAWA) 1974.

2 In addition to the HASAWA there are a number of pieces of legislation concentrating on specific aspects of health and safety at work.

3 The employer has a duty of care to the employee that includes the duty to provide a safe place of work, a safe system of work, safe equipment and safe fellow employees.

4 The employee has a duty to take reasonable care of his/her own health and safety and to co-operate with the employer in all matters relating to health and safety.

5 In assessing the employer's liability in cases of alleged work-induced stress, a key is whether the psychiatric illness caused by the stress was foreseeable.

6 Potential claims relating to the breach of health and safety legislation include damages under the tort of negligence, claims for breach of contract (eg constructive dismissal) and prosecution.

7 Processes to enforce good standards of health and safety include written statements, safety representatives, safety committees and the support of the HSE.

 Case summaries

- *Thanet District Council v Websper* (2002) EAT 1090/01 – Websper was absent from work for 12 months with stress that was found to be related to his job. His employer offered him alternative work, but within the same division, which Websper held would not help address his problems. The employer offered him no other work and he resigned. The EAT held that by not offering an alternative job the employer had not provided a safe system of work.

- *Barlow v Borough of Broxbourne* (2003) EWHC 50 (QB) – Barlow broke down in tears at work, left and did not return. It became apparent that he had been suffering from stress and depression – but he had not told his employers this. His claim for damages relating to the employer's negligence failed because he had not given any indication that he was struggling and his situation was therefore not reasonably foreseeable.

- *Dugmore v Swansea NHS Trust* (2003) IRLR 164 – A nurse developed an allergy to latex

gloves. She was given vinyl gloves to wear but still came into contact with latex, which resulted in an illness developing. This was a breach of the COSHH Regulations.

- *Morland v London Borough of Tower Hamlets* (2003) High Court 1.5.03 – Morland was a school inspector and had complained about the amount of work he had. However, his work was interspersed with quieter periods – and he had an annual holiday entitlement of seven weeks per year. The High Court did not think that his overall workload was excessive. He did have a breakdown and took up a claim for damages against his employer. However, he also had a range of personal problems. The High Court rejected his claims on the basis that his breakdown had not been reasonably foreseeable and the injury was not solely caused by his work.

- *Hone v Six Continents Retail Ltd* (2006) IRLR 49 – Hone was a licence house manager for five years. He complained that he did not have

(Continued)

(Continued)

adequate support and was working 90-hour weeks. It was agreed an assistant should be appointed, but this never occurred. He received £21,840 in damages for psychological injury because the injuries were foreseeable.

- *Johnstone v Bloomsbury Health Authority (1992) QB 333* – Johnstone was a junior doctor who was contracted to work 40 hours per week, plus up to a further 48 hours overtime. He successfully claimed that the hours he was required to work were damaging to his health.

❓ Examples to work through

1 In a factory, guards are in place against all the saws – large industrial saws that are used to cut through metal. However, some of the employees find that the guards slow down the processes and routinely tie them back. The supervisors are aware that this practice takes place and insist that the ties are removed from time to time. An employee, working on a machine with the guard tied back, cuts off three of his fingers. He takes up a claim against the organisation for negligence. What is the likely result?

2 You work in a busy call centre where staff turnover and absence is high. As a result of this, employees regularly work overtime and extra shifts. Employees moan about this all the time, but there have been no formal complaints. One employee has been absent for three months and today has submitted a claim for damages in relation to a stress-induced illness. What will she have to show to be successful?

3 The trade union-appointed safety representative has recently attended two training courses on his duties. He has now requested that he be allowed to attend a further four-day course. The employer does not believe that this is necessary and has refused the request. What is the likely outcome?

Case study 12.1

You work for a building firm. The organisation employs 120 builders on permanent contracts and then a number of additional builders and other tradespeople on temporary contracts as and when they are required. Three situations have arisen that require your attention:

1 The permanent employees have asked the organisation to recognise the ABC trade union. Three builders have been to see the management to put forward the request. They have claimed that over 60 per cent of the builders have now joined the ABC trade union, although management do not believe that this is correct. What should you do?

2 One of your project managers has recently left the organisation and gone to work for a competitor. You have heard that he has started work on tendering for jobs that your organisation is also tendering for. You

(Continued)

(Continued)

have been told that he is using confidential information that he had while working for you, about prices and materials, in putting forward the tenders. What action can you take?

3 One of the builders hates wearing a hard hat! He is bald and he claims that the hard hat rubs on his head, giving him sore patches. He has been given clear instructions that he must wear it regardless. However, the supervisor knows that he often removes it when working. Yesterday he was not wearing the hat, some bricks fell and hit him and he is now in hospital with a fractured skull and concussion. Who is liable for his injuries?

13
Study skills in employment law

13.1 Introduction

Many students have studied a range of different business- or HR-related topics when they start an employment law module. They soon find there are some very specific skills required when studying and preparing assessed work for employment law. In this chapter we look at some of those skills.

13.2 Finding information

Employment law is an ever-changing area of study. New laws are introduced and new judgments are made in important cases on a regular basis. It is very important, therefore, to ensure that the work that you present is correct and up to date. To achieve this there is the need to access a range of sources to check the accuracy of the information that you are presenting.

There are a large number of employment law websites that should provide you with detailed information. However, many of these require an annual subscription to access them – and they can be quite expensive. Before deciding to take out any subscriptions, consider the following:

- If you are working, talk to the head of your HR department. A lot of organisations – particularly larger ones – already subscribe to some information sites. Find out if your organisation subscribes to anything that is of use to you and ask if you might be able to access this during the period of your study.

- Talk to your tutor/lecturer or the librarian at the place where you are studying. Again, a lot of larger organisations already subscribe to useful information sites. If you are a student registered with a college or university, you are likely to be able to access sites relevant to your studies.

- If you have no access to any sites through these two routes, look to see if any of the subscription sites have special group rates. Maybe you could group together with some of your fellow students to have group access to a site. However, before you actually make any subscriptions, make sure that you need to do so. There is a lot of information available that is accessible to everyone.

13.2.1 Case law

If you know the name of a case but just want to find out more about the details or the ruling, put the name of the case in your internet search engine. You are likely to end up with a list of sources from which you can access details. It is certainly true that some of these will relate to subscription-based websites, but there is likely to be a summary in one of the sources that you can access free of charge.

In addition, you can access the full judgment in many cases. (Most of the websites will not keep judgments beyond around 10 years.)

- If you want to read the full judgment in a case that has gone to the Employment Appeals Tribunal, these can be accessed at: www.employmentappeals.gov.uk/judgments/judgments.htm.

- Full judgments from the Supreme Court can be found at: https://www.supremecourt.uk/news/latest-judgments.html

- Full judgments from the Court of Justice of the European Union can be found at: www.curia.europa.eu

- Judgments from the European Court of Human Rights can be accessed at: www.echr.coe.int

- Judgments from the Court of Appeal can be accessed at: https://www.judiciary.gov.uk/court/court-of-appeal/

- Judgments from the Employment Tribunal have been available since February 2017 at: https://www.gov.uk/employment-tribunal-decisions

Another useful source, covering all developments in employment law, not just case law, is the Daniel Barnett website. You can register, free of charge, for regular e-mail updates on recent rulings and developments in employment law: www.danielbarnett.co.uk

A further useful source, which has a comprehensive collection of employment links, is: www.venables.co.uk

13.2.2 *Statute*

If you want to read the full details of any Acts of the UK Parliament, those from 1988 onwards are accessible at www.opsi.gov.uk/legislation/uk.htm

13.2.3 *Exploring a topic*

If you want to know more in general about a particular topic, there are a number of options available to you:

- www.cipd.co.uk (Chartered Institute of Personnel and Development)
  Some of the sources on this website are restricted to member access. However, there is a lot of useful information about all aspects of HR that is accessible to anyone.

- www.acas.org.uk (Advisory, Conciliation and Arbitration Service)
  On this website you can access a wide range of material including the Acas annual report, various research and policy documents, Acas publications (including Codes of Practice) and general advice about employment matters.

- https://www.gov.uk/government/organisations/department-for-business-energy-and-industrial-strategy (Department for Business, Energy and Industrial Strategy)
  This is the department that is responsible for employment issues. On this website you will find updates on any new legislation, consultation documents on employment matters and information about any legal changes that have recently happened or are due soon.

- www.justice.gov.uk (Ministry of Justice)
  The Employment Tribunals are part of the Ministry of Justice, and hence details about the tribunal service are found on this website. The website gives information about the process of the Employment Tribunals, as well as having the ETS annual statistics.

- www.statistics.gov.uk (Office for National Statistics)
  This is a government website where statistics on a wide range of topics can be found.

- www.cbi.org.uk (Confederation of British Industry)
  The CBI is a lobbying organisation for businesses in the UK, on national and international issues. On this website you will find its comment on a range of issues, including employment matters.

- www.tuc.org.uk (Trades Union Congress)
  The TUC is the body that represents most trade unions in the UK. The website contains information about a lot of employment matters and includes comments on developments in employment law.

13.3 Assignments

Many employment law courses require students, as part of the assessment process, to write assignments. In this section we look at some of the specific challenges that students face when writing law assignments.

13.3.1 Writing good HR or business advice

When writing about employment law there are two important objectives to achieve: 1) to give accurate and clear legal advice; 2) to apply the law to the given situation.

However, many students forget to do both. Some students write a very good legal explanation but do not apply it to the situation. Imagine you were talking to a manager who knew very little about the issue. It is important that he/she understands the law, but also that he/she understands how it can be practically applied in the organisation.

Some students go to the other extreme and write very good practical advice but forget to explain the law. An employment law assignment that does not reference any law is very unlikely to achieve a pass standard.

Being specific

When giving legal advice it is important to concentrate on the specific points that are relevant to the case. Start by identifying the key point in the question and then focus your answer on that point. For example, consider Question 3 under 'Examples to work through' at the end of Chapter 9:

> Following collective consultation regarding redundancies you have now identified the individuals who are at risk of redundancy. You have written to all of these employees asking them to come to individual meetings to discuss the situation. One employee has written back immediately stating that he does not want to 'waste his time at such a meeting – management won't change their mind'. How should you react?

This question clearly relates to the issue of redundancy. An example of the start of an answer that is not specific is:

> There are five potentially fair reasons for dismissal – conduct, capability, statutory ban, some other substantial reason and redundancy. To make a claim for unfair dismissal, an employee must have at least one continuous year's service (two years if the employee started work on or after 6 April 2012), unless the reason is one of the automatically unfair reasons that do not require a qualifying period.

Although there is nothing incorrect with the start of the answer, it is not relevant to this specific question. The immediate impression is therefore that the student does not understand the issues.

Using case law effectively

It is very important to use case law to support and illustrate the points that you are making. However, it is important to use it and not just list it. For example, let us assume that we are answering Question 1 under 'Examples to work through' at the end of Chapter 3:

Joan works as a keep-fit instructor. She teaches at a number of adult education classes. Each term she is asked which classes she wants to teach and they are advertised in the college literature. If there are enough enrolments, the classes go ahead. If there are insufficient enrolments, the class is cancelled. If she is unable to teach one week, she tells the college that she is not available and they arrange for someone else to take the class. Apply a relevant employment test and determine whether she is an employee.

Now suppose as part of the answer a student writes:

An important test is whether there is mutuality of obligation – *Carmichael v National Power* (2000).

This is certainly a useful case to refer to – but there is no explanation of why it is relevant to this particular situation. It has not added any value to the answer. There is no requirement to write out the full details of the case, but there is a requirement to use the case to help us answer the question. So a better answer would be:

An important test is whether there is mutuality of obligation. In the case of *Carmichael v National Power* (2000) it was ruled that Carmichael was not an employee because she was not obliged to do any work that was offered to her. In this case Joan is not required to carry out any work that is offered to her because she can tell the college she is not available. This would suggest that there is no mutuality of obligation.

In the second answer the student has actually used the case to illustrate the point that is being made.

Using up-to-date judgments

It is very important to ensure that you are using the most recent judgment in a case. For example, look at the case of *Dacas v Brook Street Bureau (UK) Ltd and another* (2004) in Chapter 4. Here we see a good example of a case going through the various stages of appeal, and different rulings being given at the different stages. Using an out-of-date judgment (ie the EAT ruling instead of the Court of Appeal ruling) could totally change the logic of your argument.

This case is also a good example of how later cases result in further changes. In Chapter 4 you see how cases that have come after *Dacas v Brook Street Bureau (UK) Ltd and another* have changed the approach that courts take to the employment status of agency workers and how the current ruling is applied in *James v London Borough of Greenwich* (2008) IRLR 302. Applying this case is very likely to come to a different conclusion than the Dacas case and hence it is very important that you use up-to-date material.

Note also that the age of a case does not necessarily determine its importance. Some cases (eg *Delaney v Staples* (1992) in Chapter 5) contain important rulings that no later case has yet overturned.

Referencing materials correctly

It is strongly recommended that you check with your tutor or lecturer whether there are any particular preferences relating to referencing (eg using footnotes or not). However, there are some general rules to apply.

When citing a case in an assignment you should give the names of both parties and the date of the case (in brackets after the name of the parties). For example: *Walker v Northumberland County Council* (1995). Unless there is a specific requirement from your tutor, there is no need to give the reference data in the actual assignment (for example, for the *Walker* case, IRLR 35). However, in the list of references at the end of the assignment you should give the full reference:

Walker v Northumberland County Council (1995) IRLR 35

If you have read about a case in a textbook, it is not appropriate to use the name of the textbook instead of the case. However, if you are writing about comments that the author of the textbook has written about a case, you would reference both sources. For example:

Daniels (2016) states that the question of the employment status of agency workers has been the subject of a number of cases in recent years. In the case of *James v London Borough of Greenwich* (2008) the EAT set out the following guidelines…

When citing a piece of statute, on first reference to it you should write out the full name with the date (the date does not go in brackets). If you are referring to it on a number of occasions, you can later use an abbreviation – as long as you link it to the full reference.

For example:

The Trade Union and Labour Relations (Consolidation) Act (TULRCA) 1992 defines a trade union. In addition, at section 5 of TULRCA there is a definition of the independence of a trade union.

At the end of the assignment you should have a full reference section. This should be in three parts, all listed alphabetically: 1) cases; 2) statute; 3) other sources (eg textbooks).

13.4 Examinations

The purpose of an exam is to:

- test your knowledge;
- test your understanding;
- test your ability to apply your knowledge to specific situations.

Although it is very important to have thorough knowledge, it is most important to use that knowledge correctly. You are unlikely to pass an exam just by writing down everything you know about a particular topic, with no application of the material.

13.4.1 What can be taken into the exam?

It is important to find out from your tutor/lecturer or exam board whether any books or other materials can be taken into the examination. For example, some universities or examination boards allow students to take an unmarked copy of a statute book into the exam.

Many institutions do allow some reference material to be taken into the exam because they do not want the exam to become little more than a memory test. They would prefer students to have the reference material to hand so that they can be tested on the application of the law, rather than on what they have managed to remember.

If you are allowed to take something into the exam, it is strongly recommended that you do so. Examiners will judge the standard of the work that they mark on the basis of what has been expected of students.

13.4.2 What case law do I need to remember?

The answer to this question depends on whether the exam is closed-book (you are not allowed to have any reference material with you), restricted-book (you can have specified reference material only) or open-book (you can take any reference material with you).

Closed-book

In this situation you are clearly going to have to remember some cases. Start by asking your tutor/lecturer for a recommended list of cases to learn. If there is no such list, then write down all the key topics that you have covered in the course – for example:

- dismissal;
- employment status;
- sex discrimination;
- race discrimination.

Then, for each of these topic areas, identify one to three cases that are really important in addressing potential questions. Try to remember these cases. If you can remember more, that is brilliant – but be sure that you are learning cases from across the syllabus and not just the areas you found most interesting!

If you get to the exam and find that you have forgotten the name of a case but it is crucial to your answer, then still use it. If you can remember part of the reference, then put that – it is better than nothing. For example:

In the case of — *v A E Dalton* (1987)…

It is possible that you will remember the name later in the exam and can go back and fill in the gap. If you cannot remember any of the name of the case, you could still describe the key points – but you will obviously get more marks if you can reference it correctly.

Restricted-book

Find out before the exam if you are allowed to have any marks or indexing of sections in a book you are allowed to use. For example, you might be allowed to: write notes on a book; highlight key passages; use sticky notes with section headings to help you find material quickly.

Be very sure that you have got the correct instructions. You do not want to get to the exam and find that your book is taken from you because you have not followed the instructions correctly.

Some students make the big mistake of not revising thoroughly when they are allowed to take material into an exam because they assume they can just look up the key points when they are in the exam. This is a bad error. In employment law you have to be able to apply the law as well as quote it – and you should concentrate your revision on this. Also, there is rarely surplus time in an exam and you cannot waste that time reading a book trying to find relevant information.

Open-book

Again, it is important to determine exactly what you can take into the exam and whether there are any restrictions on what you can have written on that material. Additionally, it is very important that you still revise carefully. If the examiner knows that the student has had access to a significant amount of reference material, it is likely that the examiner will simply expect a higher standard of answer.

13.4.3 How to revise

Students often ask me which is the best approach to revision. The simple answer is that there is no best approach – you have to find out what works best for you. Some of the techniques that I have seen work well are:

- Writing out key cases and statutes on index cards – using different colours for different categories of cases; students can then use these key points as memory triggers.
- Writing out diagrams linking cases to particular topics; this particularly helps those who have a visual memory.
- Copying out key points again and again until you have remembered them.
- Making a recording of key points and playing it in the car as you drive (although this can be annoying for passengers). If you do this, please make sure that your main focus is on driving safely. Alternatively you could listen to a recording whilst travelling on public transport.

Another useful approach during revision is to practise using past papers. This allows you to test your ability to write answers in the time required, to test your knowledge and also to become familiar with the structure of the exam that you are to take (assuming that it has not changed).

13.4.4 How to answer the questions

When looking at a question, start by thinking about exactly what it is asking. Make a quick note of:

- the key issue;
- the relevant statute;
- key cases that could be used.

Check whether the question is asking you to do anything particular – for example, are you being asked to give recommendations, give advice, use recent research, draw on recent case law? Whatever you are asked to do, ensure that you do it.

Finally, be sure that your answer addresses the specific question and that you do not write everything you know about the topic. Remember the point that has already been made about the need to be very specific in answering law questions.

13.4.5 Exam techniques

The aim of this chapter is to consider specific issues relating to the study of employment law and not general study techniques. However, it is worth emphasising the following points:

- Ensure that you allocate your time carefully in the exam. I have seen many students fail an exam because they spent too long on one question and then ran out of time and were unable to answer the full paper. If there are different sections in the exam paper, work out how long you have for each section and move on when your allotted time runs out. You can always go back and write more in a section if you have time at the end.
- Read the instructions carefully. Check to see if all the questions are compulsory or if you have to answer a specific number of questions in one section.
- Read the questions carefully. Answer the question that has been set – and not the one you would have liked to answer!
- Do not waste time repeating the facts that have already been given in the question.
- Write legibly.

13.5 Continuing professional development

Although we have primarily focused on academic studies in this chapter, it is worth taking a moment to think about life beyond exams and assignments. If you are going to operate as an effective adviser on employment-related matters in your organisation you will need to be thinking about your continued development, and you will need to think about the way in which you will keep your knowledge of employment law up to date.

Employment law is a fast-moving area, so you do need to put in place ways to be informed about the changes that occur. Some suggestions are:

- Sign up to the Daniel Barnett e-mail alerts
  As already noted, it is free to sign up to the e-mail alerts from Daniel Barnett (www.danielbarnett.co.uk). Those e-mails will alert you to changes in the law, major consultations and important case law.
- Get added to e-mail alerts from other providers
  Find out if the organisation where you work subscribes to providers such as HR-Inform or XpertHR. If they do, someone in the organisation will be receiving regular newsletters and alerts from them. See if you can be added to

the distribution list, or if the person who receives the e-mails would forward them to you.

- Attend an annual update
A number of organisations, including the CIPD, run day-long updates on employment law. Make it part of your personal development programme to attend one each year. This is a useful way to get an overview of all that is happening, and is an opportunity to ask questions.

Employment law is a fascinating area of study. I hope that you enjoy learning about it and I wish you every success with your studies.

GLOSSARY

Acas Arbitration, Conciliation and Advisory Service (www.acas.org.uk)

Acas Arbitration Scheme This scheme was set up to hear claims to the Employment Tribunal relating to unfair dismissal or flexible working only. It has not been a popular scheme.

Acas Code of Practice: Disciplinary and Grievance Procedures This document sets out the approach that organisations should take when managing a disciplinary or grievance procedures situation.

acceptance When one party agrees to the offer from another party. Once acceptance has taken place the contract is binding.

additional adoption leave A period of 26 weeks of adoption leave that follows ordinary adoption leave. Also referred to as AAL.

additional maternity leave A period of 26 weeks of maternity leave that follows ordinary maternity leave. Also referred to as AML.

additional paternity leave This was removed on 5 April 2015 and can no longer be taken.

agency worker Someone who is provided to work in an organisation by an employment agency.

annualised hours A work pattern that involves a set number of hours being worked a year, but the days and weeks when the hours are worked are not specified.

antenatal care Care of a pregnant woman prior to the birth of a child.

appellant Someone who brings a case appealing against an earlier decision of the courts.

associative discrimination Discrimination against someone because he/she is associated with someone with a particular protected characteristic.

automatically unfair dismissal Dismissal that relates to one of a number of reasons that will mean that the dismissal cannot be fair. In most cases there is no qualifying period of service required to bring a claim of automatically unfair dismissal.

band of reasonable responses In a dismissal situation it is accepted that different employers might apply different sanctions. The Employment Tribunal considers whether the sanction is one that is within a 'band' of reasonable responses to the situation that has occurred.

bargaining unit A group of employees who are represented by a trade union representative.

basic award This is part of the award that is given for a successful claim of unfair dismissal. It is calculated according to the age and length of service of the employee and is equivalent to a statutory redundancy payment.

breach of contract When one party to a contract does not comply with one or more of the terms within that contract.

bundle The documents that are produced for reference in an Employment Tribunal.

capability One of the five potentially fair reasons for dismissal – a lack of ability to do a job (may be due to poor health or lack of skills).

case law Law that is developed from judgments in cases that have come before the courts. It is binding if it relates to a judgment from the Court of Appeal, the Supreme Court or the Court of Justice of the European Union.

casual worker An individual who works when required and when available. This lack of obligation means that the casual worker is not an employee.

Central Arbitration Committee A body that can help organisations resolve disputes and also oversees disputes relating to the recognition of trade unions.

Certification Officer The nominal head of an organisation that holds the list of independent trade unions and rules on whether or not a trade union is independent.

claimant An individual who brings a claim to the Employment Tribunal.

closing submissions The summary of the key points of the case that are presented to the Employment Tribunal by both parties in a case.

collective agreement An agreement made between an employer and a trade union.

collective bargaining Discussions about terms and conditions of employment or other issues relating to employment carried out by trade union representatives on behalf of the employees they represent.

collective redundancy When an employer proposes to make 20 or more employees redundant within a 90-day period.

comparator An individual to whom a claimant in a discrimination claim compares himself/herself.

compensatory award An award made by an Employment Tribunal to compensate a claimant for losses as a result of a dismissal.

compulsory maternity leave A period of two (four if the woman works in a factory) weeks following the birth of a child when the woman is not allowed to work. This forms part of ordinary maternity leave.

compulsory redundancy When an employee is selected to leave the organisation for reasons of redundancy.

conditional offer An offer of employment that is made subject to certain criteria being met (eg satisfactory references).

conduct One of the five potentially fair reasons for dismissal – poor behaviour.

constructive dismissal When the actions of the employer are a fundamental breach of the contract of employment and the employee resigns in response to this breach and does so in a timely manner.

consultation The process of the employer and employee discussing issues with the aim of reaching an agreement.

continuous employment The length of time that an employee has been employed by an employer.

continuous leave One of two ways of taking shared parental leave, when one partner takes a block of leave followed by the other partner.

contract for services A relationship between an individual and an employer in which the individual is not an employee.

contract of employment The terms relating to the employment of an individual, which are legally binding.

contract of service An employment relationship.

COT3 A form used by ACAS to record the settlement of a claim by an employee against an employer. Once a COT3 has been signed, the claim cannot be pursued.

Court of Appeal Appeals against decisions in the Employment Appeal Tribunal go to this court.

Court of Justice of the European Union The highest appeal court within the European Union.

Criminal Records Bureau Merged with the Independent Safeguarding Authority on 1 December 2012 to form the Disclosure and Barring Service.

custom and practice The way in which an employer has always acted, which can become an implied term of the employment contract.

damages Money paid to compensate for the breach of contract.

decision A binding instruction to a member state of the European Union.

default retirement age Retirement at the age of 65 years. The default retirement age was phased out from 1 April 2011, with it being completely removed on 1 October 2011.

dependant leave Leave to care for a dependant (eg child, partner, elderly relative or someone who depends on the employee for help).

dependent trade union A trade union that is under control of an employer or a group of employers.

deposit An amount of money that the Employment Tribunal can ask to be paid if a claimant wants to pursue a case that the tribunal judges to have little hope of success.

detriment Action taken by the employer that has a negative impact on the employee, but is short of dismissal.

direct discrimination Treating one group less favourably because of a protected characteristic.

directions Instructions given by an Employment Tribunal to the respondent and claimant about how the tribunal will proceed, and papers and documents to be produced.

directive Objectives that a member state of the European Union is required to implement, making them part of national law.

disabled Someone who has a physical or mental impairment that has a substantial and long-term adverse effect on their ability to carry out normal day-to-day activities.

disciplinary hearing A formal meeting where allegations of a breach of discipline are put to an employee and the employee responds.

disciplinary officer The individual who conducts a disciplinary hearing.

Disclosure and Barring Service A process of checking whether applicants for a job have previous convictions that would make them unsuitable – particularly relating to work with children and vulnerable adults. Known as a DBS check.

discontinuous leave One of two ways of taking shared parental leave, when the partners take alternate periods of leave rather than one block of leave each.

discretionary terms Employment terms that are given at the employer's choice – they are not contractually binding.

dismissal Termination of the contract of employment.

duty of care The duty that an employer has to take due care of an employee.

DWP Department for Work and Pensions (https://www.gov.uk/government/organisations/department-for-work-pensions)

Early Conciliation A process, run by Acas, that must be engaged with, in the majority of cases, before a case can be brought to the Employment Tribunal.

economic entity An organised grouping of resources that has the objective of pursuing an economic activity – a term used in transfers of undertaking.

effective date of termination The date on which a contract of employment ends.

employee An individual who works under a contract of employment.

Employment Appeal Tribunal The court that hears appeals against judgments in the Employment Tribunal. Referred to as the EAT.

Employment Judge The individual who chairs an Employment Tribunal hearing.

Employment Tribunal A court where an employee can take a claim relating to an employment dispute.

Equality and Human Rights Commission The body that advises on issues relating to discrimination, equality and human rights. Formed from the merger of the Equality Opportunities Commission, the Commission for Racial Equality and the Disability Rights Commission.

ET1 The form that the claimant completes detailing his/her claim to the Employment Tribunal.

ET3 The form that the respondent completes detailing the reply to a claim to the Employment Tribunal.

European Court of Human Rights The court that hears claims relating to potential breaches of the Human Rights Act 1998.

European Works Council A body set up for consultation purposes (if sufficient employees request that this happens) when an organisation has at least 1,000 employees in the European Union, with at least 150 in two member states.

ex parte From a party.

expected week of childbirth (EWC) The week that it is expected that childbirth will occur.

express terms Terms that have been discussed and agreed as forming part of the contract of employment.

final written warning The last stage of the disciplinary procedure prior to dismissal.

first written warning The first formal stage of the disciplinary procedure.

fixed-term contract A contract that is for a specific period of time or that will end on the occurrence of a specific event.

flexible working A working pattern that is not the usual working pattern in the organisation. Those who have worked for the organisation for at least 26 continuous weeks can request flexible working.

frustration of contract When events occur that make it impossible for a contract to be performed.

fundamental breach Action by one party that breaches the contract of employment and in doing so goes to the very root of the contract.

further and better particulars Additional details that are requested in relation to a claim or response to a tribunal hearing.

future loss The estimation of an Employment Tribunal of ongoing losses that will be suffered by a claimant following dismissal.

garden leave Asking an employee to stay at home and not work while the employee remains on the payroll.

golden formula A trade union's immunity from any legal action that applies to actions that are in contemplation or furtherance of a trade dispute.

grievance A complaint by an employee about an issue relating to their employment.

guarantee payment An amount of money an employee is entitled to when the employer has no work available for a limited period of time.

harassment Unwanted conduct relating to a relevant protected characteristic, which has the purpose or effect of violating an individual's dignity or creating an intimidating, hostile, degrading, humiliating or offensive environment for that individual.

Health and Safety Executive A body that is responsible for ensuring that standards of health and safety are met and for promoting health and safety within organisations.

HR1 The form used by an employer to inform the Department for Business, Energy and Industrial Strategy of redundancies.

implied term A term that has become part of the contract of employment because of custom and practice, case law, statute, collective agreement or because it is part of work rules.

incapacity Inability to work due to illness or injury.

Independent Safeguarding Authority Merged with the Criminal Records Bureau on 1 December 2012 to form the Disclosure and Barring Service.

independent trade union A trade union that is judged not to be under the control of an employer or group of employers.

indirect discrimination When a provision, criterion or practice is applied to an individual and this is more difficult for a group with a particular protected characteristic to comply with, it is to the detriment of that individual and it is not a proportionate means of achieving a legitimate aim.

industrial action Activity that is taken by employees to disrupt the operations of an employer (eg strike, overtime ban).

injunction An order from a court that stops an individual or group from doing something.

instant dismissal Dismissal on the spot, without following any procedure.

interim injunction An order from a court that stops an individual or group from doing something for a period of time until a full hearing of the issues takes place.

investigatory officer The individual who carries out enquiries into allegations that might lead to the dismissal of an employee.

lay member One of the three people making up the panel of an Employment Tribunal.

lay off When employees are sent home because there is no work for them to do.

like work Where an employee is doing work that is the same or similar to someone else – one of the bases of an equal pay claim.

Living Wage An amount greater than the National Minimum Wage that some employers choose to pay. It is not a legal requirement (unlike the National Living Wage, which is a legal requirement).

lock-out When an employer stops employees from working.

MATB1 A certificate issued by a doctor or midwife that confirms a woman's pregnancy.

member states Countries that belong to the European Union.

mobility clause A clause in a contract of employment that allows the employer to move the employee to work at a different location.

mutual trust and confidence A fundamental term of the contract of employment, which is implied into all contracts.

NI National Insurance – payments made by both the employer and employee.

National Living Wage The lowest amount that can be paid to employees aged 25 years and above.

National Minimum Wage An amount that is the lowest wage that an employer can pay. It is specified according to three different age ranges.

night time A period that is not less than seven hours in length and includes the hours of midnight to 5 am.

night worker A worker who works at least three hours of work during night time.

notice of appearance The ET3 form that is completed by the employer in response to a claim to the Employment Tribunal.

notice period The period of time that the employer and employee are required to give to terminate a contract of employment.

occupational requirement A specific requirement of a job that allows an employer to do something that would otherwise appear to be discriminatory.

offer The starting point of forming a contract of employment. An offer is made on the understanding that it will become binding once it is accepted.

opt-out Written confirmation from an employee that he/she is prepared not to be bound by the maximum working week defined in the Working Time Regulations 1998.

oral warning Also known as a verbal warning. The first stage of the disciplinary procedure, usually an informal warning.

ordinary adoption leave A period of 26 weeks that an employee can take following the placement of a child for adoption.

ordinary maternity leave A period of 26 weeks of leave that a woman can take, starting no more than 11 weeks before the week that her baby is due.

parental leave Leave that can be taken by parents in the first 18 years of a child's life to care for that child. Maximum of 18 weeks, with no more than four weeks taken in any year.

part-time contract A contract requiring an individual to work less than the hours worked by someone doing similar work within the organisation.

paternity leave A period of up to two weeks taken by the partner of a person who has given birth or adopted a child.

pay in lieu of notice Money paid to an employee that equates to the amount that they would have earned if they had stayed in employment for their full notice period. Employment ends on receipt of the pay in lieu.

perceptive discrimination Discrimination against someone because it is perceived that they have a protected characteristic.

PILON Pay in lieu of notice.

positive action Action taken to increase the number of people from a particular protected characteristic within an organisation.

preliminary hearing A hearing prior to a full hearing in the Employment Tribunal where the tribunal considers issues such as whether the case can proceed and case management issues.

probationary period A period at the start of employment during which the employee's ability is assessed. Employment can be terminated during or at the end of this period if the employee does not meet the required standards.

protected characteristic One of the bases of discrimination set out in the Equality Act 2010 (age, disability, gender reassignment, race, religion/belief, sex, sexual orientation, marriage and civil partnership, pregnancy and maternity).

protective award An award that can be made to employees when the employer has not complied with redundancy or transfer of undertaking consultation requirements.

qualifying period of service The length of time required to bring a claim to the Employment Tribunal – currently two years for unfair dismissal claims, or one year if the employee started work before 6 April 2012.

reasonable adjustments Action that an employer is required to take to accommodate the needs of a disabled employee.

recognition A formal agreement between the employer and trade union that collective bargaining over specific issues will take place.

recoupment The paying back of benefits such as Job Seekers Allowance when an individual is given a compensatory award at an Employment Tribunal.

redacting Removing names of individuals from documents so that they cannot be identified.

red-circling Keeping an employee's rate of pay at the same rate for a period of time. Usually until others doing the same job reach the same rate of pay.

redundancy One of the potentially fair reasons for dismissal. When the job no longer exists.

re-engagement A remedy following a successful tribunal hearing where the employee returns to the organisation but in a different role.

Regina When a case is brought by the state it is listed as R v... – where R stands for Regina.

regulations Legislation that automatically becomes law in the member state because of a treaty from the European Union.

reinstatement A remedy following a successful tribunal hearing where the employee returns to his/her old job.

remedies An award in a successful unfair dismissal hearing – compensation, re-engagement or reinstatement.

remedy hearing A tribunal hearing that is held specifically to determine the amount of remedy to be awarded to a successful claimant.

restrictive covenant An express clause in a contract of employment that restricts activities of employees once they have left employment.

settlement agreement A legal agreement that confirms settlement of claims relating to a specific incident (usually termination of employment). Once a settlement agreement has been signed, the issue can no longer be pursued.

shared parental leave Can be taken when an individual entitled to statutory maternity or adoption leave opts to end that leave, and shares the leave with the partner.

some other substantial reason One of the five potentially fair reasons for dismissal.

spent conviction A conviction that no longer has to be revealed by an individual due to the time that has passed since the conviction.

statute An Act of Parliament.

Statutory Adoption Pay The amount of money that is paid to an individual taking statutory adoption leave.

statutory ban One of the five potentially fair reasons for dismissal – when an employee cannot work because it is not legal to do so.

Statutory Maternity Pay The amount of money that a woman is paid during her statutory maternity leave.

Statutory Paternity Pay The amount of money that is paid to an individual taking statutory paternity leave.

Statutory Redundancy Pay A payment made to an individual who is made redundant and has at least two years' service in the organisation. The payment is made according to age and length of service.

Statutory Sick Pay A payment made to an individual after he/she has been absent due to sickness for four consecutive days or more.

striking out When a tribunal decides that a case cannot proceed within the tribunal.

summary dismissal Dismissal without notice – typically following gross misconduct.

summary reasons A document produced by the Employment Tribunal highlighting the key reasons for a decision.

tangible assets An asset that has a physical form – eg buildings, land.

third-party harassment This was removed from the Equality Act 2010 on 1 October 2013, and hence is a claim that can no longer be taken.

tort A wrong.

Trades Union Congress The body that represents most independent trade unions. Also referred to as the TUC.

transfer of undertaking When a service or organisation transfers to another employer and the employees transfer with it.

transferee The employer to whom employees are transferred in a transfer of undertaking.

transferor The employer from whom employees are transferred in a transfer of undertaking.

treaty The primary source of all European law.

undertaking Any trade or business.

verbal warning Also known as an oral warning. The first stage of the disciplinary procedure, often an informal stage.

vicarious liability The responsibility of employers for any wrongs committed by their employees in the course of employment.

victimisation Suffering a detriment for having previously brought or supported a discrimination claim.

voluntary redundancy When an individual volunteers to be made redundant.

whistleblower Someone who complains about unlawful or wrong practices within their organisation.

without prejudice Correspondence that is entered into with the aim of settling a claim that cannot be produced as evidence in a court.

witness order An order that someone turns up at a court to give evidence.

worker An individual who either works under a contract of employment or works under any other contract where that individual agrees to personally perform work or services for another party.

working time Any time during which the employee is required to be available to the employer.

work of equal value A term within equal pay claims. A claim that, although work is different, it is of equal value and hence ought to be rewarded similarly.

work rated as equivalent A term within equal pay claims. A claim that two jobs have been given the same rating within an analytical job evaluation scheme and hence ought to be rewarded similarly.

written particulars Details of the employment that must be given to all employees within two months of them starting employment.

written warning A stage in the disciplinary procedure, usually follows a verbal warning.

wrongful dismissal Dismissal that breaches the contract of employment.

young worker An individual who is paid for working, is at least 15 years of age, is over the compulsory school leaving age and is not yet 18 years of age.

zero-hours contract A contract that is typically where the individual is required to work only when work is available, with no commitment to a certain amount of work being available.

INDEX